INVESTIGATING EUROPEAN FRAUD IN THE EU MEMBER STATES

This book offers a detailed overview of the rules regarding criminal investigations into financial-economic criminality in the EU's main legal systems. These rules have become fundamental to the effective protection of the Union's financial interests. It undertakes a comparative study of six national legislatures (Italy, Spain, France, Germany, Poland, and the UK) which serve as paradigms of the different judicial systems existing in the Union, in order to offer a complete overview of the different approaches to financial-economic investigation in the EU. The work is further enriched with cross-sectional essays that deal with more general issues, such as data-protection and the future of investigations in the view of the establishment of the European Public Prosecutor's Office (EPPO). This provides a wider perspective on the themes considered. The book also examines transnational issues, providing essential context to the EU's legislative instruments intended to protect the financial interests of the Union.

The research whose results are presented in this publication has received funding from the European Union under the Hercule III Programme.

Investigating European Fraud in the EU Member States

Edited by
Alessandro Bernardi and Daniele Negri

·HART·
PUBLISHING
OXFORD AND PORTLAND, OREGON
2017

Hart Publishing

An imprint of Bloomsbury Publishing Plc

Hart Publishing Ltd	Bloomsbury Publishing Plc
Kemp House	50 Bedford Square
Chawley Park	London
Cumnor Hill	WC1B 3DP
Oxford OX2 9PH	UK
UK	

www.hartpub.co.uk
www.bloomsbury.com

Published in North America (US and Canada) by
Hart Publishing
c/o International Specialized Book Services
920 NE 58th Avenue, Suite 300
Portland, OR 97213-3786
USA

www.isbs.com

HART PUBLISHING, the Hart/Stag logo, BLOOMSBURY and the
Diana logo are trademarks of Bloomsbury Publishing Plc

First published 2017

British Library Cataloguing-in-Publication Data

A catalogue record for this book is available from the British Library.

ISBN:	HB:	978-1-50990-359-7
	ePDF:	978-1-50990-361-0
	ePub:	978-1-50990-360-3

Library of Congress Cataloging-in-Publication Data

Names: Bernardi, Alessandro, editor. | Negri, Daniele, 1971- editor.

Title: Investigating European fraud in the EU member states / edited by
Alessandro Bernardi and Daniele Negri.

Description: Oxford [UK] ; Portland, Oregon : Hart Publishing, 2017. |
Includes bibliographical references and index.

Identifiers: LCCN 2017008371 (print) | LCCN 2017010523 (ebook) | ISBN 9781509903597
(hardback : alk. paper) | ISBN 9781509903603 (Epub)

Subjects: LCSH: Commercial crimes—European Union countries. | Commercial crimes—Investigation—
European Union countries. | White collar crime investigation—European Union countries. | Fraud
investigation—European Union countries. | Data protection—Law and legislation—
European Union countries. | Public prosecutors—European Union countries. |
Criminal justice, Administration of—European Union countries.

Classification: LCC KJE8643 .I58 2017 (print) | LCC KJE8643 (ebook) | DDC 363.25/963094—dc23

LC record available at https://lccn.loc.gov/2017008371

Typeset by Compuscript Ltd, Shannon
Printed and bound in Great Britain by TJ International Ltd, Padstow, Cornwall

To find out more about our authors and books visit www.hartpublishing.co.uk. Here you will find extracts,
author information, details of forthcoming events and the option to sign up for our newsletters.

TABLE OF CONTENTS

PART V: Final Cross-sectional Essays

NOTES ON CONTRIBUTORS

Alessandro Bernardi is Professor of Criminal Law at the University of Ferrara, where he was Coordinator of the Doctoral School on 'European Union Law and National Legal Systems' as well as of the International Doctoral School on 'Comparative Criminal Law and European Law' and on 'European Integration and Criminal Law' from 2005 to 2010, and Director of the 'European Documentation Centre' from 2003 to 2009. He took part in and coordinated various national and international research projects (among others: 'Prison Overcrowding and Alternatives to Detention', 'European Arrest Warrant', 'Competition Law Sanctioning in the European Union: The EU-Law Influence on the National Law System of Sanctions in the European Area'). He is one of the most prominent scholars of European criminal law and has authored and edited numerous publications in this field.

Martin Böse is Professor of Criminal Law, Criminal Procedure, and European and International Criminal Law at the University of Bonn. He holds a DPhil in Law from the University of Göttingen and was awarded with a postdoctoral qualification (*Habilitation*) by the University of Dresden. His main research interests lie in the fields of European criminal law, international cooperation in criminal matters and economic criminal law. He coordinated and participated in many international research projects (among others, on the establishment of a European Public Prosecutor's Office, on the evaluation of mutual trust in the EU with regard to the implementation of the European Arrest Warrant, and on conflicts of jurisdiction in criminal matters in the EU).

Olivier Cahn is Lecturer in Criminal Law at the University of Cergy-Pontoise, Sessional Lecturer at the Universities of Strasbourg and Poitiers, and Researcher at the *Centre de Recherche Sociologique sur le Droit et les Institutions Pénales*. He holds a DPhil in Private Law and Criminal Sciences from the University of Poitiers, and participated in various research projects regarding cooperation in criminal matters within the European Union, the fight against corruption, the fight against terrorism, criminal law and human rights, the maintenance of public order, and critical criminology. In 2013, he also worked with the group of experts for' Revising EU legislation on drug trafficking' of the European Commission.

Theodora Christou is Convenor of Transnational Law and Governance at the Centre for Commercial Law Studies at Queen Mary University of London and Convenor of International Human Rights Law at London School of Economics.

She was awarded a PhD from Queen Mary University of London and holds an LLM from King's College London. She is an elected member of the Executive of the Bar Human Rights Committee where she has worked on numerous human rights interventions around the world. She has given expert evidence in a number of consultations, including to: the Home Office and Ministry of Justice Review of the Balance of EU Competence in Criminal Matters; the UK Parliamentary Consultation on Female Genital; the UK Parliamentary Inquiry on Violence Against Women; the Africa Justice Foundation on 'The Rule of Law within the Post-2015 Agenda'; and the European Commission Consultation, A Green Paper on the application of EU criminal justice legislation in the field of detention.

Juan José González López is Attorney and Associated Professor of Constitutional Law at the University of Burgos. He has authored various publications in the field of criminal law, administrative law, data protection and procedural law.

Valsamis Mitsilegas is Professor of European Criminal Law, Dean for Research (Humanities and Social Sciences) and, since 2012, Head of the Department of Law at Queen Mary University of London. He has been the Director of the Queen Mary Criminal Justice Centre since 2011. From 2001 to 2005 he served as legal adviser to the House of Lords European Union Committee. His research interests and expertise lie in the fields of European criminal law; migration, asylum and borders; security and human rights, including the impact of mass surveillance on privacy; and legal responses to transnational crime, including organised crime and money laundering. He has authored six monographs and a number of articles as well as chapters in academic volumes. He is a regular adviser to EU institutions including the European Commission, the European Parliament and the EU Fundamental Rights Agency.

Francesco Morelli is Researcher in Criminal Procedure at the University of Ferrara. He holds a DPhil in criminal procedure from the same university and was a post-doc researcher at its Department of Law from 2008 to 2012. He is licensed as Associate Professor, has spoken at various national conferences, and was involved in national and international research projects. He has authored a monographic study on acquittal verdicts in the Italian criminal procedure as well as many articles published in legal reviews and collective volumes.

Daniele Negri is Professor of Criminal Procedure at the University of Ferrara and vice-Director of the Department of Law of the same university. He holds a DPhil in Criminal Procedure from the University of Bologna, has been Coordinator of the Doctoral Program in 'Comparative and Historical Law' at the University of Ferrara and is a member of the board of its Doctoral School on 'European Union Law and National Legal Systems'. Several times, he has been guest researcher at the *Max-Planck Institut für Ausländisches und Internationales Strafrecht*, in Freiburg im Breisgau, and he has authored two monographs on personal freedom and attendance of the defendant at trial as well as more than eighty publications in legal reviews and collective volumes. He took part in various national and international research projects, such as: 'European Arrest Warrant', 'Prison Overcrowding and Alternatives to Detention', 'Relationships between the National Judicial Authorities and the Investigative Agencies in the View of the EPPO: Operational Models and Best Practices in Fight against EU Frauds', and 'Improving Cooperation between EU Member States in Confiscation Procedures'.

Fabio Nicolicchia is Post-doc researcher at the University of Ferrara where he is developing a research on electronic surveillance and fundamental rights. He was awarded a DPhil in Criminal Procedure from the same university, writing a dissertation on the Italian system of corporate criminal liability. He was a visiting scholar at the School of Law of the University of Miami in 2014.

Adán Nieto Martín is Professor of Criminal Law at the Faculty of Law at the University of Castilla la Mancha. He is vice-Director of the European and International Criminal Law Institute (UCLM), vice-President of the Spanish section of AIDP (International Association of Penal Law) and a member of the Board of Editors of the *European Criminal Law Review*. He has authored of a number of publications, mainly on white collar crime, corporate criminal liability and financial-economic crime.

Celina Nowak is Professor of Criminal Law at the Kozminski University in Warsaw and Director of the Institute of Law Studies at the Polish Academy of Sciences. She holds a DPhil in Criminal Law from the Institute of Legal Studies of the Polish Academy of Sciences, and was awarded with a post-graduate diploma by the Université de Paris 1 Panthéon-Sorbonne. She has spoken at many national and international conferences, authored various scientific publications, and is editor of a number of collective volumes. In her academic career, she was beneficiary of several research scholarships granted by the Max Planck Society (Germany) as well as by the Italian and French Governments.

Introduction

The present publication falls within the framework of the research project 'Relationships between the national judicial authorities and the investigative agencies in the view of the EPPO: operational models and best practices in fight against EU frauds', co-financed by the European Commission—OLAF (Hercule III Programme—legal training and studies).

The book thus has the objective of disseminating the results of the research and provides a complete overview of the dynamics and rules regarding criminal investigations in the area of financial and economic crime in some of the main legal systems existing in the EU.

The need to protect the financial interests of the European Union also through the use of criminal sanctions is an objective highlighted in a growing number of legislative proposals at the EU level: one need only mention the 'Proposal for a Directive on the fight against fraud to the Union's financial interests by means of criminal law' (COM(2012)363 final), and the 'Proposal for a Regulation on the establishment of the European Public Prosecutor's Office' (COM(2013)534 final, Whereas n 4).

However, the future instruments for fighting crime, as well as the action of already existing EU bodies, risk being less incisive or even ineffective if some essential requirements are not met. In addition to a thorough acquaintance with the existing legislation and its implementation, a full awareness of the practical relationships between the different authorities in charge of promoting and conducting investigations on financial and economic crimes in the Member States is needed. Different actors and heterogeneous bodies with various responsibilities and powers are involved in this area, including tax authorities, law enforcement agencies and different judicial authorities, resulting in a system that cannot be easily understood from a purely national perspective and therefore needs to be explained in detail from a comparative and international viewpoint.

The present research will thus take into consideration six different national legislations, selected also on the basis of their ability to serve as paradigms of the different judicial systems existing in Europe. Members of important academic institutions in each selected country were entrusted with the task of conducting a survey of their respective legal systems. The contribution of such scholars was considered essential for the purpose of carrying out the research and to ensure the independence of the study and thus the objectivity of its results. However, the academics also took advantage of the contribution of experts in the field of economic and financial crimes with operational investigative tasks in order to include an analysis from the perspective of legal practitioners as well.

Each national system is analysed in a dedicated chapter which provides a general outline of the investigation phase, focusing on its most distinctive features. More specifically, the study was intended to go beyond a mere analysis of national rules and aims rather to provide a detailed overview of the operational models in the area of financial and economic investigations in some of the main legal systems within the EU.

First, we will consider the approach of two Member States (Italy and Spain), where the criminal justice system is characterised by a strong functional dependence between the police and public prosecutors: in both countries, the latter generally have a monopoly when it comes to instituting criminal proceedings and particular importance is given to the role of technically specialised investigative bodies.

Specific attention is subsequently dedicated to the French system, which appears to be unique in establishing specific roles and responsibilities in the fight against financial and economic offences and which has been recently amended by the entry into force of Act of Parliament 2013-1117.

Then follows an examination of the legal systems of Germany and Poland, where administrative control authorities play a large role in criminal investigations regarding financial and economic offences and are endowed with considerable investigative powers also in criminal proceedings. Finally, a non-Roman legal system is examined in order to ensure the completeness of the survey. The UK was selected as the best model for this purpose. In the UK system, prosecutors may not even be directly involved in financial investigations.

The publication concludes with two chapters which deal with general and cross-cutting issues in the field of interest.

The first addresses the general theme of data protection, whilst the last chapter of the book provides an overall summary of the outcomes of the study, with regard in particular to the future EPPO.

Concerning the latter institution, the study appears to possess a specific relevance. Without an appropriate knowledge of the current legislation, operational protocols and practices implemented in every state, the European Public Prosecutor's Office will find it difficult to coordinate and direct all the investigations at a central level and prosecute the perpetrators of offences for which the office itself is competent. In other words, once a central authority like the EPPO is capable of interfacing with individual national systems, it will be able to assure an equivalent protection of financial interests throughout the EU area. Under the current EU Commission proposal, the EPPO will entrust the most important operations to national investigation authorities, but it will not be endowed with sufficient tools for verifying the accuracy and effectiveness of their actions. This could undermine achievement of the main objective underlying the establishment of the EPPO, which is to be able to conduct effective investigations and successfully prosecute offences against EU financial interests across the entire territory of the European Union.

It is important to underline that the 'Proposal for a Regulation on the establishment of the European Public Prosecutor's Office' contains only some very general provisions regarding the investigations of the future EPPO. It is thus evident, also considering the complexity of the subject matter involved, that national provisions and practices in the field of financial and economic investigations will continue to play a fundamental role even after the creation of a European Public Prosecutor. Consequently the present survey, unlike other studies, was aimed at analysing the investigative dynamics and tools that currently exist in each Member State considered, with specific regard to financial and economic investigations, rather than at drafting a common set of European rules of criminal procedure.

The publication may thus be a useful tool for providing scholars, practitioners and European institutions with an overview of the most relevant aspects of financial economic investigations in the various Member States and raising awareness on the specific topic of the protection of the Union's financial interests.

The Editors
Prof Dr Alessandro Bernardi
Prof Dr Daniele Negri

Part I

The Fight against Financial-Economic Crime through Specialised Investigative Bodies

1

Dynamics and Operational Models of Financial-Economic Investigations in Italy

Dr FABIO NICOLICCHIA
Post-doc researcher University of Ferrara

Introductory Considerations

The dynamics and operational models characterising investigations into frauds which may potentially harm the financial interests of the European Union show a fundamental characteristic within the Italian legal order: the simultaneous presence of investigative tools and powers of a purely administrative nature along with means of investigation typical of criminal proceedings, depending on whether the specific case concerned on each occasion has the character of a mere administrative offence or relates to a fact classified as a crime under the law.

The relationship between administrative and criminal proceedings within the Italian system—principally with regard to economic and financial crime phenomena—is a topic that has already been addressed on a supranational level as well, as emblematically attested by a recent judgment of the European Court of Human Rights, which specifically set out to verify observance of the *ne bis in idem* principle enshrined in Article 4 of Protocol No 7 to the Convention in the case of a cumulative application of an administrative penalty and criminal sanctions in relation to the same facts.[1]

However, our attention here will obviously be focused mainly on analysing the investigative tools and dynamics deriving from the existence of two different systems of inquiry, whose application is concretely dependent on whether conducts potentially detrimental to the financial interests of the Union are qualified, on an internal level, as actual crimes or simple administrative violations.

---

[1] The case referred to is *Grande Stevens and others v Italy*, App Nos 18640/10, 18647/10, 18663/10, 18668/10 and 18698/104/3/2014 (ECHR 4 March 2014).

In the former case, it is almost superfluous to point out that conducts causing damage to European finances may result in the commission of offences falling within specific categories of crime. These undoubtedly include, solely by way of example, the crime of 'embezzlement to the detriment of the State', as per Article 316 *bis* of the Italian Criminal Code, as well as cases of 'undue receipt to the detriment of the State', envisaged by the subsequent Article 316 *ter*. Both provisions are in fact explicit in identifying the criminal conduct as the undue receipt of loans, funding, grants or subsidies provided by the State or—precisely—by the European Union. Of great practical relevance, moreover, is the specific case of 'fraud', punishable according to Article 640 of the Criminal Code, in particular in its aggravated form pursuant to Article 640 *bis*, which again mentions, in clear terms, subsidies provided on a European level as being among the objective elements involved in the crime. It does not seem necessary, however, to discuss at length the most frequently occurring offences liable to cause detriment to the EU budget. The simple awareness of a possible criminal relevance of such conducts is sufficient to bring out a first aspect that is of undoubted interest for the purpose of this study: any time we are dealing with behaviour the law classifies as a crime, the ensuing investigations must be conducted applying the principles and rules laid down by the Code of Criminal Procedure (CCP).

In contrast, the investigative tools falling within the scope of administrative law, and in particular the powers of assessment in respect of tax violations, will take on relevance when it is a question of conducts that do not involve criminal offences, but rather simple financial wrongdoing in tax-related matters, which is subject exclusively to administrative penalties.

Such conducts, mainly addressed within the framework of Legislative Decree No 274/2000, can be considered merely administrative violations where the amount of the evaded tax is below certain limits established by law, whilst they may take on the nature of veritable crimes when such thresholds are exceeded. It is clear that such an eventuality will give rise to the largest problems when it comes to applying sanctions, as it implies a transition from the administrative to the criminal realm, ie, the necessity of correctly classifying the actual nature of the conduct in question on each occasion.

Turning our attention first to the merely administrative realm, deferring the analysis of investigative dynamics in criminal matters to later in the discussion, we should start off by highlighting the existence of significant and penetrating powers of assessment, also of a coercive nature, a thorough acquaintance with which appears to be of extreme importance for the purposes of this analysis.[2]

---

[2] It is well known, in fact, that pursuant to Art 3(3) of Council and Parliament Regulation (EU, EURATOM) No 883/2013 concerning investigations conducted by the European Anti-Fraud Office (OLAF) and repealing Regulation (EC) No 1073/1999 of the European Parliament and of the Council and Council Regulation (Euratom) No 1074/1999 [2013] OJ L248 and to Art 7 of the Council Regulation (EURATOM, EC) No 2185/1996 concerning on-the-spot checks and inspections carried out by the Commission in order to protect the European Communities' financial interests against fraud and

One need only consider, moreover, that financial violations connected to tax evasion have often played a role as elements of complex fraudulent schemes undertaken to the detriment of EU financial interests. In light of this, the attention shown by the legislator and the competent institutions on a European level seems completely understandable.[3] At the same time, it justifies their being singled out as one of the main focuses of the present analysis.

When addressing this complex topic, therefore, it will be necessary first of all to take into consideration how the most relevant investigative powers are regulated within the administrative sphere, particularly as regards the prerogatives of the departments of the Italian Revenue Service (Agenzia delle Entrate) and of the separate tax police body (Guardia di Finanza) responsible for conducting assessments (the powers of the customs agency—Agenzia delle Dogane—and so-called state monopolies, or Monopoli di Stato, will not be a specific focus of discussion). Then we can go on to examine the investigative tools and operational models of the criminal realm, also dedicating specific attention to the concrete dynamics of transition and the relations between the two aforementioned models of assessment.

Access, Inspections and Verifications Pursuant to Presidential Decrees Nos 633/1972 and 600/1973

The powers of assessment in respect of tax offences are governed within the framework of two legislative instruments, Presidential Decrees No 633/1972 and No 600/1973, dealing respectively with value added tax and personal income tax. These two sources show a substantially homogeneous content, as is evidenced by the explicit reference in Article 33(1) of Presidential Decree No 633/1972 to the

---

other irregularities, OJ L292, the officials of the European Anti-Fraud Office are endowed with the same investigative powers as the competent national authorities of the country in which they operate. This suffices to demonstrate the absolute importance of a thorough acquaintance with the investigative tools and prerogatives existing in each Member State. On this point, recently, G Lasagni, 'Cooperazione amministrativa e circolazione probatoria nelle frodi doganali e fiscali. Il ruolo dell'Ufficio europeo per la lotta antifrode (OLAF) alla luce della direttiva OEI e del progetto EPPO' (2015) *Dir. pen. cont.*, 5.

[3] The question as to whether offences related to home state taxation should be included among the relevant categories in the draft of the so-called PIF Directive remains a highly topical issue of debate. The Court of Justice of the European Union recently highlighted the impact of VAT-related fraud on the EU budget in an important judgment. On this subject, see Case C-105/14 *Taricco and others*. On the same point, see the earlier Case C-617/10 *Åkeberg Fransson* (especially paras 24–27). On the domestic front, it is worth pointing out the very recent revision of the system of sanctions for tax-related offences implemented by Law No 158/2015. Of undoubted significance in this regard is the introduction, under Art 10 of the law just mentioned, of a provision for mandatory confiscation of the proceeds or price in the event of a criminal conviction for one of the offences envisaged under Legislative Decree No 74/2000.

rules laid down in Article 52 of Presidential Decree No 600/1973 in respect of access, inspection and verifications. It will thus be possible, as well as appropriate, to consider the rules together. Before proceeding to analyse the most relevant investigative tools, however, it is necessary first to examine who is subjectively endowed with the powers that we will go on to consider.

In this regard, it is possible to observe a dual competence: the legislation concerned is in fact explicit in attributing the powers in question to tax offices, which may be specifically identified as the assessment divisions of the Agenzia delle Entrate (Italian Revenue Service), which are supported by the action of the Guardia di Finanza, a police body specialised in conducting internal investigations into tax offences and more in general in the economic and financial spheres.[4] As for the role of the Guardia di Finanza in combating European frauds, it is very important to highlight that this police body is today expressly empowered to engage in activities aimed at preventing, seeking out and repressing such phenomena, also through forms of international operational cooperation.[5]

The existence of a dual competence in this area is specifically taken into consideration by legislative sources, which—with the aim of protecting citizens against repeated inspections—require that the authority not directly involved be given immediate notification of the commencement of verifications and inspections by whoever has initiated the inspection activity; they also provide for the possibility of submitting requests for the purpose of acquiring specific details and being informed of the results of the verifications.[6] From an operational standpoint, this result is concretely pursued also through the introduction of specific protocols which govern procedures for the coordination of inspections and exchange of data between the two authorities concerned at a local level.

As regards the concrete powers of inspection attributed to employees of the tax authorities and the tax police, the previously mentioned power of access, inspection and verification pursuant to Article 52 of Presidential Decree No 633/1972 and Article 33 of Presidential Decree No 600/1973 undoubtedly takes on a central role. These powers consist concretely in the possibility of entering and remaining on premises even without the consent of the owner or rightful occupant. In the case of premises where commercial, agricultural, artistic or professional activities are conducted, access is undoubtedly allowed for the purpose of carrying out inspections and any other inquiry deemed useful for the investigation. Such access must take place during normal work hours[7] and in such a manner as to minimise interference with the activity of whoever is undergoing inspection. Access can also

---

[4] *cf* Legislative Decree No 68/2001, Art 2(2).
[5] See again Legislative Decree No 68/2001, Art 2(2)(m) and Legislative Decree No 68/2001, Art 4(1).
[6] See especially Presidential Decree No 600/1973, Art 33(5).
[7] Access to business premises will thus undoubtedly be allowed also during night-time hours where the activity of the business is mainly concentrated during those hours.

take place in the absence of the principal or legal representative.[8] A limit is placed on the duration of the operations; these may last for 30 working days at most, though this period may be extended for another 30 days in the case of verifications of particular complexity.[9]

Different, more restrictive rules apply in the case of access to private premises where people both work and live, as well as places used exclusively as a private residence. In both cases, a specific authorisation from the public prosecutor (Procuratore della Repubblica) will be necessary, but in the latter case there must also be strong evidence that financial violations have been committed and the access can take place solely for the purpose of gathering proof of the same.[10] It should further be pointed out that the authorisation in question will also be necessary when the business premises are only adjoining and communicating with the living quarters.[11]

The operational difficulties that may potentially derive from the provision concerned are normally overcome in practice by requesting beforehand an order from the judicial authority authorising access to the place of residence, so as not to have to interrupt the operations—which could clearly undermine their outcome—should the need to access a private dwelling arise in the course of the investigation.

The specific authorisation of a judge is also required whenever it is necessary to carry out personal searches or open sealed premises or enclosures, or to examine documentation where an objection is raised on the grounds of the existence of a professional secret. More restrictive rules apply, however, when the action in question must be carried out against individuals who are acting in the capacity of lawyers, as in this case there is a more greatly felt need to protect the confidentiality of the individuals involved.[12]

Such a necessity may give rise to specific problems in the event of access to electronic data and communications stored on the premises of the individual or entity undergoing scrutiny. In this regard a fundamental distinction needs to be drawn: where the data or communications are not subject to any special measures of protection and are fully at the disposal of the party concerned, there do

---

[8] Pursuant to Presidential Decree No 633/1972, Art 51(1), only in exceptional circumstances will access to premises used for carrying on a trade or profession require the presence of the principal or his representative.

[9] This provision is set forth in Art 12(5) of Law No 212/200.

[10] Presidential Decree No 633/1972, Art 52 (1) and (2).

[11] On this point see LR Corrado, 'Locali comunicanti? E' necessaria l'autorizzazione del Procuratore' (2013) *D&G* 264.

[12] The applicable provisions are laid down in Art 103 CCP, which permits inspections and searches in lawyers' offices only when they or other persons who regularly conduct their activities in the places in question have been accused of wrongdoing, and only insofar as such activities relate to the charge made against them. Further procedural guarantees are also provided for and it is important to highlight that seizure and examination of the correspondence between the accused party and his lawyer are not permitted.

not seem to be particular limits to their direct acquisition even where specific authorisation is lacking, since they can be considered in the same category as the documentation that is freely accessible under the previously mentioned provisions.[13] However, whenever the existence of a secret is claimed, ie, the data or communications are protected by security systems, or have not yet been viewed by the individual or entity undergoing verification, and have thus not yet come into the latter's possession, it will be necessary to obtain a specific authorisation of the public prosecutor.[14]

It is worth highlighting that all of the powers taken into consideration are coercive in nature. In other words, any refusal or uncooperative attitude on the part of the inspected party will not result in the impossibility of proceeding with the inspection, which may in any case take place with or without the consent of the party concerned.

It should also be specified that in the case of administrative inquiries, it is not required that a lawyer be present while operations are ongoing.[15] It follows that the action of the inspectors cannot be paralysed by a request to wait for a lawyer to step in.

With the aim of preventing any tampering with the evidence gathered during inspections, the officials conducting the verifications have the option of seizing the documentation retrieved; however, this will be allowed only when it proves impossible to reproduce the contents of the documentation itself in the inspection report, which must be drawn up and signed by the inspectors and by the party undergoing inspection at the end of the operations. There will be no possibility, in any case, of seizing the accounting records and registers which must be maintained by law. Only copies may be made of such documentation.[16] All of the aforementioned provisions will likewise apply when physical searches are conducted on motor vehicles or means used to transport cargo, even on behalf of third parties.[17]

Investigative Acts other than Access to Business Premises: Financial Investigations

Although access, inspections and verifications taking place in accordance with Article 52 of Presidential Decree No 633/1972 and Article 33 of Presidential Decree

---

[13] Specifically, Presidential Decree No 633/1972, Art 52(7). On this point see also the following para.
[14] Presidential Decree No 633/1972, Art 52(3).
[15] Law No 212/2000, Art 12(2) provides exclusively for the option of requesting the assistance of a lawyer during access, inspection and verification by the authorities.
[16] Presidential Decree No 633/1972, Art 52 (6) and (7).
[17] Presidential Decree No 633/1972, Art 52(8).

No 600/1973 undoubtedly represent the most significant powers attributed to the national authorities when it comes to administrative investigations into financial violations, these are not the only tools available to officials in their assessment activities.

Concerning this point it should be noted, in fact, that the tax police and tax authorities have the possibility of exercising a broad array of additional powers. Article 51 of Presidential Decree No 633/1972 and Article 32 of Presidential Decree No 600/1973 are of relevance here: they establish first of all the option of inviting individuals undergoing verification to appear in order to exhibit documentation or furnish information or clarifications useful for the assessment activities.

Similarly, there is an option of sending the same individuals questionnaires, to be returned completed and signed, as a means of obtaining data and information serving to orient assessment activities, also vis-à-vis third parties.

An extremely important provision establishes the power, subject to authorisation of the regional director, or regional police commander in the case of the Guardia di Finanza, to request banks and Poste Italiane Spa (in relation to financial and credit activities), insurance companies and agencies (in relation to financial activities), financial intermediaries, investment firms, collective investment undertakings, asset management companies and trust companies, to provide data, information and documents concerning any dealings or transactions. Such requests and the responses to them must be submitted exclusively by electronic means.[18] Failure to respond to a request for information is punishable with an administrative fine. The verifying officials are also directly empowered, without the need to obtain any authorisation, to request data and information concerning the duration of life insurance contracts concluded by taxpayers, the amount of the premium and the party entitled to collect it.[19]

The above-mentioned provisions govern the procedures for carrying out what are commonly referred to as financial investigations. They have taken on increasing importance in practice insofar as investigations concerning financial violations are concerned. As is obvious, the power in question introduces a conspicuous departure from the principle of banking secrecy, evidently justified by the need to ensure the possibility of employing an effective investigative tool in the activity of combating violations of a financial nature.

---

[18] This power is expressly mentioned in Presidential Decree No 633/1972, Art 51(2)(7) and Presidential Decree No 600/1973, Art 32 No 7.

[19] Again see Presidential Decree No 633/1972, Art 32 and Presidential Decree No 600/1973, Art 51.

The Transition from the Administrative to the Criminal Realm

The Two-track Principle

After describing the main investigative tools existing on an administrative level, it is thus necessary to more specifically address the subject of the potential transition from the administrative to the criminal realm. As already mentioned in the introduction, tax and financial offences are prosecuted and sanctioned on two different levels in Italy: the administrative-tax level and—whenever a case involves a fact constituting a crime—the criminal level.

Although our system has opted, at least in theory,[20] for a perfect autonomy of the two spheres of investigation, as well as of the subsequent stages of legal proceedings,[21] it is nonetheless possible that in the course of an administrative inspection activity, elements are detected which point to the commission of a fact that the law considers a crime; this gives rise to the necessity of activating the mechanisms and instruments of criminal procedural law.

The relationship between tax-administrative and criminal procedure can be analysed from at least three different points of view, each corresponding to different stages of the procedure. The first stage is the preliminary investigative one, which takes place within the framework of administrative procedure or—if criminal wrongdoing is involved—criminal procedure; the second stage consists in the actual trial proceedings; finally, there is the question of the relationship between judgments. Of these three stages, what we are interested in examining here, obviously, is the dynamics of the first.

Different Actors for Different Proceedings

As far as both criminal and tax-related proceedings are concerned, the law designates a specific authority which is competent to carry out investigations in relation to the commission of an offence. In the former case, the prominent role will be

---

[20] cf I Caraccioli, 'Reati fiscali: ritorna la forte tentazione di resuscitare la pregiudiziale tributaria' (2000) *Il Fisco*, 13, according to whom the reform of 2000 already risked undermining the real separation between the two systems, by surreptitiously introducing a sort of preliminary tax ruling, at least for more complex cases involving the determination of tax evasion. Analogous doubts were expressed more recently by E Marello, 'Evanescenza del principio di specialità e dissoluzione del doppio binario: le ragioni per una riforma del sistema punitivo penale tributario' (2013) 12 *Rivista di Diritto Tributario* 269.

[21] For a general overview of the double-track system and its main implications, see A Di Amato, *I Reati Tributari*, in A Di Amato, R Pisano (eds), *Trattato di Diritto penale dell'impresa*, (Padova, Cedam, 2002) 142.

played by the public prosecutor, assisted in his functions by the criminal investigation department (Polizia Giudiziaria, literally 'judicial police'), whereas in the case of administrative offences—as previously noted—the position of the Agenzia delle Entrate and Guardia di Finanza will be of most relevance. Officials belonging to the former of the two authorities are endowed solely with administrative policing powers, whereas members of the Guardia di Finanza occupy a hybrid position: they can in fact take on both an administrative policing function, with the specific investigative powers previously illustrated when addressing financing violations and a criminal investigative function.

The distinction drawn is not solely a formal one, but also possesses important practical implications. Let us consider, for example, that personnel of the Italian revenue service, being in possession solely of administrative policing functions, are qualified simply as public officials. They are no doubt subject to the provisions of Article 361 of the Criminal Code (CC), which sanctions public officials who have omitted to notify or were late to notify the public prosecutor of the commission of a crime prosecutable ex officio, when evidence of the same was acquired in the performance of or as a result of their office. Officials with criminal investigation functions, and hence the members of the Guardia di Finanza, are, by contrast, subject to the stricter obligation envisaged by Article 347 CCP, which requires that they give notification of a crime without delay, providing the public prosecutor with the essential elements related to the fact and any other evidence gathered until that time and specifying the sources of evidence and the activities carried out. News of the offence must be transmitted within 48 hours after carrying out an operation for which a lawyer's presence is required, so that a strict term has been established for such cases. This simple profile appears already emblematic in itself, as it highlights the different developments from an operational standpoint, depending on who is subjectively engaged in assessment activities at the administrative level.[22]

Article 55 CCP further provides that the Polizia Giudiziaria must, also on its own initiative, acquire information about the commission of crimes, prevent any further consequences of such crimes, seek out the perpetrators, take all the necessary steps to secure the sources of evidence and gather any other elements useful for the purpose of applying criminal law. Also following the notification of a crime pursuant to Article 347 CCP, officers of the Polizia Giudiziaria thus have the task of gathering every piece of evidence that may help to reconstruct the facts and identify the guilty party, also looking for objects and traces related to the crime—as well as ensuring that they and the state of the places involved are preserved—seeking out people able to provide insight into circumstances relevant for reconstructing the facts and carrying out other investigative activities.[23]

---

[22] On the actual scope of the obligations in question see below.
[23] For a more detailed analysis of the investigative powers of the Polizia Giudiziaria during the preliminary criminal investigation, see further below.

However, these are exclusive prerogatives of the Polizia Giudiziaria as a criminal investigation unit, and once again differentiate its position considerably from that of investigators in the administrative-tax realm, although the scope of operations of the two authorities can frequently overlap.

In any case, the above-described differences clearly show the advantages connected to the dual attribution of functions and powers to the Guardia di Finanza, while further highlighting the need to define under what circumstances the investigative action must be qualified as administrative, rather than falling within the scope of application of criminal law.

This task is fulfilled by a rule contained in Article 220 of the implementing provisions of the CCP, which constitutes a veritable hinge between the administrative and criminal investigative systems.

Article 220 of the Implementing Provisions of the Code of Criminal Procedure

According to Article 220 of the implementing provisions of the CCP, 'when evidence of a crime emerges in the course of inspection or oversight activities provided for by law or decree, the acts necessary to secure the sources of evidence and gather anything else that may be useful for the application of criminal law shall be carried out in observance of the provisions of the Code'.

Article 220 thus affirms that, upon the emergence of any evidence of a crime, it will be necessary to pass from an activity of an administrative type to another governed by the CCP. In this manner it identifies the moment in which the rules to be applied will change.

If any evidence of a criminal act arises during a tax assessment, the concrete situation will differ very significantly depending on whether the inspectors of the Agenzia delle Entrate or members of the Guardia di Finanza are involved. In the latter case, no particular problems will be posed, since these officials have been assigned a criminal investigative role and will be fully justified in proceeding with their criminal investigation, obviously in observance of the relevant provisions of the CCP.[24] In contrast, if the administrative inspection activities have been carried out by the tax authorities, the provision of Article 220 seems to preclude any possibility for these officials to proceed further with their activities, as they are endowed solely with administrative competence. Upon the emergence of any evidence of a crime, therefore, they should stop any ongoing investigative activity and

---

[24] *cf* Ministry of Justice Circular No 34/638 of 18 October 1989, which reiterates that officials other than those belonging to the Polizia Giudiziaria cannot continue inspection activities applying the rules of criminal procedure.

give notice accordingly, as prescribed by the previously cited Article 361 CC and Article 331 CCP.[25]

Notwithstanding that officials of the Italian revenue service are not authorised to carry out any investigative acts governed by the CCP, some have criticised the policy just illustrated, whereby said officials should necessarily interrupt every activity and limit themselves to reporting any elements of a criminal nature to the competent authority. Such a solution, they argue, is in 'open contradiction with the decided preference our procedural law shows for the parallel nature of the different procedures',[26] which finds concrete expression in the double-track principle discussed earlier.

Therefore, an interpretation of Article 220 of the implementing provisions of the CCP that is faithful to this principle must lead to the conclusion that the emergence of any evidence of a criminal act, even if it gives rise to an obligation to abide by the provisions of the CCP, does not preclude the continuation of the administrative investigation in the forms consistent with this type of investigation. Further confirmation of this second approach is given by the fact that in the provisions previously in force, which did not yet envisage a clear separation between the criminal and administrative spheres, it was expressly acknowledged that the administrative authorities could continue their inspection activities by virtue of their powers, even after evidence of a criminal offence had emerged.[27]

Finally, it is worth noting that the guarantees of the CCP must necessarily be applied irrespective of whether the suspect was identified; the discovery of objective evidence pointing to the commission of a crime is sufficient to give rise to the obligation. This approach has found authoritative confirmation in the case law of the Court of Cassation.[28]

The Notion of 'Evidence of Crime' and *Notitia Criminis*

Once we have clarified that the precondition for applying the provisions of the CCP is the emergence of evidence of a crime, we must attempt to offer a definition

---

[25] *cf* P Dell'Anno, 'Il processo verbale di constatazione degli illeciti tributari e il nuovo processo penale' (1990) *Cassazione penale* 439. For a more complete reconstruction of the various positions on this point, see R Orlandi, *Atti e informazioni dell'autorità amministrativa nel processo penale* (Milano, Giuffrè, 1992) 154.

[26] ibid, 155.

[27] *cf* Criminal Court of Cassation Division III, 7 June 1988, in (1990) *Cassazione penale*, 1990, 1383.

[28] Criminal Court of Cassation, Joint Divisions, 28 November 2001, No 45477, with a note by G Izzo, 'Le sezioni Unite limitano l'utilizzabilità di dichiarazioni rese in sede ispettiva di vigilanza' (2002) *Il Fisco* 1178. However, some have argued that the suspect needs to be identified in order to apply the provisions of Art 220, *cf* VM Guarnelli, 'Aspetti operativi e processuali dell'attività di p.g. nel nuovo c.p.p' (1991) *Arch n proc pen* 157.

of this notion, given that the legislator has not undertaken to provide an explicit characterisation of the element in question.

Evidence can be approximately defined as an entity 'comprised between the definiteness of the term proof and the uncertainty of suspicion'.[29] Precisely in contrast with the notion of mere suspicion, it has been affirmed that evidence means a 'certain and concrete element, even if not capable of taking on absolute probative value', whilst a suspicion is simply 'a psychological sensation'.[30] The question of the distinction between evidence and suspicion is not merely nominal, since Article 220 of the implementing provisions of the CCP, whose applicability is made conditional upon the emergence of 'evidence' of a crime, would not seem to be applicable against individuals who are simply 'suspected' of committing a crime.[31]

Some have also defined evidence in negative terms as 'all elements [...] based on which the fact that a person is committing or has committed violations of criminal relevance cannot be ruled out with absolute certainty'.[32]

It cannot be denied that, despite the attempts to restrict the meaning of the notion concerned, its actual purport remains characterised by a certain degree of ambiguity. For those working on the field, therefore, identifying with certainty the relevant criteria in light of Article 220 of the implementing provisions of the CCP remains an arduous task. Without a doubt, irrespective of the tentative definitions provided by legal scholars and case law, those vested with considerable investigative powers continue to enjoy a wide margin of discretion. In this regard, it may rightly be hoped that the rights of defence will take precedence in situations of doubt and that the application of the most substantial guarantees of the CCP will be assured accordingly.[33] This is suggested not only by the evident need for guarantees to be provided to the party or parties undergoing investigation, but also in order to make sure that the elements gathered may be used in future proceedings. The penalty for violating the provisions of Article 220 is in fact the impossibility of using evidence for the purpose of criminal proceedings if the rules of procedure have not been duly observed.[34]

A further interpretive issue with very concrete practical implications concerns the relationship between the notion of evidence of a crime and *notitia criminis*, ie, notice of an alleged crime to a prosecutor. The former represents, as we have seen,

---

[29] N Bonetti, 'Gli indizi nel nuovo processo penale' (1989) *L'indice penale* 487.

[30] R Gagliardi, 'Sospetto e indizio. Presunzione e congetture' (1969) *Riv di polizia* 720.

[31] *cf* R Orlandi, *Atti e informazioni*, 38; O Dominioni, *Le parti nel processo penale (profili sistematici e problemi)* (Milano, Giuffrè, 1985) 168; G Frigo, 'Diritto di difesa e atti di polizia giudiziaria nel processo per frodi alimentari' (1969) *Giur. cost.* 2286; G Grevi, 'Attività di polizia giudiziaria degli ispettori di lavoro', (1974) *Ind pen* 244.

[32] N Furin, 'Diritto di difesa, indizi, sospetti e l'art. 220 norme att. c.p.p.' (1999) *Cassazione penale* 2723.

[33] *cf* Circular of the Guardia di Finanza No 1/2008, Vol III, p 161, which underscores the need to abide by criteria of 'particular prudence and the general rule of basing inspection activity on the choices that appear best able to safeguard the overall validity of the activity itself'.

[34] See, among others, Criminal Court of Cassation, Division III, 10 February 2010, No 15372.

a precondition for the application of Article 220 of the implementing provisions of the CCP, whilst the latter gives rise to an obligation for the Polizia Giudiziaria to notify the judicial authorities of the commission of an act constituting a crime. It seems particularly problematic to establish whether the two aspects should always be considered as coinciding, ie, whether the emergence of evidence can always be automatically be associated with notice of a crime,[35] or whether, on the contrary, the *notitia criminis* represents a subsequent, only potential outcome of the investigation, should the overall situation in terms of evidence undergo an appreciable development.

Support for this latter view seems to come from the operational guidelines provided to the Guardia di Finanza, which emphasise the distinction between the time at which evidence of a crime emerges and the time at which notice of the crime is given to a prosecutor: the former is assumed to occur prior to the manifestation of a criminal act delineated in its essential elements.[36] A logical consequence of such an approach is the necessity of applying Article 220 of the implementing provisions of the CCP before reporting the crime to the public prosecutor.

Subsequently, assuming that a crime has been reported, we should note the previously mentioned obligation for agents of the Polizia Giudiziaria to give notice thereof to the public prosecutor 'without delay', pursuant to Article 347(1) CCP, ie, within 48 hours whenever acts were committed that require the presence of the lawyer of the person undergoing investigation. It has been likewise said that all public officials have an analogous obligation to report facts serving to complete a criminal case; according to Article 331 CCP, they must submit a written report of any crimes coming to their knowledge in the course of duty or by virtue of their office.

From the standpoint of investigative dynamics, it is necessary to add that the phrasing used by the legislator as regards the time limit within which the obligation to notify must be fulfilled is vague and cannot be determined with precision. Case law suggests that such activities must be completed within a narrow margin of time, namely, as soon as possible, taking account of the normal requirements of a public office with an average workload.[37]

Crimes Discovered Instantly and Financial Violations

In the case of economic and financial investigations, the scope, not strictly defined, of the notions examined in the previous paragraph implies that in practice there

---

[35] M Bontempelli, *L'accertamento amministrativo nel sistema processuale penale* (Milano, Giuffrè, 2009) 177.
[36] Circular of the Guardia di Finanza No 1/2008, Vol III, p 159.
[37] Criminal Court of Cassation, 15 May 2007, in *CED Cass*, 236501.

may be a considerable time lapse between the time at which the tax police or public officials involved acquire elements demonstrating the criminal nature of the fact in question and the subsequent notice pursuant to Article 331 and Article 347 CCP. The complexity of the investigative assessment in relation to the case concerned entails a complex and elaborate phase of analysis, study and organisation of the data collected during the early stages of the investigation.

One need only consider, moreover, that the concrete qualification of tax offences as criminal or administrative is influenced by the transcending of certain legislatively predetermined thresholds of punishability, which as a rule are difficult to ascertain at the early stages of the investigation. As a result, therefore, it is also necessary to consider in a more specific manner the mechanisms of concretely applying Article 220 of the implementing provisions of the CCP in cases such as the one concerned.

Worth highlighting first of all is that it would be unreasonable to consider every type of illicit financial activity as relevant evidence of a crime pursuant to Article 220 based on its simple abstract potential of constituting a criminally prosecutable behaviour. If such were the case, the administrative investigation would lack any autonomy, since it would be necessary to systematically apply the provisions of the CCP.[38]

The operational guidelines of Guardia di Finanza suggest a certain margin of discretion in this respect, albeit not without recommending a high degree of prudence.[39] They state, in fact, that 'although a generalised obligation to proceed unconditionally according to Article 220 of the implementing provisions of the CCP must be ruled out [...], inspectors will nonetheless have to evaluate, especially in dubious cases, whether it is appropriate to complete the specific reports' required under the CCP.

Very recently, the Court of Cassation once again addressed the problem concerning the application of Article 220 in respect of financial violations.[40] The judges affirmed that if the guarantees provided for by the provision in question were to be applied only after it had been ascertained, normally following a considerable amount of investigative activity, that the thresholds of punishability had been transcended, the result would be a *de facto* abrogation of the legislation in question. In other words, if it were necessary to wait for the overall results of the assessment in order to determine whether the threshold had been transcended, the consequence would be that in relation to tax crimes the procedures established by Article 220 of the implementing provisions of the CCP would never have to be adopted. It follows that the authorities have an obligation to adopt the guaranteed procedures even before assessing the amount of tax evaded whenever it appears

---

[38] *cf* Circular of the Guardia di Finanza no 1/2008, Vol III, p 161.
[39] *cf* Circular of the Guardia di Finanza no 1/2008, Vol III, p 162.
[40] Criminal Court of Cassation, 3 February 2015, No 4919.

plausible, even if not yet verified, that the thresholds of punishability have been exceeded.

As previously mentioned, such an approach would also be advisable in order to safeguard the future usability of the evidence gathered.

To conclude, it seems worth commenting on a recent judgment of the European Court of Human Rights, which served to highlight the problems connected to the co-existence of administrative and criminal investigative systems in relation to the same subject matter.[41] More specifically, the judges stressed the need to guarantee the application of specific provisions which exclude the possibility of imposing penalties on anyone who refuses to supply documents or information within the framework of an administrative assessment whenever there is a possibility that criminal charges may—even only potentially—arise from the assessment. This approach obviously aims to ensure, also outside the scope of criminal proceedings, the applicability of the so-called privilege against self-incrimination in all cases in which the charges against a taxpayer undergoing inspections of an administrative nature may be potentially transformed.[42] The concern displayed in this case emblematically demonstrates the profound relationship existing between the two models of assessment taken into consideration together with the need to adopt appropriate precautionary measures to protect the rights of the person investigated and to guarantee, accordingly, that the evidence collected during the investigation will later be usable. In the Italian system, this task must undoubtedly be fulfilled by an orthodox application and interpretation of Article 220 of the implementing provisions of the CCP.

Dynamics and Tools of Criminal Investigation

Emergence of the Criminal Nature of the Fact

Attention will now be focused on the tools and dynamics more strictly tied to the sphere of criminal investigation, in reference both to cases which were qualified *ab initio* as being of a criminal nature and cases which were originally treated like mere administrative offences, but then revealed elements of a criminal nature, thus resulting in the transition discussed in the previous section.

It should be specified preliminarily that despite the fact that Italian procedural law views the acquisition of information about a crime directly by the public

---

[41] *Chambaz v Switzerland*, App No 11663/04 (ECHR 5 April 2012).

[42] On this point, see again R Orlandi, *Atti e informazioni*, 79. See also N Furin, 'Il principio della libertà dalle autoincriminazioni e la sua rilevanza in materia di infortuni sul lavoro o di malattia professionale' (1998) *Cassazione penale* 1008; A Faberi, 'Sui confini delle garanzie, autodifensive dell'accusato (accertamenti fiscali, richiesta di documenti, rischio di autoincriminazione)' (2013) 2 *Archivio Penale* 6.

prosecutor (Article 330 CCP) as entirely routine, in the realm of economic and financial crime 'autonomous' acquisitions are wholly exceptional from a concrete point of view. In nearly all cases, in fact, the *notitia criminis* is delivered to the public prosecutor by the previously mentioned criminal investigation unit (Polizia Giudiziaria) of the Guardia di Finanza. This authority, by virtue of its structural and functional characteristics and its specialisation, represents the agency of choice when it comes to finding evidence and information concerning criminal acts of an economic and financial nature.

As regards the scope of the aforesaid obligations to notify, reference should be made to what was previously noted in relation to the actual meaning to be attributed to the notion of *notitia criminis*. Here it is important to stress that once notice of a crime has been given as required under Article 347 CCP, the judicial authority will be free to make an autonomous evaluation as to whether the reported fact is criminal in nature. The evaluations made by the Polizia Giudiziaria are not in any way binding for the judiciary. A new phase of analysis of the complex technical data already scrutinised by the Guardia di Finanza may thus take place.

In light of the foregoing considerations, the present scenario is not exactly reassuring. The time it actually takes to determine whether a fact constitutes a criminal offence could in fact be used as a shield to hide behind in order to circumvent procedural rules regarding the maximum duration of preliminary investigations, or in any case to considerably lengthen the investigation phase. This possibility also appears to be favoured by the consolidated orientation which emerges from case law, whereby the judge can in no way challenge the promptness with which the public prosecutor enters the notice of crime or the name of the perpetrator in the register as per Article 335 CCP. The time it normally takes both to ascertain the criminal nature of what is in most cases a complex fact, as well as the identity of the person whom the investigative activity should be directed against, could be deliberately used to justify tardy entries, such as to delay the end of the preliminary investigations.[43]

Relations Between the Tax Police and the Public Prosecutor

In the Italian system, the general principle governing the relations between the main actors in the investigation process is that the public prosecutor has the Polizia Giudiziaria at his disposal. This criminal investigation division is subordinate to investigating magistrates from a functional viewpoint, and must therefore abide by their instructions, despite maintaining a margin of investigative autonomy

---

[43] Criminal Court of Cassation, Joint Divisions, 30 June 2000, in (2000) *Cassazione penale*, 2000, 3259; Court of Cassation, Joint Divisions, 24 September 2009, Lattanzi, (2010) *Giur it*, 1401 ff.; for a legal scholar's view see E Zappulla, 'Notizia di reato', in *Enc Dir*, Annali Vol V (Milano, Giuffrè, 2012) 915.

even following the intervention of the public prosecutor in the investigation (Article 109 of the Constitution, Articles 56 and 327 CCP).[44]

In the case of economic and financial crime, however, the relationship tends to be inverted: if anything, it is the magistrate who is to some extent subject to the determinations and evaluations of the Polizia Giudiziaria.[45]

The reasons for this distortion of the legal framework are substantially to be found in the level of specialised technical competences in the field of economic and tax-related crimes: at least in the majority of cases, the public prosecutor's competences are not comparable to those at the disposal of the Guardia di Finanza. In this regard, it is worth stressing the high degree of technical complexity that normally characterises investigations in the subject matter considered. To this we may add that the Guardia di Finanza has frequently already carried out administrative policing tasks in relation to the facts concerned before their relevance as criminal offences emerged, and this contributes to ensuring that its officers will have thorough acquaintance with the reality in question. Given the aforementioned inversion of the relationship between the public prosecutor and the Polizia Giudiziaria, the judicial authority may not be capable of leading the investigation in a proactive manner. This is true both as far as the investigative options are concerned, and as regards the choices relating to prosecution of the case. Essentially, such fundamental aspects in the evolution of the procedural process are in some respects left up to the initiative of the Polizia Giudiziaria, so that there is sometimes a concrete risk of the prosecutor's office submitting to the opinion of the police.

This is made concretely possible given that—notwithstanding the general principle of the functional dependence of the police on the judiciary—the former maintain a sphere of 'autonomous' action.[46] Moreover, authorisations and guidelines of a vague and generic character issued by the judicial authority are considered legitimate. Though this vagueness cannot be construed as giving a blank cheque, there is nothing to stop the prosecutor from granting broad powers, such as to leave truly vast spaces of manoeuvre to the Polizia Giudiziaria, which will turn to the magistrate solely for the purpose of requesting any authorisations that may be needed to carry out specific acts.[47]

In order to prevent the relations between the public prosecutor and the Polizia Giudiziaria from arriving at an equilibrium that is so remote from the legislative design, public prosecutors' offices should themselves set up internal

---

[44] For an in-depth analysis, see G Della Casa-Voena, 'Soggetti', in Conso-Grevi (eds), *Compendio di procedura penale*, 7th edn (Padova, Cedam, 2014) 88; F Caprioli, 'Indagini preliminari e udienza preliminare' in Conso-Grevi (eds), *Compendio di procedura penale*, 7th edn (Padova, Cedam, 2014) 522.

[45] On this subject see E Amodio, 'I reati economici nel prisma dell'accertamento processuale' (2008) *Riv it dir proc pen.* 1496.

[46] *cf* Article 348(3) CCP, according to which the Polizia Giudiziaria 'carries out, on its own initiative, all other investigative activities serving to ascertain crimes, promptly informing the public prosecutor thereof'.

[47] E Amodio, I reati economici, 1502–1503.

divisions specialised in tax, economic and financial crime, as has actually occurred in some local jurisdictions. In such a case, the judicial authority would be capable of proactively taking the lead of investigations in this highly complex technical field.

Moreover, although the Guardia di Finanza undoubtedly enjoys a somewhat privileged position in respect of wrongdoing occurring in economic and financial contexts, the fact that its criminal investigative arm, the Polizia Giudiziaria, concretely directs the investigations could arouse some concerns as far as ensuring abidance by constitutional principles is concerned. It must not be forgotten, after all, that the executive power stands at the top of the hierarchical structure of the police. The fact that an organisation of such a nature can concretely determine how investigations are conducted and cases are prosecuted is strongly inconsistent with the principle enshrined in Article 112 of the Constitution. This fundamental provision, whilst constitutionalising the principle of mandatory prosecution, simultaneously attributes an exclusive monopoly over the relevant decisions to the public prosecutor.[48]

The Main Tools of Investigation

General Overview

The investigative tools normally employed in investigations into economic and financial crimes do not differ in any specific way from those used in investigations concerning other criminal phenomena. It is nonetheless worth offering some reflections on this topic, taking into account the most important investigative tools.

In the first place, there is a need to maintain a distinction between purely investigative tools and tools for combating crime, such as, for example, *sequestro preventivo* (precautionary seizure), whose ultimate purpose is the confiscation of assets of equivalent value (Article 321(2) CCP, Article 322 *ter* CC). This and other forms of compensation for wrongdoing are on a different level from investigative tools and their principal aim is to allocate and impose penalties.[49] It is nonetheless worth highlighting the particular importance that precautionary seizure, executed precisely, with a view to future confiscation of an equivalent amount, is destined to have, in particular with reference to tax-related offences. The reason lies in the structure of these crimes, in which the profit consists in a negative entity (the savings

---

[48] On this subject see G Spangher, *Trattato di procedura penale*, vol III (Torino, Utet, 2009) 267.

[49] Criminal Court of Cassation, 14 May 2015, in *CED. Cass.*, 260176; Criminal Court of Cassation, 23 October 2014, in *CED Cass*, 260901; Criminal Court of Cassation, 27 October 2006, in (2007) *Cassazione penale* 2884, with a note by C Bonzano, 'Sull'inapplicabilità del sequestro preventivo al profitto che l'ente ha tratto dal reato'.

achieved by the taxpayer by violating tax collection laws), so that 'ordinary' confiscation measures may be difficult to enforce.[50]

Turning our attention, therefore, to the actual means of investigation, it should be pointed out first of all that the transition to a criminal investigation will result in the adoption of tools that are significantly more incisive than the ones typical of an administrative investigation. Accordingly, the legislator will clearly be concerned about providing adequate guarantees so as to balance the needs of the criminal investigation with the protection of the rights of the person being investigated.

More specifically, the most relevant activities are governed by the provisions of Article 244 *et seq* CCP, which firstly address inspection, an activity aimed at ascertaining the traces and other physical effects of the crime. It is normally ordered by the judicial authority, which must state the grounds for the inspection. However, except in the case of personal inspections, when it is a question of carrying out activities designed to preserve traces or things pertinent to the crime (Article 354(1) CCP), or of assessing and recording the same to avoid the risk of them being modified, tampered with or lost pending the intervention of the public prosecutor (Article 354(2) CCP), the Polizia Giudiziaria can act autonomously without the need for any specific authorisation,[51] unlike in the case of access as per the provisions of Presidential Decrees Nos 633/1972 and 600/1973, where it is necessary to obtain at least the authorisation of the director of the office.

A further evidence-gathering tool at the disposal of criminal investigators is the *perquisizione* (search: Article 247 *et seq* CCP). It is mainly aimed at finding material evidence of the crime[52] or things pertinent to the case, where there are justified reasons to believe them to be concealed on the person or in a specific place.[53] Searches as provided for under Article 247 *et seq.* CCP thus have a definitely broader scope than access taking place during administrative assessments. The latter are limited to the premises where the investigated party has his place of business or home, or motor vehicles or boats. A search, by contrast, can generically regard any place where there are reasonable grounds for believing that material evidence of the crime or other things pertinent thereto are to be found. In criminal investigations, moreover, the investigators are also specifically authorised to conduct personal searches (Articles 247 and 249 CCP) as well as performing searches on information systems (Article 247(1) *bis* CCP).

---

[50] S Eusepi, 'Reati tributari, sequestro preventivo e fondo patrimoniale' (2014) *Riv Dir Trib* 347.

[51] The officers of the Polizia Giudiziaria must complete a report detailing the operations carried out, to be made available to the public prosecutor, Art 357(2) letter (e), 4 CCP.

[52] Falling under this heading, pursuant to Art 253(2) CCP, are 'things on which or by means of which the crime was committed, as well as things that constitute the product, profit or price'.

[53] Searches can also be ordered in view of the arrest of the suspect or fugitive, Art 247(1) CCP. It should be noted that the Code of Civil Procedure lays down particular provisions for cases in which a search or inspection must be carried out in the office of a lawyer; on this point see fn 12 above.

Searches, like inspections, must be ordered by the public prosecutor with a warrant stating the reason for the search.[54] However, the CCP provides that the Polizia Giudiziaria can also conduct a search without a warrant issued by the prosecutor if someone is caught in the act of committing a crime or has fled and there are grounds for believing that things or traces pertinent to the crime are concealed on his person or in a certain place and risk being eliminated or lost (Article 352(1) CCP). The Polizia Giudiziaria may conduct a search when executing a warrant of detention or in relation to crimes for which arrest is mandatory as in the case of *flagrante delicto*, that is, when it is necessary to detain a person suspected of a crime and there are particular reasons of urgency (Article 352(2) CCP).

In either case, in observance of constitutional rules, a report of the activities carried out must be sent to the public prosecutor within 48 hours at most; he will then have to validate it within the next 48 hours (Article 352(4) CCP).

As in the case of inspections, it is necessary to report the absence of any prior authorisation issued to the Polizia Giudiziaria in the cases considered. A further element that distinguishes searches from access to premises on the occasion of tax assessments is the interval of time in which the latter may take place. Article 251 CCP specifies a period of between 7 hours and 20 hours within which the activity may be carried out inside a home or in indoor premises adjacent to it, although it further allows the possibility of departing from this rule in cases of urgency, if thus authorised in writing by the judicial authority, or else—in the case of a search on the initiative of the Polizia Giudiziaria—any time when a delay in carrying out the activity could prejudice the result (Article 352(3) CCP).

Searches represent a typical example of a 'surprise' activity, ie, an action whose outcome would be fatally compromised were the suspect to be notified of it in advance. Therefore, the assistance of defence counsel is guaranteed to the extent that the suspect's lawyer, who has the right to be present, but without being notified in advance, is readily available. This aspect further distinguishes the search from its administrative counterpart, where the presence of a lawyer to assist the party concerned is not provided for even as a possibility.

Seizure (Article 253 *et seq* CPP) is a measure closely tied and consequent to the search for evidence just described; indeed, it relates to the same things that were looked for during the search. The prosecutor orders a seizure by means of a warrant stating the grounds, but its concrete execution can be delegated to officials of the Polizia Giudiziaria. If the police discover the *corpus delicti* or things pertinent to it during a search or an urgently conducted assessment they can autonomously seize them (Article 354(2) CCP); they must send a report of the seizure to the public prosecutor within 48 hours, and the latter in turn must validate it or order

---

[54] If it is a matter of looking for specific things, pursuant to Art 248 CCP the activity in question must be preceded by a hand-over request. Whenever the thing being looked for is handed over spontaneously, a search will be conducted only when it is deemed useful for the sake of completeness of the investigation.

the return of the seized property within the following 48 hours (Article 355 CCP). If the seizure is not validated within the time limit established by law, it will lose all effect.

The CCP also lays down rules for specific types of seizure, which differ either in terms of their object (eg correspondence), or because of the need to balance the requirements of the investigation with those protected by legislation on professional, official or state secrets.[55] Here it should be pointed out that, notwithstanding the provisions of Article 52(7) of Presidential Decree No 633/1972, seizures need not be limited to cases in which it is impossible to reproduce the relevant documents, nor do there exist any particular restrictions against seizing the accounting records or registers that must be mandatorily kept by those engaging in business activities.

One investigative tool that deserves special consideration, given its particular significance, is the seizure of digital evidence. A number of authors[56] have in fact emphasised the importance that computer data have taken on today, not only in the framework of investigations into crimes in which the suspect conduct targets information systems, but also in relation to commonly occurring cases, often regarding economic and financial crime phenomena.[57]

An attempt to overcome the challenges and problems posed by digital evidence—due to its wholly peculiar nature—may be seen in the approach adopted with Law No 48/2008,[58] which sought to broaden the scope of provisions related to inspections, searches and seizures to include the search for and gathering of digital evidence. However, the legislation in question has left some fundamental questions unresolved.

One problem of great relevance lies in the fact that the authenticity of computer data directly depends, to a much larger extent than in the case of traditional evidence, on the methods and techniques used to search for and seize them.[59] Given the intangible nature of digital information, the knowledge it provides may be considered reliable only when it has been acquired in strict observance of the best practices of computer forensic science. The Italian legislator limits himself to making a generic reference to the latter, well aware that the instrument of

---

[55] For the rules governing such cases, see Art 254 *et seq* CCP.

[56] R Orlandi, 'Questioni attuali in tema di processo penale e informatica' (2009) *Riv Dir proc* 129; E Amodio, 'I reati economici', 1496; L Lupària, 'Processo penale e scienza informatica: anatomia di una trasformazione epocale', in Lupària-Ziccardi (eds), *Investigazione penale e tecnologia informatica* (Milano, Giuffrè, 2007) 131.

[57] See, in particular, E Amodio, 'I reati economici', 1496, according to which, in particular, computer-related investigations today represent the '*preferred* tool' in investigations into economic crime, especially, but not only, when a business is involved.

[58] *cf* Vitale, 'La nuova disciplina delle ispezioni e delle perquisizioni in ambiente informatico o telematico' (2008) *Dir. internet* 506; A Macrillò, 'Le nuove disposizioni in tema di sequestro probatorio e di custodia ed assicurazione dei dati informatici' (2008) *Dir internet* 511.

[59] E Lorenzetto, 'Utilizzabilità di dati informatici incorporati su computer in sequestro: dal contenitore al contenuto, passando per la copia' (2010) *Cassazione penale* 1522.

legislation is too rigid to be adapted to a science that is constantly developing and evolving.

However, case law reveals an inclination to recognise that evidence gathered in violation of these standards can nonetheless be admissible, though the probative value of such evidence may be reduced.[60] In the absence of any specific provision of law, legal scholars have arrived at analogous conclusions.[61]

Precisely because inobservance of the above-mentioned best practices is not subject to a penalty of inadmissibility of the digital evidence gathered, it seems extremely important to ensure that the parties concerned can effectively participate at the time the evidence itself is acquired. The preferable solution seems to be to guarantee the right to have a lawyer present during technical operations on electronic media, albeit without the right to advance notice,[62] while ensuring the protection of the right to a fair hearing. To this end, it is essential that the operations carried out be fully documented using audio-visual means so as to provide the defence with tools for carrying out a subsequent verification.

Lastly, it is worth underlining the difficulties encountered when it comes to fitting some investigative actions into the legal paradigm of investigative means when items of digital evidence are involved. This category includes, in particular, emails: insofar as they constitute a form of communication, they could become an element of evidence following an interception of electronic communication flows (Article 266 *bis* CCP), or simply an object of seizure.

The *discrimen* identified in this respect, according to a distinction already partly drawn in reference to access and inspections under administrative procedures, regards the question as to whether the intended recipient of the email is acquainted with its content.

If the email is in transit, or, rather, was delivered to the recipient's address but the latter did not open it, the strictest rules governing interception will apply, namely, seizure on the premises of the provider of IT or Internet services, in the event that the email is temporarily stored there (Articles 254 and 254 *bis* CCP).[63] If, on the other hand, the email recipient has already viewed the contents, the procedural instrument that can be used to acquire it is seizure pursuant to Article 253 CCP. The problem arising from the aforementioned hermeneutic reconstruction is the difficulty that may be associated with the apparently simple task of establishing whether the email was opened or not, especially when particular reading protocols were used.[64]

---

[60] Court of Bologna, 2 July 2005, (2006) *Dir internet* 2006, 153.

[61] M Daniele, 'Indagini informatiche lesive della riservatezza. Verso un'inutilizzabilità convenzionale?' (2013) *Cassazione penale* 367–368; M Daniele, 'La prova digitale nel processo penale' (2011) *Dir pen e proc* 294–295; Braghò, 'L'ispezione e la perquisizione di dati, informazioni e programmi informatici', in L Lupària (ed), *Sistema penale e criminalità informatica* (Milano, Giuffrè, 2009) 190.

[62] M Daniele, 'La prova digitale', 298.

[63] R Orlandi, 'Questioni attuali', 134.

[64] What comes to mind, in this respect, is web mail services enabling users to view e-mail content without leaving any trace, L Marafioti, 'Digital evidence e processo penale' (2011) *Cassazione penale* 4509 ff; R Orlandi, 'Questioni attuali' 135.

Finally, of undoubted importance from an investigative standpoint are the activities conducted for the purpose of obtaining statements from the person undergoing investigation or others who are more or less 'third parties' in the proceedings; once again, the rules laid down in criminal law are much more detailed than those generally outlined in Article 51(2) 2 of Presidential Decree No 633/1972 and Article 31(2) of Presidential Decree No 600/1973.

As far as the investigations of the public prosecutor are concerned, a central role is played by the interrogation of the person undergoing investigation, which takes place following an invitation to appear, with the right to have a lawyer present (see, in particular, Articles 364, 375 and 376 CCP). The provisions in question provide for a whole series of guarantees, consisting, specifically, in warnings that the statements given could be used against him, the option of exercising the right of silence, and the fact of taking on a role as witness upon making statements concerning the responsibilities of others.[65] In the absence of such warnings, the statements given may be deemed inadmissible as evidence (Article 64 CCP). Another provision of fundamental importance requires that formal charges be set forth in a clear, precise manner (Article 65(1) CCP).

The public prosecutor can thus take the statements of persons informed about the facts (Article 362), and thus not only of individuals engaging in business, trades or professions, as is the case in administrative proceedings. Such persons are obligated to respond according to the truth, and are subject to criminal penalties (Article 371 *bis* CC). Special provisions apply for those who are suspects or defendants in connected proceedings; they are principally aimed at protecting the accused from the risk of self-incrimination which may arise when they give statements concerning the responsibility of others (Article 363 CCP).

The Polizia Giudiziaria can also acquire information from the suspect in situations other than those in which the public prosecutor delegates them to conduct interrogations (Article 370(1) CCP). The rules set forth in Article 350 CCP envisage three different cases: the first four paragraphs provide that the Polizia Giudiziaria can obtain summary information from the suspect, who is free, and whose lawyer must be present, in observance of Article 64, but without the need to formally state the charges resulting from the investigations conducted. Paragraph (5) of the aforementioned article allows the police to acquire information about the place and immediately after the fact;[66] the following paragraph prohibits any documentation and use thereof other than that of facilitating the investigations in the period immediately following the crime. Finally, pursuant to Article 350(7) CCP, the Polizia Giudiziaria can receive the spontaneous statements of the suspect.[67]

---

[65] Notwithstanding the incompatibilities provided for under Art 197 CCP and the guarantees provided under Art 197 *bis* CCP.

[66] Even though the suspect is *in vinculis* whether or not his lawyer is present.

[67] The presence of a lawyer is not obligatory in this case.

2

Investigating Economic Crimes in Spain: An Attempt to Find Order in Chaos[1]

PROF DR ADÁN NIETO MARTÍN
Professor of Criminal Law
University of Castilla La Mancha

DR JUAN JOSÉ GONZÁLEZ LÓPEZ
PhD in Law
Attorney in the Regional Government of Castilla León

Opening Remarks

No matter how hard one tries it is often difficult to explain to somebody, in a somewhat understandable way, the Spanish approach to the investigation of economic crimes. If we had to explain the Spanish model of economic crime investigation to a foreign colleague, we would probably be discouraged trying to convey the actual role of the judge, the police, the public prosecutor, or of the various government agencies that might get involved. We can always stay within the comfort zone provided by the 'law in books,' ie simply putting forward the model provided in the Spanish Code of Criminal Procedure (hereinafter, LECr). However, this amounts to speaking of words whilst moving away from reality; it would amount to *magic legalism*. In broad terms, the model contained in the LECr, which revolves around the investigating judge, has been left for very specific cases or substantially modified in the 'law in action' sphere. Aside from other problems, this model was designed for a very different kind of criminality. In other words, it was for criminal

[1] This paper is framed within the research project 'Relationships between the national judicial authorities and the investigative agencies in the view of the EPPO: operational models and best practices in fight against EU frauds'. This is why there are certain specifications which might be unnecessary for most Spanish readers.

offences which were less complex and much easier to investigate.[2] Indeed, there have been legislative amendments, which do not fit in the original model, that have increasingly modified the Code of Criminal Procedure, subsequently blurring the original model.

This paper contends that there is not a single model or approach to economic crime investigation in Spain. Prior to the trial stage of economic offences, the investigation thereof is conducted on the basis of various investigation models, which have been implemented in practice through something similar to customary law or professional routines. All actors involved acknowledge and accept, to some degree, these customary elements.

Both the people, the singular actors and the bodies involved play a very prominent role in shaping these aspects of economic crime investigation. For instance, the role of singular actors involved in the investigation is essential when it comes to enabling cooperation between the actors taking part in the investigation (judges, police officers, public prosecutors, or government agencies). The development of the investigation largely depends on how a given police officer and the public prosecutor get along. Government bodies or agencies involved also play a significant role regarding the model to be followed. Things change depending on whether the investigation is carried out from the outset by police officers or by the Guardia Civil, who is highly specialised in the investigation of economic offences, or by the Spanish Prosecutor's Office against Corruption. Along these lines, the Spanish Tax Agency plays a very prominent role in the investigation of tax offences, but this does not normally happen in other investigations. In sum, the investigation roadmap varies depending on the actors and agencies taking part in it.

The purpose of this paper is to understand and give an account of the complex scenario of the investigation of economic crimes, having in mind three main objectives. First, to provide an overview of the various models and subsequently to discuss the advantages and disadvantages thereof. It is necessary to be fully aware of the reality in view of the urgent and never-ending reform of the criminal procedure. It has been taken for granted that the best model entails a public prosecutor leading the investigation whilst a judge plays a more rights-based role.[3] However, as will be shown below, after examining the complexity of the investigation stage, this is only a possibility.[4] In fact, comparative law shows that there is not a single

---

[2] On the original model provided by the LECr, EG Orbaneja, *Comentarios a la Ley de Enjuiciamiento Criminal* (Barcelona, Bosch, 1947) *passim*, and M Pastor López, *El proceso de persecución: análisis del concepto, naturaleza y específicas funciones de la instrucción criminal* (Valencia, Universidad de Valencia: Secretariado de Publicaciones, 1979) *passim*.

[3] In light of the large bibliography on the debate on the lead of the investigation by the Public Prosecutor's Office, we must highlight, in order to summarise the view of many reputed scholars, the following work: E Bacigalupo, V Gimeno Sendra, V Moreno Catena and E Torres-Dulce Lifante, *La posición del fiscal en la investigación penal: la reforma de la Ley de Enjuiciamiento Criminal* (Cisur Menor Navarra, Thomson/Aranzadi, 2005) *passim*.

[4] As pointed out in JA Martín Pallín, '¿Tiene futuro el juez de instrucción?' (2001) 5 *Anuario de la Facultad de Derecho de la Universidad Autónoma de Madrid* 158, 'beyond outlines and abstract designs is day to day reality, which shows in a very expressive and realistic manner that there are not two

approach to the investigation of economic crimes. In countries similar to Spain, government agencies play a major role (which differs from country to country yet it is a very significant role in all cases) concerning the initiation or the lead of the investigation.[5] It is a mistaken point of departure to design the criminal procedure only counting on three actors: judges, police officers, and public prosecutors.

The second objective has a supranational nature. The European Public Prosecutor's Office seems close, and thus it is necessary to come up with a way to link together and fit supranational investigations in this convoluted mosaic of actors and professional routines.[6] If the conclusion to be drawn from this paper is that there are diverse investigation models depending on the actors involved, the establishment of the European Public Prosecutor's Office will give rise to its own investigation approach, with its own practices, routines and synergies. However, it must be noted that it will take some time until this supranational sub-system fits into the current frame and shapes its own tailored procedure.

Finally, there is a transversal objective focused on the application of the right of defence within the various models. As will be discussed below, adopting one model or the other has a very significant impact on rights such as those related to the *nemo tenetur* principle[7] or on the possibility to exercise the rights of defence right from the initiation of the investigation, pursuant to Article 118 LECr.[8]

This work will follow this outline: firstly we will discuss the actors involved in the investigation of economic crimes, subsequently providing a brief overview

---

identical judicial investigations. Reality evidences that each judicial investigation has very distinct features. Also, it is different to investigate a theft than a corporate crime or environmental offences, tax frauds or other complex crimes. The legislator has to be aware of this prior to getting entangled in amendments'.

[5] See P Beauvais and Y Muller, in Fauvarque and B Cosson (eds), *Les procédures répressives contre la grand délinquance économique et financière, en Le Droit Comparé au XXI Siècle. Enjeux et Défis. Journées Internationales de la Société de Législation Comparé 8–9 Avril 2015*, (Paris, Société de Législation Comparée, 2015) 215. For instance, in Germany, the tax crime investigation is conducted mainly by tax authorities (§§ 339(1), 386(2) Tax Order and § 161 StPO, unless the facts amount to additional tax crimes. The same thing happens regarding customs offences, where the investigation can be carried out by the Customs Agency, which is particularly important for custom frauds, which affect the financial interests of the EU.

[6] *cf* mainly regarding the way to structure the relationships between the EU Public Prosecutor and the national prosecutors, A Nieto Martin, M Wade, M Muñoz De Morales, 'Federal Criminal Law and the European Public Prosecutor's Office' in K Ligeti (ed), *Toward a Prosecutor for the European Union: A Comparative Analysis*, Vol I (Oxford, Hart, 2013) 781; on the establishment of the EPPO, see also the reflections on the matter by the working group: *European Criminal Policy Initiative* in Asp (ed), *The European Public Prosecutor's Office. Legal and Criminal Policy Perspectives*, (Stockholm University, 2015).

[7] A Blumenberg and A Nieto Martin, 'Nemo tenetur se ipsum accusare en el Derecho penal económico europeo' in A Nieto Martín and Diez Picazo (eds), *Los derechos fundamentales en el derecho penal europeo* (Madrid, Civitas, 2010) 397. A posterior version of this work was published in C Fall, E Müller, H Satzger, S Swoboda, *Ein menschengerechtes Strafrecht als Lebensaufgabe. Festschrift für Werner Beulke zum 70 Gegurstag* (Heidelberg, CF Müller, 2015).

[8] Actually, this provision, which was amended in the 1970s, is the first major amendment to the inquisitive system provided in the LECr, where the potential suspect only became an actual suspect after the prosecution order was issued.

of each of the actors' roles in accordance with the provisions of the LECr. In the second part of the paper we will try to make some sense of the mosaic of actors and practices, trying to clarify the various approaches to crime investigation depending on the criminal offence and on the body or agency leading the investigation.

The Actors

As opposed to other legal systems, the Spanish legal system does not provide for any specific noteworthy procedural requirements regarding the investigation of economic crimes.[9] Theoretically, the investigation model applicable to a theft and a complex market abuse is the same. The existing particularities of economic crimes have led to the establishment of various specialised bodies within the Public Prosecutor's Office and the law enforcement agencies. In addition, the Spanish National High Court (Audiencia Nacional), although it is not a specialised body, undertakes the investigation of the most significant cases.

Investigation Judges

Under the LECr, investigation judges are responsible for 'investigating' the case: they carry out the necessary investigative measures to inquire about the crimes and to record the commission of crimes and the guilt of criminals (Article 299 LECr). Investigating judges are scattered all across the country. They belong to 'judicial districts'. A political district (in Spain they are called provinces), may include several judicial districts. A court has jurisdiction over a case based on the place where the crime was committed, ie in Spain the principle of territoriality applies.

Notwithstanding the foregoing, as to economic offences this general rule has two significant exceptions. First, jurisdiction rules change when the investigated person holds public office and is granted a special status, pursuant to which only higher courts have jurisdiction to hear his or her case (in Spanish: *aforamiento*, and the person granted this special status is designated as *aforado*). According to recent research, there are more than 20,000 *aforados* in Spain, out of which 3,000 are politicians holding office.[10] For the purposes of this work, it must be noted that the largest group of *aforados* is made up of politicians holding office, ie the President, Ministers and Members of Parliament, along with senior civil servants holding national, regional, or local governmental offices. When they hold office

---

[9] On the investigation of economic offences, see A Gutiérrez Zarza, *Investigación y enjuiciamiento de los delitos económicos* (Madrid, Colex, 2000) *passim*, and E Solaz Solaz, *La instrucción de los delitos económicos y contra la Hacienda Pública* (Madrid, Consejo General del Poder Judicial, 2005) *passim*.

[10] JL Gòmez Colomer and I Esparza, *Tratado jurisprudencial de aforamientos procesales* (Valencia, Tirant lo Blanch, 2009).

at a national level, the Supreme Court has jurisdiction over the cases involving these aforados. However, if a regional officeholder with this special status was to be judged, Regional High Courts (Tribunales Superiores de Justicia) would have jurisdiction to hear the case. In both cases the competent court shall appoint an 'investigating judge' to investigate the case, who will subsequently not be in court at the trial stage. This exception must be highlighted, since large-scale corruption cases involving the national or regional government (or national or regional Members of Parliament) are investigated by these investigating judges.

The National High Court (Audiencia Nacional, and hereinafter AN) amounts to the second exception, which is much better known. The National High Court is a kind of superior court which regarding economic crimes has jurisdiction to hear cross-regional economic offences; either involving injured parties who are scattered across the country or because the case affects the national economy or business transactions at a national level. The jurisdiction of the High Court is governed by a very vague legal framework, regarding both the crimes under its competence as well as the criteria for jurisdiction concerning these crimes. Supreme Court's case law has not been able to shed light on this issue.[11] Thus, the National High Court's jurisdiction often depends on the interest of any of the parties in widening the scope of the case in order to 'take it out' of the provincial courts, or on the interest of the provincial courts themselves to investigate and prosecute the offence. When the case falls within the jurisdiction of the National High Court (AN), it must be investigated by the six Central Investigating Courts (Juzgados Centrales de Instrucción), with national jurisdiction, based in Madrid.

For the purposes of this paper, it must be underlined that this small number of investigating judges—six—must investigate the most complex cases in Spain. These are not only economic crimes or corruption cases, but also drug-trafficking, organised crime or terrorism are matters within their competence. Indeed, the AN has jurisdiction to hear all crimes committed outside Spain falling under its competence pursuant to the principles of universal jurisdiction, active personality or protection of interests. But, of course, the question that arises is: how can these 'super investigating judges' personally lead several extremely complex investigations at a time as provided by the LECr?

Public Prosecutors

Pursuant to Article 124(1) of the Spanish Constitution (hereinafter, CE), public prosecutors are entrusted with 'promoting the action of justice in defence of legality'. Moreover, in the context of criminal investigation, they are legally entrusted with a twofold duty: in connection with the crime, they must initiate

---

[11] In this regard, E Velasco Núñez, 'La competencia de la Audiencia Nacional en delitos económicos' (2012) 7932 *Diario La Ley*.

criminal proceedings and they must bring a civil action where appropriate; additionally, they must require the relevant judicial authority to adopt as many precautionary measures and to order measures of inquiry, in order to develop a clear record of the facts.[12] There is a public prosecutor's office in each province, but district public prosecutor's offices can be created within each judicial district.[13]

Within the frame of the most widely applied criminal procedure, ie the summary criminal procedure, the public prosecutor may conduct a 'preliminary investigation' (under Article 773(2) LECr). Carrying out such preliminary investigation has also become a common practice within the ordinary criminal procedure.[14] In other words, public prosecutors may conduct a prior investigation aside from the investigating judge. They are entitled to carry out investigative measures insofar as these investigative tasks do not affect fundamental rights, with some exceptions.[15] However, it must be noted that it is not mandatory for the public prosecutor to carry out these investigative measures. Additionally, as will be seen below, as soon as the investigating judge comes in, the public prosecutor is no longer allowed to conduct the abovementioned investigation. From then onwards, his or her investigative tasks are limited to cooperation and promotion.

There is no data on when this preliminary investigation is conducted nor on when the investigating judge starts to investigate the crime right away. In any event, and in order to ascertain the possibility that public prosecutors have to perform investigative tasks, it must be taken into account that public prosecutors in Spain have few resources at their disposal, although the number of public prosecutors is similar to that of other European countries.[16]

In addition to the said provincial public prosecutor's offices (one in each province), there are a series of specialised public prosecutor's offices with a national scope. For the purpose of this paper, the Public Prosecutor's Office against Corruption and Organised Crime (Fiscalía contra la Corrupción y la Criminalidad Organisada), established in 1995 is particularly remarkable.[17] It prosecutes particularly large-scale economic offences. It is based in Madrid and it has delegated

---

[12] Art 3, paras 4 and 5, of Act 50/1981, of 30 December, on the Statute of the Public Prosecutor's Office (hereinafter, EOMF).

[13] Art 18(3) EOMF.

[14] Fiscalía General del Estado (Public Prosecutor's Office), Circular 4/2013, on investigative measures, 4.

[15] On preliminary investigation, see JM Isaguirre Guerricagoitia, *La investigación preliminar del Ministerio Fiscal. La intervención de las partes en la misma*, (Navarra, Aranzadi, Elcano, 2001) *passim*. Regarding the investigative measures that may be adopted by the public prosecutor in the context of the preliminary investigation, see Fiscalía General del Estado (Public Prosecutor's Office), Circular 4/2013, on investigative measures, *passim*, and M Aguilera Morales, *Las diligencias de investigación fiscal* (Navarra, Thomson/Aranzadi Cisur Menor, 2015) 141.

[16] On other EU countries: Italy: 1900 prosecutors (in 2012), 3.2 x 100,000 people; Portugal: 1698 (in 2014): 14.9 x 100,000 people; France: 1938 (in 2015) 2.9 x 100,000 people; Germany: 5,245 (in 2012) 6.5 x 100,000 people; Spain: 2,473 (February 2015) 5.3 x 100,000 people. *cf* J Gimeno Bevià, *El Ministerio Fiscal director de la investigación criminal. Un análisis teórico y práctico de la situación en los países de nuestro entorno*, Observatorio de Justicia Civil y Penal, Europeo e Internacional UCLM (forthcoming).

[17] Arts 12(h) and 19(4) EOMF.

prosecutors in the most important Spanish provinces. These delegated prosecutors are 'double headed', since they report to the provincial prosecutor's office as well as to the Public Prosecutor's Office against Corruption.

As with the AN, the competences of the Prosecutor's Office against Corruption are not provided for very thoroughly. On the one hand, as stated above, they are responsible for a long list of crimes. On the other, any offence that falls under their competence must have a 'large scale'. This large-scale nature must be determined by the State Prosecutor General. It is worth noting that the State Prosecutor General is appointed on the motion of the Government. Although it performs its duties impartially and objectively, since the 'Caesar's wife' doctrine, his impartiality could be called into question. The decision of entrusting the Prosecutor's Office against Corruption with the case is not open to appeal.

Judicial Police

Pursuant to Article 547 of Organic Act 6/1985 of 1 July on the Judiciary (hereinafter, LOPJ) and under Article 126 of the Spanish Constitution (CE), the judicial police are entrusted with *assisting* investigating judges and prosecutors (when they perform investigative tasks) in their functions of investigating crimes and finding and seizing the criminal. The judicial police force is made up of police officers (regardless of whether they are national, regional or local police officers), but also of civil servants from other government agencies, such as tax authority officials from the Revenue and Customs Agency.[18]

The assisting duties entrusted to the judicial police are framed within a hierarchical relationship. The judicial police report to the judicial branch and thus judges and prosecutors can give instructions to the judicial police. Far from being guidelines, these instructions must be precise in terms of 'content' and 'circumstances'. Both judges and public prosecutors control all of the investigation activities performed by the judicial police, and in the event of insubordination or non-compliance, they are entitled to initiate disciplinary proceedings. In other words, in accordance with the investigation model of the 'law in books', judicial police officers are simply responsible for assisting judges and prosecutors. Their scope for investigation is very narrow. However, it must be stated that, unlike in other legal systems, the Spanish judicial police do not specifically report to a particular court or prosecutor's office.[19] Although there are a few exceptions (for instance, the Public Prosecutor's office against corruption), judicial police units must be available to any judge that may require their assistance.

---

[18] On judicial police, R Martínez Pérez, *Policía Judicial y Constitución* (Navarra, Aranzadi, 2001) *passim*, and P Martín García, *La actuación de la policía judicial en el proceso penal* (Madrid, Marcial Pons, 2006) *passim*. Particularly concerning the Revenue and Customs Agency, see, A Fernández Vázquez, 'El Servicio de Vigilancia Aduanera: problemática sobre su consideración como policía judicial' (2009) 2088 *Boletín del Ministerio de Justicia* 1838–1853.

[19] Arts 23 *et seq* of Royal Decree 769/1987, of 19 June, regulating Judicial Police.

In order to account for the organisation of judicial police in Spain we can resort to the notions of 'double headed' and 'single headed.' There are police officers that are permanently performing judicial police duties. These are police servants that report at all times to judges and prosecutors. These police officers, although they act under the instructions of judges, report to the Ministry of the Interior. In fact, the Ministry of the Interior determines the number of these 'permanent' judicial police officers, following consultations with the General Council of the Judiciary (Consejo General del Poder Judicial) and the General Prosecutor's Office (Fiscalía General del Estado).

In addition to these 'single headed' judicial police officers, there are some 'double headed' ones. First, if an investigating judge deems insufficient the number of judicial police officers available thereto, he or she is entitled to request more officers (Article 29 of Royal Decree 769/1987). Accordingly, if a judge requires assistance, certain police officers who are not performing judicial police duties at all times may become available to the judge to carry out such duties. However, for the purposes of this paper, the most remarkable 'double headed' civil servants are the Revenue and Customs Agency members. In tax fraud cases, these officials may perform judicial police duties. Any judge or prosecutor may ask for their assistance, and, just like the judicial police, they may perform prevention duties.[20]

Concerning the investigation of economic crimes in Spain in the last few years, one of the most significant factors is the establishment of highly specialised police units in the investigation of economic criminal offences. These specialised units are the following: Judicial Police Commission of the National Police Department (Comisaría General de Policía Judicial del Cuerpo Nacional de Policía), the Fiscal and Economic Crime Unit (Unidad Central de Delincuencia Económica y Fiscal (UDEF)), which is also made up of sub-units (brigades) specialised in the prosecution of certain crimes—among others, money laundering, corruption, asset recovery, or currency counterfeiting. For instance, there is a Fiscal and Economic Crime Brigade (Brigada Central de Delincuencia Económica y Fiscal) responsible for the investigation of tax crimes, crimes against social security, and more importantly, offences against the EU's financial interests. There is a special unit within the abovementioned UDEF performing judicial police duties for the Prosecutor's Office against Corruption on a permanent basis.[21] The second specialised police unit belongs to the Guardia Civil. Its Central Operating Unit is headquartered in Madrid, and it is entrusted with the investigation and prosecution of organised crime and economic and international offences. This unit takes care, among other crimes, of money laundering or the criminal offence of smuggling.

The question of who acts (either one specialised unit or the other) is somewhat hazardous; it depends on who is the first to receive the notitia criminis, ie, on

---

[20] Unanimous non-jurisdictional agreement of the Second Chamber of the Supreme Court adopted on 14 November 2003. Opposed to the consideration of the Customs Surveillance Service as judicial police: O Morales García and V Ferreres Comella, 'El Servicio de Vigilancia Aduanera como policía judicial: la dimensión constitucional del problema' (2015) 8666 *Diario La Ley* 16 December, 1–18.

[21] Art 23 of Royal Decree 769/1987.

who is the first to gain knowledge of the commission of the crime. If the judge or the prosecutor led the investigation from the beginning, they would actually have room for choosing the unit that is going to perform judicial police duties.

Government Agencies and the Duty to Cooperate of Civil Servants

Except in a few other cases, which do not fall within the scope of this paper (environmental agents, for instance), the only civil servants aside from police officers that can act as judicial police are the tax authority officials mentioned above. The remaining civil servants have the duty to assist in the investigation. It must be pointed out that they must report any facts that could amount to criminal offences. This obligation to report possible criminal activity is more stringent (Article 262 LECr) than the reporting obligation incumbent upon citizens in general (Article 259 LECr). Accordingly, penalties applicable to civil servants who fail to report criminal activity of which they gain knowledge by virtue of their office, are more serious than those that may be imposed on individuals.

The National Court of Auditors (Tribunal de Cuentas), alongside equivalent regional bodies, plays a very prominent role as to the investigation of economic crimes. It is entrusted with the economic and financial monitoring of the public sector. The duty entrusted thereto places this body in a unique position to find out about crimes. The particularity of the National Court of Auditors lies in the fact that it has a prosecutor on staff, which probably helps to detect crimes and to promptly 'report and pass on the facts of the case' to the competent authorities.[22] This does not necessarily mean that criminal activity detected in the Court of Auditors is subsequently investigated in an efficient manner.

The duty to report incumbent upon public authorities entails the duty to 'report and pass on the facts of the case.' Pursuant to this rule, civil servants with competence to impose administrative penalties must stop the penalty procedure and report the facts to the public prosecutor immediately. This rule is contained in many administrative law provisions, and it is a central tool to comply with the *ne bis in idem* principle applicable to criminal and administrative sanctions. Additionally, the application of this rule must be governed by the principle of immediacy in the criminal procedure. After the facts have been passed on by the government agencies involved, it will be within the competence of the prosecutor to decide whether or not to move forward with the investigation, for instance, by carrying out preliminary investigative tasks.

It is also of interest to tackle the Commission for the Prevention of Money Laundering and Monetary Offences (Comisión de Prevención del Blanqueo de Capitales e Infracciones Monetarias). This body, which reports to the State

---

[22] Art 16 of Act 7/1988, of 5 April, on the functioning of the National Court of Auditors.

Secretariat for Economic Affairs,[23] is halfway between the judicial assistance duties entrusted to judicial police, and those reporting and cooperation obligations incumbent upon public authorities as a whole. Its supporting agency is the Commission's Executive Service (SEPBLAC), which must be the addressee of any suspicions to be reported by those to whom money laundering rules and regulations apply. Among others, the Commission is entrusted with the following duties: to 'cooperate with law enforcement authorities' and to 'ensure prompt assistance' concerning money laundering and terrorism financing. The SEPBLAC carries out police intelligence functions on the basis of the information provided thereto. It must submit reports to judges, prosecutors and the judicial police. The fact that judicial police are listed right by judges and prosecutors could be a miswording of the law, which might evidence that, against the original model provided by the LECr, judicial police officers actually perform their own autonomous investigation duties.

The Investigation Model According to the LECR

Aside from the 'inquisitorial vs adversarial' controversy concerning the Code of Criminal Procedure's approach, the truth is that the Spanish LECr has a very straightforward model as to the allocation of competences amongst the actors involved. It goes without saying that the main role is played by the investigating judge. Public prosecutors have a secondary yet prominent role, and there are various supporting actors: judicial police officers or government agencies. The judge leads the investigation, and has exclusive competence to adopt any measures directly affecting fundamental rights. At first the prosecutor has some room to carry out investigative tasks. However, once the trial stage begins, public prosecutors must help judges in moving forward with the procedure. Judicial police assist under the direction of judges and prosecutors. A more in-depth analysis of this competence allocation scenario is provided below. We examine how these actors interact in three different situations that may appear in the context of an investigation.

Initiation by Judicial Police

As has been stated, judicial police officers are led by the investigating judge or the public prosecutor. Nonetheless, the LECr allows the judicial police to carry out very specific investigative acts. This can be due to two reasons. On the one hand,

---

[23] Arts 44–48 of Act 10/2010, of 28 April, on the Prevention of Money Laundering and Terrorism Financing.

to the fact that police officers might gain knowledge of the facts before the judge or the prosecutor (through criminal complaints or confidential reports); on the other, it may be due to practical reasons (police officers are normally able to arrive early to the crime scene). In these situations, judicial police officers are allowed to adopt by themselves as many measures as may be necessary to gather any evidence that may disappear (Articles 282 and 770 LECr) prior to the judge's or prosecutor's intervention. It must be highlighted that the widening of the scope of police measures that may be carried out by police officers on an autonomous basis has been enshrined in the LECr, following the enactment of Organic Act 13/2015 of 5 October, amending the Code of Criminal Procedure to strengthen procedural safeguards and to regulate technological investigation measures.[24] Notwithstanding the foregoing, the last amendment carried out in 2015 still provides for the obligation of reporting any measures adopted by the judicial police to the judge or to the Public Prosecutor's Office within 24 hours.[25]

The narrow scope of this autonomous investigation by the judicial police is further evidenced by the fact that the results obtained from such investigation must be declared in the official police statement. The value of this statement is similar to that of a criminal complaint filed by any citizen, notwithstanding the evidentiary value of certain measures adopted and duly certified in the official police statement (Article 297 LECr). Along these lines, the narrow scope of judicial police investigation in the law is also shown by the difficulties encountered thereby to access data held by government agencies or certain private entities such as banks.[26]

Additionally, Article 286 LECr provides for the withdrawal of prevention measures when the investigating judge gets involved. In connection with the foregoing, termination of autonomous investigative action by the police is made conditional on the type of investigative tasks to be performed, since those requiring judicial authorisation (entry, search and seizure or communication surveillance, among others) automatically entail the initiation of criminal proceedings, thus the investigation is passed on to the competent judicial authority.

---

[24] That has happened with the infiltrated agents in the Internet (Supreme Court Ruling, Criminal Chamber, 767/2007, of 3 October), in Art 282 *bis* (6), regarding the IMSI-catcher (Ruling 249/2008, of 20 May), in Art 588 *ter* (1), regarding the capture of images and sounds (Ruling 1733/2002, of 14 October), in Art 588 *quinquies* (a), regarding the use of a GPS (Ruling 798/2013, of 5 November), in Article 588 *quinquies* (b). On these means of investigation, see J Pérez Gil (ed), *El proceso penal en la sociedad de la información. Las nuevas tecnologías para investigar y probar el delito* (Madrid, La Ley, 2012) *passim*.

[25] Art 295 LECr. Act 41/2015, of 5 October, amending the Code of Criminal Procedure to speed up criminal procedures and to strengthen procedural safeguards, which amended this provision, still provides for the reporting obligation within 24 hours, unless an event of *force majeure* occurs or unless the criminal is unknown, in which case the obligation to submit the official police statement does not apply, unless any of the circumstances provided in Art 284(2) LECr (as modified by Act 41/2015) occur.

[26] On this issue, see L Martín Velasco, 'La investigación policial en el blanqueo de capitales' in JL González Cussac, *Financiación del terrorismo, blanqueo de capitales y secreto bancario: un análisis crítico* (Valencia, Tirant lo Blanch, 2009) 244, and JJ López Ortega, 'Derecho Penal y corrupción: las garantías en los instrumentos penales de investigación y enjuiciamiento' in A Jareño Leal and A Doval País (eds), *Corrupción pública, prueba y delito: cuestiones de libertad e intimidad* (Navarra, Thomson/Aranzadi, Cizur Menor, 2015) 194 and 195.

In sum, the *law in books* of the criminal procedure is designed to narrow the scope of autonomous investigation of judicial police, so the latter is immediately available to judges and prosecutors. This same rule applies when Revenue and Customs Agency members perform judicial police duties.

Initiation by the Public Prosecutor's Office

As is well-known, within the frame of the most widely applied criminal procedure, ie, the summary criminal procedure, public prosecutors may conduct a preliminary investigation, which is also applied in the remaining procedures. Autonomous investigation, which is prior to judicial investigation, is governed by the 'report and pass on the facts of the case' rule. This rule brings along the duty of government agencies to report to the prosecutor any facts that could amount to a crime. Although nothing prevents government agencies from reporting those facts directly to the judge, it is common practice to inform the public prosecutor.

This investigation enables the public prosecutor to adopt certain measures by himself, inasmuch as they do not affect fundamental rights (with a few exceptions, like detention). There is a qualitative difference between this preliminary investigation and the extremely narrow scope of judicial police activities. The existing difference lies in the kind of investigative action allowed. The prosecutor may access the database autonomously, and he or she can even use undercover agents to access information. Furthermore, the principle of immediacy in the criminal procedure does not apply to this case. However, the preliminary investigative tasks carried out by the prosecutor cannot last more than six months, unless the crime falls within the competence of the Prosecutor's Office against Corruption, in which case there is a 12-month deadline. In addition to the foregoing, within this preliminary investigation the prosecutor can be assisted by the judicial police, which at this stage has identical obligations towards the prosecutor and the judge (Article 31 of Organic Act 2/1986, of 13 March, on Law Enforcement Authorities). At this stage, judicial police officers can perform a similar kind of investigative action as the one that may be required from the judge (Article 28 of Royal Decree 769/1987).

Insofar as the measures that may be adopted by the public prosecutor are much more stringent than those that may be implemented by the police, at this point we must highlight the principles of proportionality, defence and due process, and the adversarial principle (Article 5(3) of the Statute of the Public Prosecutor's Office). Thus, once the identification of a suspect is sufficiently reliable, it should be common practice to inform the relevant suspect of the existence of an investigation. Indeed, according to the Public Prosecutor's Office, upon due identification of the subject, if the prosecutor decides not to take a statement therefrom, the right thing to do would be to pass on the case to the judge in order for him or her to declare the investigative secrecy (all judicial records of the case must remain secret) in order not to frustrate the investigation. In other words, the person responsible for adequately weighing the rights of defence and the efficiency of criminal procedures is the judge, and not the prosecutor.

Preliminary investigation shall terminate, in some cases, when the prosecutor considers that the facts do not amount to a crime and thus closes the investigation. This closure does not equal the situation in which the judge closes the case. In fact, the injured party may withdraw the criminal complaint at any time, filing a petition before the investigating judge. In some other cases, the investigation shall terminate when the investigating judge is requested to continue with the proceedings or, better said, to initiate the proceedings, since the prosecutor's investigation is prior to the procedure (pre-procedural).

In any event, the public prosecutor must close his or her autonomous investigation when he or she becomes aware that the investigating judge has begun to investigate the case. Thus, the judge and the prosecutor must not perform investigative tasks simultaneously. If this were the case, the prosecutor's investigation would be encroaching upon the powers of the judge, and thus it would have to be considered null and void.

Initiation by the Investigating Judge

As has been stated, the investigating judge must lead the investigation, although he or she must not necessarily perform it. In the original model provided by the LECr, the judge may have also been thought of as responsible for carrying out any investigative action. However, and although to this day the judge may delegate investigative powers, the truth is that as we pointed out above, the judge has to specify the investigative action to be performed. Indeed, the rule aims at providing a list of the measures that the judge (or the prosecutor in the context of his or her preliminary investigation) can entrust to the judicial police: visual inspection, tracking the suspect, gathering evidence, finding out about home addresses, or drafting solvency reports. Although this rule is open-ended, it provides for measures 'of a similar nature' to that of those expressly provided.[27]

We have moved beyond this narrow provisions. In fact, police officers use any investigative means at their disposal, which is the result of new technologies and the wide array of possibilities offered thereby. As we shall see below, this variety of means of investigation currently available to the police has altered their relationship with judges and their role as investigators.

There is less comprehensive regulation on how judges can profit from the Revenue and Customs Agency, aside from the fact that they can take advantage of its means when investigating possible tax frauds. In these cases a strong cooperation is provided for; some sort of 'investigation within the investigation'.

It is worth examining the interaction between judges and prosecutors once the former are done with their preliminary investigation. As has been stated, once the

---

[27] Art 28 of Royal Decree 769/1987.

investigating judge comes into the scene, he or she begins to lead the investigation. From then onwards, the prosecutor is entrusted with cooperation duties, and he or she is also able to propose measures related to the investigation or to securing evidence, as he or she sees fit.

The term 'cooperation' does not mean that the prosecutor reports to the judge with no autonomy or that it becomes an *amicus curiae*. One of the most surprising features of the Spanish criminal procedure is that the prosecutor can even oppose the investigation led by the judge, thus becoming a *de facto* public defender. This might happen when the public prosecutor considers that the facts do not amount to a criminal offence or that the investigated persons are not guilty. We cannot get further into these cases, but the controversial issue in this regard is under which conditions may the judge continue with the investigation.[28]

Conversely, although the investigating judge has exclusive competence over preventive or investigative measures affecting fundamental rights, concerning pre-trial detention the prosecutor is supposed to counterbalance the judge. It is the prosecutor or any of the parties who must request pre-trial detention to the investigating judge, who decides on it after hearing the parties. This is colloquially called 'mini-court hearing'.[29]

In sum, in a procedure at the trial stage the prosecutor can play various roles: to cooperate with the investigating judge, to become a true prosecutor by requesting pre-trial detention to the investigating judge (who is suddenly impartial again), or to become some sort of 'public defender.'

Beyond the Law: Investigation Models in Practice

So much for 'law in books,' ie the model that can be inferred from the wording of the LECr as well as from the myriad of rules and regulations governing the Spanish criminal procedure. Currently this 'legal approach' is probably just one more model, and not the main one, particularly concerning economic crime investigation. Practice, or, more accurately, practical needs, have given rise to alternative investigation approaches. The feature shared by these models is that the investigating judge is no longer the leading actor, and both the secondary yet important actor (public prosecutor) and even the abovementioned supporting actors (police officers, tax authorities) have assumed the leading role. When dealing with these models it must be taken into account that we are not confronted with clear-cut investigation patterns. They are far from Weberian models. They are actually

---

[28] See Supreme Court Rulings 1045/2007 and 54/2008. On this controversial issue, see Gimeno Sendra, 'La doctrina del TS sobre la acusación popular: los casos "Botín" y "Atutxa"' (2008) 6970 *La Ley*.
[29] 5.2 EOMF.

trends stemming from professional routines which are in compliance with the law, at least formally speaking.

The Investigation led by the Prosecutor's Office, Particularly by the Prosecutor's Office against Corruption

This first model may use a twofold coverage. First of all, it uses the cover provided by preliminary investigation, which as has been pointed out can be carried out by the public prosecutor prior to the initiation of the criminal procedure (which only begins when the judge gains knowledge of the crime and decides to initiate proceedings). Secondly, it may profit from the umbrella provided by the prosecutor's prominent role in the investigation. In the first case the investigation is led by the public prosecutor, and the judge does not get involved. This non-intervention is due to the fact that as soon as a judge steps in, criminal proceedings must be initiated and thus the judge becomes the true leader of the procedure. However, in the second case, the judge is formally entrusted with leading the investigation, yet the prosecutor becomes a *de facto* leader of the investigation because of the proposal and driving duties allocated thereto.[30]

In order for the public prosecutor to initiate the investigation, he or she must have gained knowledge of the *notitia criminis* (of the commission of a crime). Therefore, such initiation largely depends on the decisions of other actors involved (government agencies, police officers or citizens). Moreover, even if the prosecutor is the first to become aware of the criminal act, he or she might decide to pass on the case to the judge, thus giving rise to the trial stage, since the preliminary investigation is not mandatory. Although we lack data in this regard, it is likely that the specialised public prosecutor's offices (for the purposes of this paper the Prosecutor's Office against Corruption) are the ones which more frequently undertake in-depth preliminary investigations. In other instances, it is unlikely that prosecutors are able to carry out thorough preliminary investigations given the scarcity of the resources available. The Prosecutor's Office against Corruption is entitled to carry out a more comprehensive preliminary investigation (it has a 12-month time period). Additionally, it has an office and is assisted by expert groups. Thus, the following mainly addresses investigations in which this specialised prosecutor's office has been involved.

There are several factors that could make preliminary investigations more attractive and efficient at first sight. Firstly, it must be stated that the investigation carried out by the Prosecutor's Office against Corruption, which is not limited by the principle of territorial jurisdiction of judges, can be more effective

---

[30] The situation in this second case is discussed in JJ López Ortega, *Derecho Penal*, 186.

(when strictly performed) than standard judicial investigation when it comes to finding out facts. Secondly, it can also be more swift and efficient because it is carried out in a secretive manner, ie, the potential suspects (they are not yet deemed as actual suspects) are not aware of this investigation. This avoids difficulties attached to the involvement of lawyers in this process. However, there is a downside to this effectiveness, since most proceedings tend to be repeated in order to ensure protection of the rights of defence.

Thirdly, effectiveness is enhanced. This is because within this domain the main investigative acts are related to obtaining information, and the public prosecutor, pursuant to Articles 11(2)(d) and 22 of the Spanish Organic Act on Data Protection and in accordance with settled case law, may autonomously collect personal data with no prior judicial authorisation and without getting the judge involved. This 'easily' obtained information can help support the criminal charge.[31] To add to these investigative measures, we must take into account those that can be carried out by the prosecutor in a somewhat autonomous way alongside the judicial police available to the prosecutor. As we will see below, one of the consequences attached to the appearance of new technologies as admissible means of evidence is that the police have been further empowered.

If a thorough investigation has been carried out, the prosecutor will most likely remain the main actor in the investigation once the trial stage begins. Having regard to the Prosecutor's Office against Corruption expertise and technical support, rather than helping the investigation to move forward, it will probably end up being a *de facto* leader thereof. The exact time when the trial stage begins remains uncertain. On the one hand, there is no clear boundary, although certain investigative measures can only be adopted by the judge. On the other, the individualisation of a specific suspect, and thus the time for the judge to come into the scene, is open to interpretation.

The Investigation Led by the Police

The second economic crime investigation model is led by the police, and particularly by the specialised units mentioned above (UDECO-UDEF).[32] The police may initiate the investigation once they gain knowledge of the crime, and thus in most

---

[31] In this regard, see J Pérez Gil and JJ González López, 'Cesión de datos personales para la investigación penal. Una propuesta para su inmediata inclusión en la Ley de Enjuiciamiento Criminal,' (2010) 7401 *Diario La Ley* 13 May, 1–14.

[32] As pointed out in LM Vallés Causada, *La policía judicial en la obtención de inteligencia sobre comunicaciones electrónicas para el proceso penal*, Tesis Doctoral, (Madrid, UNED, 2013) 244, 'in many works cited in this paper, there seems to be an underlying consideration of the judicial police as a mere enforcer of judicial decisions. It appears that the judge "truly investigates" and that the only duty entrusted to judicial police officers is to implement certain measures under the direction of judges. This is not how it works in practice, and it should not be like that. The judicial police has an immense capacity for many things, and thus it must be legally engaged in the criminal procedure. And, by the way, the judicial police does investigate'.

cases it depends on the decisions made by other parties (government agencies, police officers, or citizens), or on anonymous criminal complaints, which are allowed in Spain.[33]

This model is the result of various factors. The first of them is the high competence and qualification of these units, which are very well trained and thus more capable of conducting an investigation than most judges and prosecutors. This simply stems from the training given to the two different authorities as well as from the respective professional backgrounds. Judges and prosecutors are barely trained to investigate. Their knowledge on investigation comes from their experience. Self-evidently, they have trouble leading a complex investigation.

The second factor is that new technologies have brought along a wide array of investigation possibilities that were not available to police officers before. New technologies amount to means of evidence that escape from regulation. In addition, they evolve so incredibly fast that any attempt to regulate them becomes obsolete right from the outset. Police units take advantage of this 'unregulated domain'. With the acquiescence of judges, police officers have widened the means of investigation at their disposal. This 'unregulated domain' is a battleground, where efforts have been made. Indeed, police officers have put in their best efforts to gain ground: for instance, they struggle to gain access to private or public databases with no need for a prior judicial authorisation. The fact that there is a Code of Criminal Procedure in force where means of evidence were under regulated (at least until the 2015 amendment), has triggered the appearance of this no man's land which is being conquered by the police.

The scope of police investigation should end when a measure affecting fundamental rights has to be adopted, when preventive measures are required, or even when citizens or government agencies are reluctant to cooperate with the police, not allowing them to access their databases. At that point, the judge must necessarily become involved in the investigation, ie, the investigation must be 'judicialised'. However, as it happened with prosecutors who played the leading role, this 'judicialisation' does not necessarily entail that the judge becomes the main character of the investigation at the expense of the prosecutor. The judge can still lag behind the police officer that has investigated the case. In any event, the intervention of

---

[33] It must be underlined that case law has deemed acceptable anonymous criminal complaints. However, they must be carefully weighed and assessed. In this connection, Supreme Court Ruling (Criminal Chamber) of 11 April 2013, which refers to previous decisions, makes the following claim: 'Everything suggests that when it comes to confidential information, where the disclosing party is not identified, a careful and strict weighing and assessment must be performed. The addressee of the information must assess the reliability, credibility and adequacy thereof for the purposes of initiating criminal proceedings. A system which did not worry about delays in the procedure and which initiated criminal proceedings following every anonymous complaint, it would hurt not only social living but also citizens' fundamental rights, since it would empower the government to investigate any citizen. However, the foregoing does not prevent confidential information to give rise to the duty to investigate any apparently criminal acts of which the judge, the prosecutor or law enforcement authorities gain knowledge by virtue of their office, provided that the accuracy, consistency and credibility of such confidential information has been verified.'

the judge ensures that a secret investigation of which the suspect is unaware is not going to be conducted. This is actually the aspect of police investigations which raises the most concerns.

There is a third factor leading to the extension of autonomous police investigation as opposed to judicial investigation: the police organisation provides greater flexibility. Judges are linked with a given territory, and when they leave it (and they simply have to go to another province) they must resort to the judicial assistance provisions contained in the LECr. Police officers, just as prosecutors (particularly prosecutors from the Office against Corruption) are a federal and hierarchical body that may act in the whole country and which exchange information easily. This advantage is furthered when dealing with cross-border investigations. International police cooperation is much more dynamic, informal and smooth than judicial cooperation in spite of the efforts made within the European Union.

The fourth and decisive factor that has led to this model is the softening of the principle of immediacy enshrined in the LECr. As has been seen, the legal model provides that any inquiry made autonomously must be reported to the judge within 24 hours. However, this rule has been softened or is simply formally fulfilled in a way which is openly contrary to the spirit of the LECr. The judge is periodically notified through a fax, a mail, or a phone call, and he or she gives room for the performance of the investigation by the police officers. This means of communication has replaced the official police statement, which is still issued, yet (following a long investigation) it has become a mere report on the criminal act and the crime scene. As can be seen, within this model the judge no longer leads as provided by the LECr. The judge rather monitors or controls, ie, it has become a protectionist judge playing a more rights-based role.

The transformation undergone by the principle of immediacy and the role of judges has a lot to do with personal factors. This is to say, with who is the judge or prosecutor responsible for the case. They will assume the leading role provided in the LECr if any of them becomes interested or has time and resources. Otherwise they will be much more passive, and it might get to the point where the police officer tells the judge what to ask when taking a statement. This leading role of the police (and maybe of certain prosecutors too) can help to explain why the High Court has not collapsed, in spite of the fact that it only has six investigating judges. The presence of specialised judicial police units or of the Prosecutor's Office against Corruption (which has more resources and thus a greater capacity to help in moving forward the procedure) explains why these investigating judges have been able to deal with the most significant and complex cases in the country.

The furtherance of police investigative powers allows police officers to practice some sort of *forum shopping*. As the investigation advances, the police officer may visit a prosecutor to get him or her involved in the investigation by having him or her perform preliminary investigative action. Maybe following this preliminary investigation they can both see the judge. However, the police officer might also resort directly to the judge, and thus the prosecutor would become a mere spectator of the investigation, simply acknowledging any information given thereto and subsequently making the charge at the hearing. There is another possibility; the judge might disagree with the lines of investigation put forward by the police, but it is still evidenced that each of the actors' roles are dependent on personal aspects and not on legal provisions.

Obviously, the police investigation model is focused on efficiency rather than on protection of rights and guarantees, and therefore it raises several concerns from the perspective of fundamental rights such as the right of defence. As has been discussed, it can take a long time until the suspect becomes aware of the investigation. This is far from transparent and thus very worrying, particularly if we take into account that the ultimate investigator according to this model is the executive power to which the police department reports. There is not even an attempt to be impartial as it happens with the Public Prosecutor's Office. We should be concerned with the lack of transparency. We must worry about what is being investigated, but even more worrying is what is not investigated.[34] What happens when the police gain knowledge of certain information and decide not to investigate it or to follow a specific trace? As is well-known, any procedure is nothing but a way to structure reality, and whoever is granted the powers to investigate without major controls can structure reality as he or she sees fit.

As can be seen, although the investigation approach is in compliance with the wording of the LECr, it is contrary to the spirit of the law. The Code of Criminal Procedure provides for 'urgent' or 'precautionary' action by the judicial police, yet not for a long-lasting investigation. In addition to the foregoing, this approach is not clearly in line with the right of defence and it lacks transparency.

The Investigation led by the Tax Agency

The approach pursuant to which the Tax Agency or other government agencies investigate a crime amounts to a sub-model within the previous police model. Let's recall that the principle of cooperation governs the relationships between public authorities, just like the 'report and pass on the facts of the case' rule (a variation of the principle of immediacy) applies to government agencies with the power to impose sanctions. The correct application of this rule entails that in cases where it is unclear whether the facts amount to a crime, the facts must be reported to the prosecutor, and he or she will decide whether or not to file a criminal complaint. Actually, the difference between administrative and criminal penalties is sometimes blurred. As to tax crimes, in addition to the amount (which can be open to discussion), it all depends on whether we are confronted with a wilful or negligent act. In other words, it depends on whether we consider there has been an error of fact (in which case administrative sanctions will be imposed because it was a negligent act) or an error of law (in which case a reduced criminal penalty shall be imposed).

---

[34] They are rated as 'opaque and uncontrolled investigations' in JJ López Ortega, *Derecho Penal*, 186.

In sum, this model is implemented in a way which, although it is not contrary to the wording of legal texts, is once again questionable in terms of the spirit of the law. The Tax Agency, and particularly its Tax Fraud Unit, is cautious when it comes to reporting and passing on the facts of the case to prosecutors.[35] Consequently, the common practice has become to make sure that any facts reported to the prosecutor actually amount to a criminal offence. The tax inspector who finds out about the possible fraud reports the case to the Tax Fraud Unit within the Spanish Tax Agency. If this Unit considers that there is enough to the case, it drafts a report on it, which must be submitted to the prosecutor alongside the tax record. Otherwise it requests the inspector to continue with the investigation, in order to subsequently make the decision of passing on the case to the prosecutor once the criminal nature of the case has been verified. In the event of large-scale tax frauds, this unit is replaced by a more powerful one: the National Fraud Investigation Office (ONIF),[36] which specialises in large fortunes, and is closely connected with the Prosecutor's Office against Corruption.

This interpretation of the 'pass on the case' rule entails reversing the roles. The decision on the criminal nature of tax frauds is ultimately made by the Tax Agency. In addition, the Tax Agency also carries out most investigation acts, assisted where appropriate by the Revenue and Customs Agency, which becomes a tax police force under the control of the Tax Agency and a judicial police body under the direction of judges and public prosecutors.

Sometimes, specialised police forces assist the Tax Agency. Instead of reporting the case to the prosecutor, there can be leaks to the police to draw their attention to a particularly complex tax fraud. In any event, judicial intervention in this model is also slow, unless (as it always happens) such intervention is necessary to adopt a measure affecting fundamental rights.

The issues posed by this sub-model are similar to those posed by the police model. On the one hand, there is the lack of protection and guarantees, mainly because the Tax Agency acts as an inspection authority when investigating the case and not as an 'investigator'. Game rules change completely, because the Tax Agency's position as an inspection authority enables it to ask suspects to cooperate, and in the event of non-cooperation the Tax Agency can threaten suspects with sanctions.[37] The risks for the right not to incriminate oneself are clear.

---

[35] On this particular application of the 'pass on the case' rule, see A Gil Martínez, 'Instrucción de los delitos fiscales y contra la Hacienda Pública' in E Solaz Solaz (ed), *La instrucción*, 321.

[36] See Art 2(1) of the Decision of 24 March 1992 issued by the Spanish Tax Agency.

[37] The National High Court Ruling (Administrative Chamber) of 22 June 2011 points out that 'the right not to incriminate oneself is applicable as soon as the sanction procedure is initiated, which does not preclude any prior administrative inquiries.' However, it is a controversial issue, as pointed out in JA Sanz Díaz-Palacios, 'Las Sentencias del Tribunal Constitucional 18/2005 y 68/2006 y los pronunci-amientos del Tribunal de Estrasburgo Shannon, Weh y Allen. Reflexiones sobre inspección tributaria y autoincriminación' (2006) 20 *Impuestos*, October, 259. On that point, see A Nieto García, '«Nemo tenetur se ipsum accusare» en el Derecho Penal económico europeo,' in LM Díez-Picazo and A Nieto Martín (eds), *Los derechos fundamentales en el Derecho Penal europeo*, (Navarra, Thomson Reuters, Cizur Menor, 2010) 397.

The violation of this right becomes even more likely when judges or prosecutors profit from the Tax Agency's inspections to further their investigation of the case.

In addition to the lack of safeguards, there is a serious transparency issue. Again, the investigation is in the hands of the executive branch of government (the Ministry of Finance), who ultimately decides whether to submit the case to a criminal court or to leave it on the shelf. The 'pass on the case' rule, in addition to ensuring compliance with the *ne bis in idem* principle, is also essential to preserve transparency.

At this point, the question is why the investigation of economic crimes is so slow. This slowness seems inconsistent with the smoothness and efficiency of the police model of investigation or that of tax crimes. As has been seen, in this model the rights of defence are somewhat unprotected; there are not any lawyers hindering the actions of government officials. The procedure is so slow because upon 'judicialisation' of the case, legal counselling appears and part of the proceedings has to be repeated (with long and complex statements). The judge, the prosecutor and, above all, the police, know how everything is going to end, but it is necessary to redo the whole thing, or at least the most important parts thereof, before the judge. Within this model, at court hearings the inspectors themselves are often summoned as experts.

The Inquisitive/All-star Judge

Although Alaya and other judges in Spain might not like this designation, the fourth approach to investigation of economic crimes is the 'all-star judge model'. These all-star judges lead the investigation in accordance with the LECr. Pursuant to this model, the investigating judge does not 'authorise' but rather 'decides' on the adoption of investigative measures. In other words, since they are the leaders of the investigation, they do not need the parties to request the adoption of any of those measures. All-star judges are entitled to adopt as many measures as they deem appropriate to find out about the crime and seize the criminal on their own authority. This fourth model is the closest to the original model provided in the LECr. The judge truly leads the investigation assisted by judicial police officers. It is not that the judicial police are deprived of initiative, and neither is the public prosecutor, but the judge assumes the leading role, since he or she is fully aware of the case, drives the investigation, and decides on his own to adopt investigative measures; at least most of them.

However, as has been seen, practice and case law show that those measures limiting fundamental rights are adopted by the judge on the motion of the police or the public prosecutor. Thus, the investigating judge is increasingly becoming to play a 'rights-based role'.[38] Furthermore, it is usual that judicial investigation becomes

---

[38] It must be highlighted that the LECr 2015 amendment, although it mentions the judicial 'authorisation' to adopt measures affecting fundamental rights, does not completely forget about the original LECr model, since it provides for the possibility of adopting those measures '*ex officio.*'

the result of a combination of judicial initiatives in the adoption of certain measures (statement of the accused or witness statements) with other actors' initiatives (judicial police or prosecutors). This, taken to the extreme, is evidenced by the delegation of the leading role to the police or the Public Prosecutor's Office. Even the most stringent measures, such as preventive detention, can only be ordered by the judge if they have been requested by the prosecutor or by any of the parties.

Therefore, since we are now used to more current and softer investigating judges, often similar to protectionist rights-oriented judges, sudden re-appearances of inquisitive judges are horrifying; just like watching a ghost. An investigation without a truly impartial judge is not in line with our legal sensitivity. We demand investigating judges that decide on investigative measures proposed by the true main characters of an investigation, ie, prosecutors or government agencies under the guise of investigators.[39] On the one hand, it is dramatic that these investigators are not independent, since they all report to the executive branch of government. On the other hand, it is also discouraging that the only independent actor in this context, the judge, when he or she actually starts leading the investigation and gets involved, ceases to be impartial. In sum, currently it is hard to find sufficiently independent investigators or otherwise highly impartial judges.

In addition to the anachronistic nature of the LECr model, the appearance of the inquisitive judge, depending on his or her ability to compromise, can lead to a struggle for the lead that could end up hindering or curtailing lines of investigation proposed by other actors (judicial police or public prosecutors, for instance). In any event, it is not a very smooth model, since lawyers are fully involved therein and criminal proceedings are significantly slowed down.

Closing Remarks

From the foregoing it can be inferred that in practice there are four models, or at least three if the intervention of government agencies is considered to be a sub-model. Some of those models are far from the original approach provided in the LECr or from the modern trends of the formal criminal procedure. These models are not mutually exclusive. In fact, they can be implemented in a consecutive manner or they can even overlap. Hence, theoretically, the inspection (investigation) conducted by government agencies can be followed by the judicial police investigation, who can become aware of what has been investigated by the

---

[39] This situation is not new. This is evidenced in G Cámara Villar, 'Justicia y política en la España democrática. Una reflexión a propósito de los llamados jueces estrellas y la judicialización de la política' (2007) 47 *Revista de Derecho Político* 27–52. Along those lines, see the various works contained in M Marchena Gòmez (ed), *El juez instructor y el juez de garantías: posibles alternativas* (Madrid, Consejo General del Poder Judicial, 2002).

government agency, subsequently submitting the official police statement to the Public Prosecutor's Office. Public prosecutors could conduct a preliminary investigation prior to the judicial investigation. In practice, government agencies can be asked to perform an ancillary inspection to complement the criminal investigation, thus triggering a controversy among the police, the public prosecutor and the judge (already at the trial stage) regarding the right direction of the investigation.

There is some sort of tension between pre-trial action and the measures adopted at the trial stage. The first is performed by judicial police or public prosecutors, and is very swift and necessary to find out about the facts. The second entail adequate safeguards, yet they are slow and complex. Conversely, pre-trial measures are not mandatory, and sometimes their procedural efficiency is blurred, it can be questioned, and these measures do not seem to be protective of rights of defence. On the contrary, measures adopted at the trial stage do not seem very efficient as to the discovery of crimes and seizure of criminals, they are often hindered by the involvement of lawyers, and they tend to be long. The success of the investigation often depends on the importance that pre-trial action had in each case. However, these pre-trial measures are prior to the trial stage, ie, they are apart from the formal procedure provided for the investigation of crimes, and thus there are certain inevitable consequences regarding the lack of evidentiary value attached to these pre-trial measures. The success of the investigation largely depends on the degree of specialisation and on the overall approach. These aspects cause many investigations to fail, because investigations are conducted by non-specialised bodies or because the 'pass on the case' rule has been impartially applied.

The context examined herein leads to a great degree of uncertainty, since there is no criterion that allows us to know on an *a priori* basis who will get involved in the procedure and to what extent. These factors are dependent on a large amount of variables, among which we can remark on the attitude of the actors involved, who control whether or not other actors are included in the investigation, or the good relationship between the actors involved. This uncertain context does not seem like the best scenario for the establishment of the European Public Prosecutor, who will have to learn to get along in this convoluted mosaic of rules, professional routines and actors; also designated as the Spanish criminal procedure. The position of the delegated prosecutor is decisive under these circumstances, and the OLAF must provide guidance to the European Public Prosecutor with regards to those government agencies involved in the investigation. Both actors have to be able to welcome the EU Public Prosecutor to economic crime investigation so the latter can find order in chaos.

Part II

Establishing Specific Competences in Prosecuting Financial-Economic Crime

3

Criminal Investigations in Financial-Economic Matters in France

DR OLIVIER CAHN
Lecturer, University of Cergy-Pontoise
LEJEP-PSC, CESDIP-CNRS, ARPE

Introduction

In France, criminal investigations are mainly conducted by the public prosecution service (ministère public, also called parquet). Law enforcement forces in charge of the investigation of economic crimes act under its authority (Article 12 of the Code of Criminal Procedure (CCP)). The district prosecutor (procureur de la République) receives complaints and denunciations, supervises the inquiry and has control over police investigations.[1] At the end of the inquiry, when the district prosecutor considers the elements collected as likely to constitute a criminal offence, he/she owes discretionary jurisdiction to decide whether to initiate a prosecution, to implement alternative proceedings[2] or to drop the case without

[1] Art 12-1 CCP provides that the district prosecutor enjoys a discretionary power to choose which judicial police unit shall be entrusted with the inquiry. Besides, Art 41 CCP reads: 'The district prosecutor institutes or causes to be taken any step necessary for the discovery and prosecution of violations of the criminal law. To this end, he directs the activity of the judicial police officers and agents within the area of jurisdiction of his court.' According to the French Constitutional Council decision 2011-625 DC of 11 March 2011, police forces shall in any event remain subjected to the direction and supervision of a judicial authority. Besides, felony or 'complex' misdemeanor cases should be left to an investigating judge who will then supervise a judicial investigation (information judiciaire). The investigating judge being statutorily independent, he/she could hardly be subjected to the authority of the EPPO. However, considering that current practice, as far as economic and financial crimes are concerned, is to restrict as much as legally possible the submission of cases to investigating judges (cf infra), this distinctive feature of the French criminal justice system is likely to have only limited incidence on effective cooperation between French authorities and the European prosecutors.

[2] Public prosecutors may thus deal with offences through either conditional suspension ('composition pénale') or appearance on prior admission of guilt (comparution sur reconnaissance préalable de culpabilité)—which both empower the prosecutor, when the suspect admits committing the offence, to offer the offender a sentence that, if accepted, will only have to be approved by the trial judge.

taking any further action (Article 40-1 CCP). The district prosecutor is vested with the power of committing the case to trial and, once the case is brought before a tribunal, of requesting that the law be enforced and a sentence passed (Article 31 CCP).

Until the early 1990s, the French criminal justice system showed little interest in financial and economic crimes. The explanations are complex but mainly consist in the weakness of structured criminal organisations on national territory,[3] the prevailing of a largely state-controlled economy and both the low attractiveness of the Paris stock-market and a then poorly developed financial system, an almost complete absence of community interest for white-collar crimes, the weight of history—discreetly called geo-political strategies,[4]—political ambiguousness[5] and the relative (in)dependence of prosecution authorities.[6]

As a consequence of both international pressure—brought about by, on the one hand, the Council of Europe, OECD, and Palerme UN Conventions and, on the other hand, the first instruments on UE financial interests protection and on corruption fighting—and cohabitation[7] phases which allowed some emancipation of the judiciary, concern for economic and financial crimes has slowly grown in France. Under the constant influence of the European Union and as a reaction to both recurrent scandals involving national companies or politicians and the 2008 financial crisis, the French legislator has enacted a material and procedural penal apparatus aimed at curbing economic and financial crime that, at least on paper, now appears satisfactory.

A plethora of administrative and judicial authorities are in charge of enforcing (derogatory) powers to curb a substantial number of crimes that cover all forms

---

[3] Except for *mutatis mutandis* in Corsica, there is no equivalent in French penal history of such a phenomenon as the Italian mafias. France has for long been more affected by investments made on the national territory by criminal groups and/or corrupted people than by their activities.

[4] For example, the so-called 'françafrique' system: basically, for more than 50 years, French highest authorities have been dealing with former colonies' dictators, maintaining their corruption and sometimes (militarily) intervening to protect their regime in exchange for privileges offered to French companies in procurement contracts and votes at the United Nations.

[5] Until the coming into force of the OECD convention, implemented by a 2000 Act of Parliament, French companies practising corruption abroad were granted tax credits of an equivalent amount (so-called 'confessional' procedure). Until an Act of Parliament of 11 March 1988, there were no rules to govern the funding of political parties in France. Furthermore, at national level, 'politician' is traditionally regarded as a full time permanent employment in France and, since an Act of Parliament of 1982, France has had a decentralised political organisation.

[6] Although made up of professional magistrates, the French prosecution service is, according to Art 30 of the code of criminal procedure (code de procédure pénale) subordinated to the minister of Justice's authority. A ministry of Justice circular of 2012 and an Act of Parliament of 2013 formally secure their independence and forbid direct ministerial interventions in individual cases. Nonetheless, prosecutors are still appointed by a government decision, which is not bound by the opinion of the Magistracy Superior Council (Conseil supérieur de la magistrature).

[7] A situation which occurs when, in a general election, another party than the president's gets the majority, resulting in antagonism between the two heads of the executive.

of economic and financial misbehaviours such as fraud,[8] bribery[9] and ancillary offences.[10] Although they are increasingly approximated, the powers and assignments given to these authorities somehow diverge. Furthermore, their cooperation is affected both by some contradictions between enforcement agencies' purposes[11] and by the different objectives of the various ministerial supervisions of these entities, which affects dynamics of transition between administrative investigations and criminal ones and dynamics of cooperation between enforcement forces involved in economic and financial crime investigations.

The specifications assigned to this study imply the presentation of the provisions of the French code of criminal procedure that establish authorities with competence to fight economic and financial crimes. The focus should be put, on the one hand, on the entities mainly involved in the investigative phase and their relationships and, on the other hand, on the special powers they owe to fulfil their duties, with a view to illustrate the dynamics of financial—economic investigations in France and the main operational models that hereby come out. This presentation is furthermore aimed at illustrating the particular features of the French criminal justice system with regard to the foreseeable relationships that may come out of the collaboration between French national judicial and law enforcement authorities and both the European Anti-Fraud Office (OLAF) and the European Public Prosecutor Office, when the later is established.[12] In accordance with the

---

[8] Swindling (escroquerie): Art 313-1–313-3 Criminal Code, then CC; Art 313-7 and 313-8 CC (alternative and supplementary sentences); rules governing criminal liability of legal entities and sentences (Art 313-9); breach of trust (abus de confiance): Art 314-1–314-3 CC, Art 314-10 and 314-11 CC (alternative and supplementary sentences), Art 314-12 and 314-13 CC (rules governing criminal liability of legal entities and sentences); unlawful acquisition of an interest (prise illégale d'intérêts): Art 432-12 and 432-13 CC; Art 432-17 CC (alternative and supplementary sentences); favoritism in public procurement contracts (favoritisme): Art 432-14 CC, Art 432-17 CC (alternative and supplementary sentences); misappropriation of public funds (détournement de fonds publics): Art 432-15 CC; customs and excise frauds: Arts 408–440 Customs Code; tax frauds: Arts 1741, 1743 and 1789 General Tax Code.

[9] Active corruption of a national public authority by an individual (Art 433-1 and 433-2 CC); passive corruption by a national public authority (Art 432-11 CC); active and passive corruption of magistrates or individual acting on behalf of a judicial authority (Art 434-9 CC); active and passive corruption of private individuals (Art 445-1–445-4 CC); active and passive corruption of a foreign civil servant, a foreign elected representative ou a member of an international public organisation (Art 435-1–435-6-1 CC); active and passive corruption of foreign or international courts magistrates and employees (Art 435-7 and 435-11 CC); Arts 432-17, 433-22 and 433-23 and 435-14 CC (alternative and supplementary sentences); Arts 433-25 and 435-15 CC (rules governing criminal liability of legal entities and sentences).

[10] Receiving and possession of stolen goods (recel): Art 321-1–321-5 CC, Art 321-9–321-11 CC (alternative and supplementary sentences), Art 321-12 (rules governing criminal liability of legal entities and sentences); money laundering (blanchiment): Art 324-1–324-6-1 CC, Art 324-7 and 324-8 CC (alternative and supplementary sentences), Art 324-9 CC (rules governing criminal liability of legal entities and sentences); forgery (faux): Art 441-1–441-12 CC.

[11] For example, contradictions between the aims of customs and interests of customs officers and those of police forces in the fight against transnational traffics.

[12] EU Commission's proposal for a Council regulation on the establishment of the European Public Prosecutor's Office, COM(2013)534 final.

requirements of the editors, the scientific material has been collected through a systematic analysis of relevant legal provisions complemented with academic literature and interviews of practitioners.[13]

The presentation of French operational models and practices in the investigations of economic and financial crimes involves dealing with the complexity of the institutional framework from the powers vested to investigation and prosecution authorities.

Complexity of the Institutional Framework

Through an Act of Parliament of 6 August 1975, the French legislator has enacted in the CCP a Title XIII dedicated to prosecution, investigation and trial of offences in economic and financial matters. The purpose was to improve repressive efficiency through the directing of serious and/or complex cases towards specialised judicial authorities, mainly within Paris' tribunal de grande instance. Over the years, this title has been significantly amended (notably by Acts of Parliament 2004-204 of 9 March 2004 and 2013-1117 of 6 December 2013 and 2016-1691 of 9 December 2016), giving rise to intricacies in the distribution of proceedings between the various courts likely to claim their jurisdiction. Besides, institutional complexity is further accentuated by the institution, prior to the penal apparatus, of extensive mechanisms of prevention and detection of offences. Finally, two specificities of economic and financial crimes contribute to the complexification: such criminality is damaging to economy and public funds and most of the time it is clever and sophisticated. It therefore requires from the authorities a high level of specialisation to detect, investigate and prosecute cases. As a consequence, the legislator has chosen to involve in the penal process *lato sensu* not only the usual actors (police forces, prosecution services and criminal courts) but, indeed, all the participants—both civil servants and private individuals/entities—in economic and financial activities.

The result is an exuberant bureaucracy aimed at preventing and detecting or investigating and prosecuting economic and financial crimes.

Prevention and Detection Institutions

As far as prevention and detection of economic and finance crimes are concerned, a *summa divisio* can be made between administrative institutions and private individuals/entities associated with these assignments.

---

[13] Interviews with some of the contributors of the international colloquium *Les polices fiscales—Regards croisés sur les moyens de lutte contre la fraude fiscale*, University of Cergy-Pontoise, 20 March 2015 (proceedings published in *REIDF*, 2015/1, 7-173) and with E Houlette, Financial Republic Prosecutor, head of the National Financial Prosecution Service, Paris, 25 September 2015.

As regards administrative authorities, those in charge of controlling civil servants and political entities may be told from those in charge of supervising private operators.

The prevention and detection of economic and financial crimes likely to be perpetrated by civil servants and political entities are mainly assigned to specialised administrative bodies such as:

— the prevention of corruption central service (Service Central de Prévention de la Corruption), which is an inter-ministerial service supervised by the minister of Justice and directed by a judicial magistrate. It is in charge, on the one hand, of centralising information, providing professional training and helping public authorities and private companies to set up ethic compliant policies and, on the other hand, of providing advice to the government in the definition of anti-corruption legislation. Furthermore, it is associated with the Council of Europe GRECO and to the OECD working groups on corruption and, although it owes no investigation powers, it is a contact point for OLAF and Eurojust;[14]

— following the coming into force of Act of Parliament 2016-1691, the SCPC has been replaced by the Agence française anticorruption, which will retain the prerogatives of its predecessor but will further be entrusted with controlling the efficiency of the prevention of corruption programmes set by both public authorities and major companies. Besides, when in the performance of its duties, the agency will gain knowledge of the existence of an offence to probity, it will have to notify forthwith the district prosecutor and/or the Financial public prosecutor of the offence and to transmit to him/her any relevant information or documents. Finally, the agency will be in charge of supervising the implementation of the compliance programmes that may be imposed, through a public interest judicial convention, by the district prosecutor or the Financial public prosecutor, onto companies after they admitted their involvement in acts of international corruption;

— the transparency high authority (haute autorité de la transparence): established by Act of Parliament 2013-1117, it is in charge of checking the patrimonial declarations and the declarations of interests that members of the government and of the national and European Parliaments, presidents of local authorities, President of the Republic's and ministers' staffs, members of independent administrative authorities and administrators of public companies have to fill in when taking and leaving office. The authority collaborates with the French Inland Revenue and owes a power of injunction;

— the election campaign accounts national commission (commission nationale des comptes de campagne) which is in charge of a posteriori assessing election campaign accounts and supervising political parties' funding. It owes no investigation prerogatives;

---

[14] M Barrau, 'Un instrument de lutte contre la corruption: le SCPC' (5/2006) *AJ Pénal, Dossier—La lutte contre la corruption*, 202–204.

— the revenue court (Cour des comptes) and the revenue regional chambers (chambres régionales des comptes), which are administrative courts, owing injunction and investigation prerogatives and in charge of assessing national and local public authorities accounts.[15]

Since the implementation of the third Anti-Money Laundering Directive,[16] the prevention and detection of economic crimes likely to be committed by private entities together with the control of their compliance with their duties towards the financial intelligence unit is entrusted to independent administrative authorities, mainly the resolution and prudential control authority (autorité de contrôle prudentiel et de résolution), which supervises the insurance business and the financial market authority (autorité des marchés financiers), which supervises the banking sector. Both owe investigative prerogatives (such as the right to order the disclosure of documents or the right to carry out hearings and questionings; independent administrative authorities inspectors also enjoy a right to visit workplaces) and power to pass administrative sanctions.

However, the detection of economic and financial offences perpetrated by private economic operators is mainly entrusted to the French financial intelligence unit (service de traitement du renseignement et d'action contre les circuits financiers clandestins—TRACFIN). It is a Ministry of Economy service in charge of processing the suspect transaction reports made by professionals subjected to such an obligation.[17] According to Article L561-1 Monetary and Financial Code, 'Individuals and legal entities other than those referred to in Article L561-2 who, in the normal course of their business, execute, supervise or recommend transactions giving rise to capital movements, shall be required to declare to the district Prosecutor any transactions they have knowledge of that involve sums which they know to be the proceeds of an offence referred to in Article L562-15' (offences punished by a minimum of one year imprisonment, offences of terrorism financing and tax fraud). Besides, according to Article L561-15 of the same code, all financial institutions and regulated professions listed in Article L561-2 MFC shall declare to TRACFIN the sums entered in their books or the transactions relating to sums which they know, suspect or have good reasons for suspecting are the proceeds of an offence punishable by a custodial sentence of more than one year or are destined for terrorist financing, without being held liable for such reporting. According to Article L561-23, II, MFC 'where (TRACFIN) investigations reveal acts likely to relate to the laundering of the proceeds of an offence punishable by a custodial sentence in excess of one year or to terrorist financing, (…), the unit shall refer the matter to the district prosecutor via a memorandum'. When investigating a suspicion report, TRACFIN is allowed to require from financial institutions

---

[15] Art R135-3 et R241-25 du Code des juridictions financiers.

[16] Ordonnance 2009-104 du 30 janvier 2009 relative à la prévention de l'utilisation du système financier aux fins de blanchiment de capitaux et de financement du terrorisme, JORF 31 janvier 2009, 1819.

[17] Art L561-2 and L561-15, I, monetary and financial code.

and professionals listed in Article L561-2 the disclosure of the documents they retain that the unit thinks pertinent to the claim, and shall receive, on the initiative of the administrations of the State, of local authorities, of public institutions, of revenue courts and of any other entity tasked with a public service mission all the information required to perform its duties or shall obtain it at its request (Articles L561-26 and L521-27 MFC). Besides, according to Article L561-31, TRACFIN may communicate to its counterparts abroad, at their request or on its own initiative, the information it holds relating to sums or transactions whose object seems to be the laundering of the proceeds of an offence punishable by a custodial sentence of more than one year or the financing of terrorism, subject to reciprocity and to the following conditions: (a) the foreign authorities must be subject to confidentiality obligations which are at least equivalent, and (b) the processing of the information communicated must guarantee adequate protection of privacy and of fundamental human rights and freedoms. Nonetheless, such information shall not be communicated if criminal proceedings have been instituted in France on the basis of the same acts or if this should compromise sovereignty, national interests, security or public order.

Nonetheless, the way TRACFIN fulfils its duties is currently a matter of concern. The bankers we have questioned have confirmed that their compliance services now systematically report suspicious transactions to TRACFIN. A former fixed-term contract agent who worked three years for TRACFIN confirmed that during that period of time, his hierarchy never agreed to submit to the district prosecutor cases involving a French multinational company or a high rank politician he reported on. Furthermore, considering the reluctance of TRACFIN to submit cases to prosecution services or to communicate spontaneously probatory elements at its disposal, the national financial prosecution service[18] has systematically taken up the practice to send a request when undertaking a new case, ordering TRACFIN to transmit the relevant elements available to them. Explanations of TRACFIN difficulties to cooperate with criminal courts may probably be found in the hybrid nature of the agency, which was originally aimed to support penal authorities judicial actions but which, in the meantime, is also part of the French intelligence community established by Act of Parliament 2015-912 of 24 July 2015.

Besides, according to Article 40(2) CCP, constituted authorities, public officers or civil servants who, in the performance of their duties, have gained knowledge of the existence of a felony or of a misdemeanour have to notify forthwith the district prosecutor of the offence and to transmit to him/her any relevant information, official reports or documents. Nonetheless, the OECD notes the 'rare use' of this prerogative.[19]

---

[18] See below.
[19] OCDE, Rapport de phase 3 sur la mise en oeuvre par la France de la Convention de l'OCDE sur la lutte contre la corruption, octobre 2012, §.171.

Finally, some administrative authorities' inspection may enable them to detect economic and financial offences. To perform their investigations, they are granted powers, even coercive ones, that allow them to overcome resistance from subjected people.

Decree 2009-1535 has vested the Competition, Consumption and Frauds Repression General Directorate (Direction Générale de la Concurrence, de la Consommation et de la Répression des Fraudes—DGCCRF) with the power to control the compliance of people working in real-estate business with AML/TF requirements and sanction breaches of their duty of vigilance or their obligations to report suspicious transactions and comply with the freezing of assets orders. To perform this duty, agents enjoy coercive access to the workplace of people under investigation, the right to hear and question them and the possibility to examine documentation, including computer data, retrieved during access. On DGCCRF agents' demand, people working in the real-estate business do have to disclose documents and information required without being allowed to invoke for legal professional secrecy. Article L574-4 MFC makes refusal to answer information demands, obstruction to control and communication of false/erroneous information a criminal offence. Non-compliance with AML/TF duties recorded by DGCCRF agents expose the perpetrator to administrative penalties passed by the ministry of Economy Sanctions National Commission[20] which owes jurisdiction to sanction non-financial business professionals who do not resort to the jurisdiction of another administrative authority. Furthermore, according to Article R561-41 MFC, the Commission shall report the most serious cases to the public prosecutor.

According to the customs code, in the performance of their inspections, customs officers enjoy powers to 'visit' modes of transport (Articles 60–63); to search and seize in workplaces (Article 63 *ter*); to use illicit origin evidence when such evidence is 'legally' handed over by judicial authorities or through administrative assistance (Article 63E); subjected to a liberty and custody judge's warrant, to search and seize in private dwellings (Article 64); to disclosure (*communication*) of documents detained by State or local authorities and administrations, social security and unemployment services and some private legal entities (Articles 64A and 65); to control beneficiaries of EU subsidies and compliance with EU single market rules on free movement of goods (Articles 65A, A *bis* and B) and to access private legal entities data bases for customs inspection purposes (Article 67 *sexies*).

Within the public funds general directorate (direction générale des finances publiques—DGFiP), five nationwide jurisdiction directorates are entrusted with the fight against tax fraud, namely the national and international tax investigation directorate (direction des vérifications nationales et internationales—DVNI), the tax investigations national directorate (direction nationale des enquêtes

---

[20] Arts L561-37–L561-44 and R561-43–R561-50 MFC.

fiscales—DNEF), the tax investigations of tax statements national directorate (direction nationale des vérifications de situations fiscales—DNVSF), the general services and expatriates directorate (direction des résidents à l'étranger et des services généraux—DRESG) and the large companies directorate (direction des grandes entreprises—DGE). They have all developed a vast number of sub-groups such as the general tax investigation squads (brigades de vérification générale) within the DVNI or the inter-regional intervention squads (brigades inter-régionales d'intervention) of the DNEF. At local level, tax investigations are carried out by the tax inspection specialised directorates (directions spécialisées de contrôle fiscal—DIRCOFI) and the public funds regional and departmental services (services régionaux et départementaux des finances publiques), the latter being sub-divided in specialised services including departmental tax investigation squads (brigades départementales de vérification—BDV) and tax inspection and research squad (brigade de contrôle et de recherche—BCR). A liaison officer is in charge of the cooperation between the DGFiP services and TRACFIN. Furthermore, a collaboration protocol between the DGFiP and the customs investigation and inspection services of the customs and indirect taxes general directorate (direction générale des Douanes et des droits indirects—DGDDI) of 3 March 2011 allows crossed access to databases and exchange of information. At a political/strategic level, the coordination of governmental action is decided by the anti-fraud national committee (comité national de lutte contre la fraude), presided by the Prime Minister.

As far as investigations on tax offences are concerned, tax officers are, according to the Tax Proceedings Book (livre des procédures fiscales—TPB), allowed to implement powers to require from financial institutions the disclosure of a taxpayer bank account records (Article L10-0A); to use illicit origin evidence in tax procedures when such evidence is 'legally' handed over by judicial authorities or through administrative assistance (Article L10-0AA); to get involved in investigations launched by a district prosecutor on offences of non-justification of resources (Article L10B); subjected to a liberty and custody judge's authorisation and supervision, to search and seize in workplaces and private dwellings (Article L16B); to visit workplaces and require the disclosure of relevant documents related to (intra UE) VAT (Article L80F and L80I) and to require from inspected people, public prosecution services, State or local authorities and public legal entities, the resolution and prudential control authority and the financial markets authority, the disclosure of relevant documents and information (Articles L81, L82C, L83, L84D and L84E). Furthermore, according to Article L238 TPB, tax officers records are endowed with a reinforced probative value that binds trial courts. Finally, according to Articles L141A and L142 TPB, tax officers are allowed to disclose elements collected in the course of their investigations on request of a district prosecutor, an investigating judge or a court of justice. According to Article L135 TPB, tax and customs officers are obliged to answer demands made by police and *gendarmerie* officers relating to financial, tax and customs information and documents involving a criminal implication contained in their databases or files without professional secrecy being invokable, whenever the information requested is related to lucrative activities likely to impair law and order or public security.

As regards private individuals/entities associated with the prevention and detection of economic and financial offences can be mentioned, on the one hand, there are the disciplinary organs in charge of the supervision of the so-called 'regulated professions' (mainly Bar associations, notary chambers, auctioneer chambers, auditor associations and chartered account associations), on the other hand, the auditors who, according to Article L823-12 commercial code, are obliged to notify the district prosecutor of offences they have gained knowledge of in the performance of their duties. Furthermore, Act of Parliament 2013-1117 has provided for a general protection of whistleblowers which now extends to all forms of economic crimes that would resort to the jurisdiction of the EPPO (Article L1132-3-3 labour code) and has amended the Act of Parliament 83-634 to extend the protection to civil servants.[21] In the meantime, it provides for an attenuation of the sentence incurred by criminal turned informers in money laundering, corruption and influence peddling cases. Finally, attention should be paid to the role likely to be played by non-governmental organisations. Act of Parliament 2013-1117 has enacted Article 2-23 CCP that allows any lawfully registered association proposing through its constitution to fight corruption and economic crimes to exercise the rights granted to the civil party in respect of these offences.[22] Eventually, the protection of whistleblowers is substantially strengthened by articles 6 to 16 of Act of Parliament 2016-1691 which provides for a legal definition of the 'lanceur d'alerte' and improve both his/her defences against accusations of breach of professional secrecy and against subsequent dismissal procedures.

Once detected, economic and financial crimes will be investigated and prosecuted by other specialised authorities.

Investigation and Prosecution Authorities

Within the French criminal justice system, criminal investigations are carried out by administrative law enforcement authorities whereas prosecutions are launched by judicial magistrates in the public prosecution service.

---

[21] Arts L1161-1 and L1132-3-3 labour code and Art 6 *ter* A, Act of Parliament 83-634 *portant droits et obligations des fonctionnaires*.
[22] Unfortunately, the legislator did not amend Art 85 of the same Code that allows petition to become a civil party by filing a complaint with the competent investigating judge only after a previous complaint has been addressed to the public prosecutor for more than three months.

Law Enforcement Authorities

The assignment of cases to law enforcement authorities depends on how serious and complex each case is.[23]

Cases which are regarded as either trivial or simple are dealt with by local police and gendarmerie. Such cases hardly require cooperation with OLAF or the EPPO.

In practice, two central offices (offices centraux) of the judicial police central directorate (direction centrale de la police judiciaire—DCPJ) are mainly in charge of dealing with inquiries into economic and financial cases.

The central office for the repression of serious financial criminality (office central pour la répression de la grande délinquance financière—OCRGDF) is mainly in charge of money laundering, terrorism financing and fraud cases. It was established in 1990 and is responsible for coordinating activities of police and gendarmerie units in complex cases. It is usually in charge of investigations resulting from TRACFIN denunciations. Like all central squads, it is also entrusted with international cooperation, especially with Europol and Interpol.

Besides, decree 2013-960 of 25 October 2013 has established the central office for the fight against corruption and financial and tax offences (office central de lutte contre la corruption et les infractions financières et fiscales—OCLCIFF). The gendarmerie and the Ministry of Economy are 'associated' with the activities of the office which regroups national police, gendarmerie and tax judicial police officers. Article 2 of the decree provides that the office jurisdiction covers business criminal law offences (mainly corruption), tax offences listed in Article 28-2 CCP, breach of probity or political parties funding rule offences, and ancillary offences, including money laundering, when cases are or appear to be of 'great complexity'. The office gathers the national squad for the fight against tax criminality (brigade nationale de répression de la délinquance fiscale—BNRDF) and the national squad for the fight against corruption and financial crime (brigade nationale de lutte contre la corruption et la criminalité financière—BNLCCF). According to Article 4, it is competent to carry out judicial inquiries on demand of judicial authorities or on its own initiative, to assist on their request national police and national gendarmerie units in their investigations, to coordinate on the whole national territory operational judicial police investigations that fall within its jurisdiction, to handle abroad proceedings related to its jurisdiction and cooperate with foreign police forces, and to collect and centralise intelligence that fall within its jurisdiction from police and gendarmerie forces, customs, tax services judicial authorities and the DGCCRF in its area of competence, both for operational and documentary

---

[23] V Lemoine, 'Les aspects policiers de la lutte contre la corruption' (2012) *Droit pénal et procédure pénale, Dossier: Les manquements au devoir de probité* 23; JP Philippe, 'La lutte contre la corruption, le point de vue du policier à partir du retour d'expérience de plusieurs enquêtes' (2008) *Dossier—La lutte contre la corruption* 1095.

purposes. All enforcement agencies attached to the Ministries of Interior, Justice and Economy are to cooperate with the office and provide it with relevant materials collected in the course of their activities. Article 8 specifies that in its area of competence, the office is the designated central contact point for international cooperation and that it is allowed to develop and maintain operational liaisons both with homologous specialised services abroad and international organisations enforcement institutions. It is eventually in charge of contributing to the identification and freezing of criminal assets in tax and corruption offences and therefore cooperates with the criminal assets identification platform (plateforme d'identification des avoirs criminels) of the DCPJ. The OCLCIFF gathers about 90 officers and within the DCPJ is aimed at becoming the main interlocutor of the financial district prosecutor (procureur de la République financier).

According to the nature of the case investigated, three other central offices may be involved, namely the central office for the fight against counterfeited currencies (office central pour la répression du faux-monnayage), the central office for the fight against information technology and communication criminality (office central de lutte contre la criminalité liée aux technologies de l'information et de la communication) and the central office for the fight against organized crime (office central de lutte contre le crime organisé).

Besides, some specialised administrative agencies are involved.

Two Ministry of Economy services are vested with investigation powers, similar to those enjoyed by judicial police officers and, to a certain extent, with powers to sanction offences.

According to Article 28-1 CCP, 'I. Category A and B customs officers specifically designated by order of the Ministers of Justice and of Finance, (…), may be authorised to carry out judicial inquiries when required by a district prosecutor or on letters rogatory from an investigating judge. For the exercise of the duties specified under this article, these agents are competent to act on any part of the national territory. They are competent to seek out and establish: 1 offences under the customs code; 2 offences relating to indirect taxation, VAT fraud (…); 3 offences relating to the protection of the financial interests of the European Union; (…); 5 offences provided for under articles 324-1 to 324-9 of the criminal code; (…); 7 offences related to offences set out under 1 to 6. (…) IV. To carry out judicial inquiries and to receive letters rogatory, customs officers designated under I above must be personally authorised by a decision of the prosecutor general. This authorisation is made by the prosecutor general before the Court of Appeal in their jurisdiction. (…) V. For the performance of the duties mentioned in I and II above, customs officers come under the direction of the district prosecutor and are supervised by the prosecutor general (owing territorial jurisdiction).[24]

---

[24] CConst déc 84-184 DC du 29 décembre 1984, Rec p 94: Customs and tax investigations must be carried under supervision of a judicial authority as the Judiciary is according to Art 66 of the French Constitution entrusted with the protection of individual liberty.

VI. Where, when required by the district prosecutor or when acting under letter rogatory of an investigating judge, the customs officers referred to under I and II above carry out judicial inquiries, they owe the same prerogatives and obligations than those owed by judicial police officers[25] (…); VIII. Customs officers referred to under I and II as above may not, under penalty of nullity, exercise any other powers or carry out any other acts apart from those specified under the present Code and in the context of the matters with which they are entrusted by the judicial authority'. In the performance of their judicial police investigations, customs officers may further, under supervision of a district prosecutor, implement controlled delivery or infiltration operations and surveillance of persons suspected of customs offences on the whole of national territory while under point VIII. of this provision, the minister of Justice may authorise foreign customs officers to take part in surveillance operations on French soil under the supervision of French customs officers (Article 67 *bis*); subjected to either the district prosecutor's or the liberty and custody judge's authorisation, they may use tracking and tracing devices (Article 67 *bis*-2) and under preliminary authorisation of the minister of Justice and subjected to a decision made by a district prosecutor set up customs special joint investigation teams (Article 67 *ter*A).

As a consequence of the 2008 financial crisis, a judicial investigation procedure has been implemented to repress tax fraud offences.[26] According to Article 28-2 CCP, 'I. Category A and B tax officers specifically designated by order of the Ministers of Justice and of Budget, (…), may be authorised to carry out judicial inquiries when required by a district prosecutor or on an investigating judge's letters rogatory. To perform duties specified under this article, these agents are competent to act on any part of the national territory. They are competent to seek out and establish offences under articles 1741 and 1743 of the General Tax Code and money laundering ancillary offences when presumptions as stated in 1 to 5 of article L228 Tax Proceedings Book do exist. II. To carry out judicial inquiries and to receive letters rogatory, tax officers designated under I above must be personally authorised by a decision of the prosecutor general. (…) III. To perform duties mentioned in I and II above, tax officers exclusively come under the direction of the district prosecutor and are supervised by the prosecutor general (…). They are placed within the ministry of Interior. IV. Where, when required by the district prosecutor or when acting under an investigating judge letters rogatory, the tax officers referred to under I and II above carry out judicial inquiries, they owe the same prerogatives and obligations than those owed by judicial police officers (…). V. Tax officers referred to under I and II as above may not, under penalty of nullity, exercise any other powers or carry out any other acts apart from those specified under the present code and in the context of the matters with which they are entrusted by the judicial authority. VI. Tax officers authorised under II above shall not take part

---

[25] *cf* below.
[26] Art 23 Act of Parliament 2009-1674 of 30 December 2009 and decree 2010-914 of 3 August 2010.

in tax inspection proceedings during their period of authorisation nor take part to judicial inquiry on tax cases they have inspected before being authorised …'. As stated above, Article 28-2 CCP tax judicial police officers (BNRDF) have been merged within the OCLCIFF. The BNRDF gathers 22 national judicial police officers and 27 public funds agents (tax inspectors authorised as tax judicial officers) and is in charge of carrying out investigations on tax offences, using the special powers enlisted in Articles L228 and L188B TPB and 28-2 CCP.[27] This allows combining the abilities and capacities of both administrations. The functional integration of tax officers within the DCPJ is aimed at providing judicial police authorities with a 'supplemental technical support'[28] complementing pre-existing law enforcement organs that already gather under DCPJ authority Ministry of Economy and Ministry of Interior civil servants such as the economic investigation national squad (brigade national d'enquêtes économiques), the economic investigation regional groups (groupes régionaux d'enquêtes économiques) or the regional intervention groups (groupes d'intervention régionaux)[29] but without entrusting tax officers with judicial police powers. The squad owes jurisdiction to collect evidence on, and to record, offences enlisted in Article 28-2 CCP. It is vested with the power to coordinate judicial police investigations at national and operational levels, to cooperate with foreign authorities and, when legally allowed, investigate abroad; to centralise and circulate intelligence; to provide criminal analysis and assistance to other enforcement authorities (mainly national police and gendarmerie). Finally, the BNRDF systematically extends its inquiries to patrimonial investigations with a view to allowing seizures of criminal assets. Thus, judicial investigations allow to freeze suspects' assets and preserve effective possibilities of confiscations by trial courts.[30] Articles L16-0 BA and L252 B-1 TPB and L252 B GTC allow the Public Accountant to take protective measures without requesting a judicial order on the sole ground of tax flagrante delicto statements.

The DCPJ is entrusted with the global coordination of the various forces involved in the enforcement of the fight against economic crime as defined by the Act of Parliament 2013-1117.

Judicial Authorities

Cases which are regarded as either trivial or simple are dealt with at local level and submitted to the economic and financial sections of the *tribunaux de grande instance* prosecution services. Again, they hardly require cooperation with OLAF or the EPPO.

---

[27] cf below.
[28] L Ayrault, 'La pénalisation de la lutte contre la fraude fiscal' (2015/1) *REIDF* 39–40.
[29] Circulaire interministérielle du 22 mai 2002, NOR: INTC0200129C.
[30] G Hézard, 'Présentation de la brigade nationale de répression de la délinquance fiscale—Une idée audacieuse et originale pour le renforcement de la lutte contre la grande fraude fiscale' (2015/1) *REIDF* 65–66.

Article 704 CCP provides for inter-regional jurisdictions specialised in economic and financial cases (juridiction inter-régionale spécialisée—JIRS), in charge of dealing with cases 'of a great complexity'—meaning cases which involve a large number of perpetrators, accomplices or victims or committed on a large territorial scale, exceeding the geographical jurisdiction of a single court of appeal. The eight current JIRS owe jurisdiction to investigate, prosecute and, when dealing with misdemeanours, try offences provided for at Articles 222-38, 223-15-2, 313-1 and 313-2, 313-6, 314-1 and 314-2, 323-1–323-4, 324-1 and 324-2, 432-10–432-15, 433-1 and 433-2, 434-9, 435-1 and 435-2, 442-1–442-8 and 450-2-1 CC; misdemeanours provided for in the commercial code and the MFC; misdemeanours provided for at Articles 1741–1753 *bis* A of the general tax code and in the customs code, and ancillary offences. The territorial jurisdiction of the JIRS extends to the jurisdiction of several appeal courts. Article 704-1 specifies that 'for the prosecution, the investigation and, in the case of misdemeanours, the trial of the offences set out in article 704 and their ancillary offences, the district prosecutor, the investigating judge and the specialised correctional tribunal specified in the same article have a jurisdiction that is concurrent with that deriving from' ordinary rules governing jurisdiction and that 'where they hold jurisdiction for the prosecution and investigation of offences falling within the scope of article 704, the district prosecutor and the investigating judge exercise their duties over the whole territorial area determined pursuant to article 704'. Articles 704-2–704-4 provide for the settlement of conflicts of jurisdiction. In practice, JIRS enjoy a pre-emptive right over other jurisdictions, which they exercise under the control of the general prosecutor to the Court of Appeal they are attached to.

The national financial prosecution service (Parquet national financier—PNF), headed by the financial Republic prosecutor (procureur de la république financier—PRF) has been instituted within Paris tribunal de grande instance by Act of Parliament 2013-1117. According to the impact study attached to the 2013 draft Act of Parliament, the PNF has been designed to gather 22 magistrates in charge of an average of 260 procedures a year, each magistrate being more specifically in charge of an average of eight most serious cases. Today, the PNF gathers 16 magistrates, 14 of whom have operational activities, one is in charge of the general secretariat (and deals with organisation and communication issues) while the PRF supervises all cases and deals with strategic issues. Since it started its activities, 673 cases have been submitted to the PNF and 285 are currently on-going. All the magistrates appointed at the PNF have been selected on previous experience that qualifies them to deal with economic and financial cases (one is a former investigating judge at the financial pole of the Paris tribunal de grande instance, that has for a few years been seconded to the competition authority and the Ministry of Finance general inspection before joining the PNF, four magistrates were previously attached to the Paris financial prosecution service, one stems from the financial customs, another comes from the economic and financial cases department of the Ministry of Justice, one was attached at the Court of cassation documentation and studies section and with an highly academic background in economics, one is a former deputy prosecutor at an inter-regional specialised jurisdiction, another is a former prosecutor before the Paris Court of appeal economic chamber and the others are former investigating judges specialising in economic and financial cases). From 1 October 2015, four specialised assistants[31] will join the team: two tax administrators—one of whom comes from the Bastia tribunal de grande instance economic and financial pole where he was mainly in charge of the freezing of criminal assets procedures—a stock exchange expert and a chartered accountant.[32]

According to Article 705 CCP, the PNF owes jurisdiction to deal with cases of 'great complexity' which, in the words of the ministry of Justice circular (31 January 2014), mainly results from the existence of extraterritorial elements, the intricacy of the means used to perpetrate the fraud or offence and the 'visibility' of the company or agent involved in the crime. As far as this issue is concerned, the PRF faces two main difficulties: on the one hand, the necessity to select the more serious cases among the important number of cases referred to the PNF by district prosecutors (who consider they are ill-equipped to deal with economic and financial crimes)[33] to make sure that the service will not get overwhelmed and, on the other hand, the necessity to deprive defence lawyers of the argument that the PNF is passing over the legal definition of its jurisdiction. The same provision reads: 'The PRF, the investigating judges and the Paris specialized correctional tribunal have a jurisdiction that is concurrent with that deriving from' ordinary rules governing jurisdiction, including those of the JIRS, 'to investigate, prosecute and, in the case of misdemeanours, try the following offences' (corruption, VAT fraud, tax fraud, money laundering, favouritism and ancillary offences). The PNF and the investigating judges attached to it owe nationwide jurisdiction. Besides, the PNF and Paris specialised correctional tribunal owe exclusive jurisdiction to investigate, prosecute and try insider dealing cases and other stock market offences. Articles 705-2–705-4 deal with the settlement of conflicts of jurisdiction which are ultimately left to the decision of the Criminal Chamber of the Court of Cassation. Contrary to what could have been apprehended, the concurrent jurisdiction with courts owing territorial jurisdiction owed by the PNF has given rise to very few positive conflicts of jurisdiction that were all rapidly settled by the Paris general prosecutor.[34] As far as operational aspects are concerned, the PRF regards

---

[31] Art 706 CCP.

[32] The PNF develops a systematic practice of (pre-trial) freezing and/or seizure of criminal assets (since 2014, 65 million euros have been impounded). Besides the recent appointment of a tax administrator expert whose activities will be mainly dedicated to this aim, instructions are given to police forces to systematically investigate the 'patrimonial environment' of suspects with a view to allowing an early crystallisation.

[33] The lack of both human means and expertise somehow impairs the efficiency of the fight against business criminality at a local level in France.

[34] Certainly, through its prerogative to settle conflicts of jurisdiction resulting from the implementation of his/her pre-emptive right by the Financial District Prosecutor, the Criminal Chamber of the Court of cassation may act as the ultimate authority to coordinate the activity of the different judi-

the French model as 'well thought out'. The restrictive *ratione materiae* jurisdiction allows focusing on serious cases whereas the autonomy given to the PNF allows restoring the Prosecutor's role as 'inquiry director' directly involved in the investigations. In practice, since the PRF has started her activities, she has pre-empted all relevant complex corruption and economic crimes cases. So the PRF may certainly be amongst the main interlocutors of the EPPO in France and that it might even be designated as delegated EPPO.

Regarding the rules governing the allocation of cases to police forces, the PNF mainly refers cases to the OCLCIFF[35] when the case appears of 'great complexity' and/or of national dimension (the case may then be co-submitted to the OCLCIFF and the local judicial police regional directorate—direction régionale de la police judiciaire). A substantial number of cases are also referred to the financial squad (brigade financière), particularly stock market cases, and to the economic criminality squad[36] (brigade de répression de la délinquance économique—BRDE) of the Paris Préfecture de police. Accessorily, some investigations are referred to the judicial customs national service (service national des douanes judiciaires) or to the gendarmerie (an agreement has recently been concluded between the PNF and the gendarmerie director; the force will mainly be involved in investigations carried out in French overseas territories). On the other hand, the PNF practice is to limit as much as possible the submission of cases to investigating judges who are overwhelmed by the number of cases they have to deal with. Furthermore, pragmatic experience does not confirm that business criminal law cases dealt with by investigating judges better thrive before trial courts. As successive reforms since 2004 have vested prosecutors in preliminary inquiries with powers similar to those owed by investigating judges and as the police officers that will in practice be put in charge of carrying out the investigations are the same, the submission of a case to an investigating judge is felt necessary only when prosecutors consider that coercive measures that can only be ordered by an investigating judge should be implemented (for example, pre-trial probation). Finally, despite the provisions of Article L811-3 of the interior security code (code de la sécurité intérieure), enacted by Act of Parliament 2015-912 of 24 July 2015, that allows French specialised

---

cial authorities involved in the investigation of the most complex cases. Nonetheless, in its report to the Minister of Justice, the Commission on public prosecution modernisation identifies a difficulty that has not yet been solved by the legislator: no authority is legally in charge of settling conflicts of jurisdiction between a 'JIRS' and a prosecutor, located in a different Court of appeal, who would owe jurisdiction according to ordinary rules of procedure. Indeed, no legal mechanism is provided for the settlement of conflicting decisions made by two prosecutors general when they arise. Since an Act of Parliament of 25 July 2013, the minister of Justice has been deprived of his/her prerogative to give instructions in such a situation. The Commission recommends that the 'JIRS' general prosecutor be put in charge of settling the conflict. Obviously it would not provide any solution if two different JIRS claim for jurisdiction.

[35] Décret 2013-960 du 25 octobre 2013 portant création d'un office central de lutte contre la corruption et les infractions financières et fiscales, JORF 0251 du 27 octobre 2013, texte No 6.

[36] Cases involving elements concentrated exclusively in the Paris Court of appeal jurisdiction.

intelligence services to enforce special techniques to collect intelligence with a view to protecting '3 France major economic, industrial and scientific interests' or to '6 preventing organized criminality', the PNF keeps very limited relationships with the internal security general directorate (Direction générale de la sécurité intérieure—DGSI): right now, it is only requested to transmit information on the 'environment' of 'sensitive' companies or individuals involved in cases. Nevertheless, although the DGSI activities are currently focused on counter-terrorism, the new legislation is promising and the PRF does not exclude appealing more to this force in the future.

Currently, the main concern of the PRF is the dependence of the PNF towards on specialised police forces *lato sensu* which are all under dimensioned and therefore not always able to carry out in due time acts requested by prosecutors. For example, the tax administration refers to prosecutors an average of 100 cases per year when the OCLCIFF is, depending on the complexity of cases, only able to deal with 30 to 40 cases a year. Furthermore, neither the OCLCIFF nor the BRDE are exclusively dedicated to the PNF. Both also carry out investigations under investigating judges' letters rogatory or other prosecutors' requests. As the OCLCIFF and BRDE directors enjoy a completely free hand to assign cases to their officers, the efficiency of PNF work may sometimes be affected by the concentration of police means on other priorities. Besides, a recurrent difficulty[37] remains: the fight against economic and financial criminality is not regarded as a priority by French political authorities. For more than ten years, it has mainly been thought out by the Ministry of Interior as incidental to the fight against organised crime. Furthermore, the mobilisation of the required forces is currently affected by the massive appointment of police officers to counter-terrorism forces or activities. It is all the more a handicap since the PRF expects prosecutors to get more and more personally involved in acts of investigation—they already take part in searches and are expected to get more systematically involved in hearings and questionings— with a view to setting up a more efficient time management in procedures. This is corroborated by the conclusions of a recent report on the 'modernisation of prosecution services' from the commission appointed by the Minister of Justice.[38] It points out that action priorities of police forces are too often assigned by the Minister of Interior, without taking into consideration the penal policy carried out by the district prosecutor within his/her jurisdiction. As a consequence, the commission further recommends the strengthening of the functional authority of public prosecution services over judicial police forces. Eventually, the Commission suggests the secondment of police and gendarmerie liaison officers to the public

---

[37] See O Cahn, *La politique criminelle de lutte contre la corruption en France ou la théorie du chapon*, in *Politique(s) criminelle(s)—Mélanges en l'honneur de Christine Lazerges* (Paris, Dalloz, 2014) 497–522.

[38] Commission de modernisation de l'action publique (sous la présidence de Jean-Louis NADAL, procureur général honoraire près la Cour de cassation), *Rapport à Mme la garde des sceaux, ministre de la Justice—Refonder le ministère public*, Novembre 2013, recommandations 38 and 39.

prosecution services to ease the collaboration between the two entities. A more efficient remedy could certainly be found in other EU Member States' criminal justice systems in which economic and financial prosecution services have dedicated police and tax officers at their disposal and under their sole authority. This is nonetheless unlikely to happen in France as the Ministry of Interior systematically opposes the uniting of the judicial police with the Ministry of Justice.

Powers of Investigation
and Prosecution Authorities

As a consequence of the mere specificities of economic and financial offences, hardly any investigation is carried out under *in flagrante delicto* proceedings. Investigative bodies become aware of offences merely through the reporting of an offence or a complaint from the victim. Currently, in most cases, the district prosecutor orders a preliminary inquiry. Judicial police then act under his/her supervision.[39] Police forces nonetheless enjoy autonomy in the conduction of investigations as, according to Article 12 CCP, in the absence of any specific instructions from the district prosecutor, officers are left free to decide the appropriate means they should implement to carry out their investigations.

Following Act of Parliament 2013-1117, important (coercive) powers have been made available to the law enforcement authorities involved in the investigation of economic and financial crimes. Nevertheless, obstacles remain that are likely to impair the efficiency of the penal apparatus.

Special (Derogatory) Powers of Investigation[40]

On the one hand, the powers available for the investigation of economic and financial offences are those enforceable by police forces in preliminary investigations. Article 76 provides for searches, house visits and seizures, either with the express consent of the person in whose residence the search is carried out or subjected to an authorisation granted by the liberty and custody judge at the request of the district prosecutor. Under identical conditions, judicial police officers may, during the course of a seizure, access any data relevant to the inquiry stored in a computer system set up within the premises where the seizure is carried out or in another computer system, provided the data is accessible from the initial

---

[39] Or under an investigating judge supervision when occasionally the case is submitted to such a magistrate.

[40] See J Tricot, 'France' in K Ligeti, *Toward a Prosecutor for the European Union: A Comparative Analysis*, vol. I (Oxford, Hart, 2013). CCP provisions are for those in force before 2005, quoted from Prof JR Spencer, *Code of criminal procedure*, http://www.legifrance.gouv.fr/Traductions/en-English.

system. Data capture may be made; furthermore, computer storage equipment may be seized and placed in judicial safekeeping (Article 76-3). Post interception is governed by the rules on search and seizure. However, Act of Parliament 2009-928[41] has significantly increased the range of confidential classification on ground of national defence and enacted Article 56-4 CCP that submits searches and seizure in classified premises and of classified documents to a prior authorisation of the Executive. Article 77 deals with police questioning and police custody. In its decision 2013-679 DC of 4 December 2013,[42] the Constitutional Council found inconsistent with the Constitution the enforcement of four-day long derogatory police custody (Article 706-88 CCP) when dealing with such offences. As a consequence, police custody cannot exceed 48 hours when investigating economic and financial offences and access to legal advice and council assistance should not be postponed. According to Article 61-1 CCP, enacted by Act of Parliament 2014-535, anyone who may plausibly be suspected of committing or trying to commit an offence shall not be questioned unless he/she has been given notice of the legal qualification, time and place of the offence he/she is suspected of, his/her right to leave the police station at any time, his/her right to be assisted by a translator, his/her right to remain silent and his/her right to be assisted by a lawyer. Any person summoned to questioning by a police officer is compelled to appear. At the end of the hearing, an official record of the statements and the questions asked must be drawn up immediately and signed. Confrontations may also take place. The district prosecutor or the police officer may call on any qualified person (who will take an oath when he/she is inscribed on the official list or, if not, each time he/she is called upon) 'if any technical or scientific reports or examinations need to be carried out' (CCP, Articles 60 and 77-1). The *Cour de cassation* considers that the technical or scientific tasks requested by the prosecutor are of the same nature as those ordered by the investigating judge to the expert. According to Article 77-1-1, police officers may, upon prior authorisation from the district prosecutor, order any person, establishment or organisation, whether public or private, or any public services liable to possess any documents relevant to the inquiry, including those produced from a registered computer or data processing system, to disclose them. This measure applies to banking information and transactions. Since Act of Parliament 2002-1094 of 29 August 2002, agents of tax and customs directorates and DGCCRF have also been compelled to disclose to police officers, at their request, any information or documents. Professional secrecy cannot be put forward not to comply with this order.[43] Finally, Article 77-1-2 allows judicial police officers, on the authorisation of the district prosecutor, to require public organisations or private legal persons

---

[41] Art L2312-1 and L2312-4 defense code and Art 413-9–413-11 CC.

[42] CConst., décision 2013-679 DC du 4 décembre 2013, Loi relative à la lutte contre la fraude fiscale et la grande délinquance économique et financière, considérant 77.

[43] Nonetheless, when information required relates to lawyers, doctors and journalists, the transmission of documents is subjected to their prior consent.

to make helpful information available, when stored in one or several computer or data processing systems they administer. For the needs of discovery and reporting of offences, Act of Parliament 2001-1062 of 15 November 2001 requires telecommunications operators to keep subscribers' or users' identification data and calls' technical characteristics at the disposal of the judicial authorities for one year. Upon prior authorisation from the liberty and custody judge, the public prosecutor may order judicial police officers to require telecommunications operators to take without delay all appropriate measures to retain information consulted by users for a period that cannot exceed one year. Articles 695-9-1 *et seq* CCP adapt French criminal procedure to the requirements of the EU Council's Framework Decision 2003/577/JHA of 22 July 2003 on the freezing of assets. Finally, Act of Parliament 2010-768 of 9 July 2010 allows investigating judges or liberty and custody judges, on the request of prosecutors, to order criminal protective seizures at investigation stage with a view to guaranteeing the enforcement of confiscation complementary sentences trial courts may pass. All kinds of goods and assets may be 'frozen'. Assets seized during investigations are left in the care of the agence de gestion et de recouvrement des avoirs saisis et confisqués (AGRASC).[44] Orders are subjected only to proportionality requirements.[45]

On the other hand, Act of Parliament 2013-1117 has enacted Articles 706-1-1 and 706-1-2 CCP that provide for the possibility of enforcing the derogatory provisions of Articles 706-80–706-87 and 706-95–706-103, 706-105 and 706-106 to investigate, prosecute and try offences, respectively of corruption, tax fraud offences and money laundering ancillary offences and of misuse of corporate assets.[46] Besides, Act of Parliament 2015-993 of 17 August 2015 has enacted Article 706-73-1 CPP that makes the same special powers available to law enforcement forces investigating swindling, some labour offences and ancillary offences, when committed by an organised group.

Article 706-80 CCP provides for '*surveillance*' measures, both 'tailing' and controlled deliveries. It allows judicial police officers, acting within the framework of a preliminary police inquiry to extend the measure to the whole national territory, after informing the prosecutor (although his authorisation is not required).

According to Article 706-81 *et seq* CCP, that provide for 'infiltration' measures, police officers are granted, on authorisation from the district prosecutor, the power to keep under surveillance persons suspected of committing a felony or a misdemeanour by passing themselves off as one of their fellow perpetrators, accomplices or receivers. To this end, officers may use an assumed identity and

---

[44] Arts 131-21 and 131-39 CC and 706-141–706-164 CCP; T Ballot, 'Réflexions sur les sanctions patrimoniales à la lumière du recouvrement des avoirs issus de la corruption transnationale' (2013) *RSC*, 321

[45] Cons const déc No 2010-66 QPC du 26 november 2010; ECHR, 26 february 2009, *Grifhorst v France*, App. n. 28336/02 et ECHR, 4 november 2014, *Aboufadda v France*, App No 28457/10.

[46] Arts L 241-3 and L 242-6 commercial code.

commit, when necessary, some offences limitedly enumerated in the provision. The infiltration operation is limited to a maximum of four months, renewable.

Article 706-95 allows police officers to carry out interceptions of communications within the framework of a preliminary inquiry. The measure must be authorised by an order from the liberty and custody judge, at the request of the prosecutor, for a maximum period of 15 days, renewable once under the same conditions of form and duration. Special safeguards are provided in respect of certain professions or functions (Members of Parliament, magistrates, lawyers).

Articles 706-96–706-102 CCP provide for the taking of audiovisual recordings in vehicles and dwellings. An investigating judge, after hearing the opinion of the prosecutor, may by means of a reasoned decision authorise judicial police officers acting under letters rogatory to install any appropriate technical device to detect, retain, transmit or record words spoken or images of people in private places or vehicles. The authorisation is given for a maximum period of four months, renewable.

According to Articles 706-102-1–706-102-9, enacted by Act of Parliament 2011-267, an investigating judge, after hearing the opinion of the prosecutor, may by means of a reasoned decision authorise judicial police officers acting under letters rogatory to install any appropriate technical device to access in any places, record, retain and transmit data as they appear on the screen for the user of an automated data processing system, as they are introduced in an automated data processing system by input characters or as they are received or transmitted by audiovisual peripherals. Operations are carried out under the authority and supervision of the investigating judge. The authorisation is given for a maximum period of four months, renewable.

Article 706-73 CCP allows the liberty and custody judge, on request of the district prosecutor, to order protective measures on goods belonging to a person under judicial information.

Furthermore, Act of Parliament 2014-372 provides for tracking and tracing objects and individuals measures and adapting French law to the requirements of European standards.[47] According to Articles 230-32 *et seq* CCP, in misdemeanors investigations when the sentence incurred is of a minimum of three years, tracking and tracing devices can be implemented for 15 days under authorisation from the district prosecutor. Renewal for a month is subjected to the authorisation of the liberty and custody judge on request of the district prosecutor. Operations are carried out under the supervision of the magistrate that authorised them.

It appears that the PNF is making moderate use of investigation special techniques whereas, up till now, inquiries have not been impaired by the constitutional prohibition of derogatory custodies. The only difficulty lies in legal limits governing the interception of communications in private corruption cases. Nonetheless, according to the PRF, the fairly uncommon enforcement of special

[47] ECHR, 2 September 2010, *Uzun v Germany*, App. n. 35623/05.

techniques is mainly due to the recent creation of a service that still has to set up and develop its own practices and the use of these prerogatives will certainly increase in the future.

Finally, according to Article 695-9-31 CCP, implementing the framework-decision 2006/960/JAI, police forces, customs and tax officers designated by the minister of Justice are, on their initiative, allowed to exchange information in their possession with their counterparts in another EU Member State with a view to preventing a criminal offence, collecting evidence of a criminal offence or identifying perpetrators. Similar prerogatives are given to the French assets recovery office under Article 695-9-50 *et seq* CCP for the implementation of Council decision 2007/845/JHA of 6 December 2007. According to the PRF, international cooperation with other EU Member States is satisfactory, although it needs strengthening. Nonetheless, cooperation with Switzerland is regarded as more difficult, local authorities remaining reluctant to satisfy foreign authorities' requests. Amongst EU tools, exchange of intelligence mechanisms and joint investigation teams are regarded as noticeable improvements. Some need for approximation of practices and simplification of the mechanisms is nonetheless pointed out. In September 2015, a first case was referred to the PNF by OLAF. Finally, the PNF has currently no contact with EUROJUST.[48] International cooperation issues have been settled through French liaison magistrates in other EU Member States and the PNF has not yet faced conflicts of jurisdiction with judicial authorities in another Member State.

Furthermore, Act of Parliament 2016-1691 enacts a new article 41-1-2 CCP which provides that, until the initiation of public proceedings, the district prosecutor may offer legal entities suspected of being involved in corruption, money laundering or tax fraud offences, to conclude a public interest judicial convention aimed at imposing them legal obligations such as to pay the Treasury a public interest fine and/or to submit themselves, for a period of time of three years maximum, to a compliance programme under the supervision of the Agence française anti-corruption. The costs involved by the implementation of the programme, as designed by the agency, shall entirely be borne by the legal entity. The convention is subjected to a validation order made by a criminal court. It involves a deferred prosecution agreement and the public prosecutor's right of action is extinguished by the fulfillment of the legal obligations.

According to Article 20, 2, of the Act of Parliament 2012-354, tax judicial police agents are, under the supervision of the public prosecutor or on letters rogatory delivered by an investigating judge allowed to implement the powers owed by judicial police officers in preliminary investigations, whereas following Act of Parliament 2013-1117, they may implement the special derogatory prerogatives aimed at curbing organised crime. Article 63 of Act of Parliament 2010-1658 extends the jurisdiction of the force to offences related to fraud. Besides, Article L228 TPB provides that, subject to three conditions (the existence of

---

[48] The PRF has planned a visit to make herself known there.

blatant presumptions of fraud, the seriousness of the fraud and the risk of evidence decline), the DGFiP may refer the case to the tax offences commission (commission des infractions fiscales—CIF) that may allow the administration to refer the case to the prosecutor, who may then decide the launch of an investigation by the tax judicial police. In other words, this complaint on suspicion procedure allows the law enforcement authorities to resort to Article 28-2 CCP judicial police prerogatives when the revenue services, using their ordinary administrative powers, have collected evidence of a fraud which is not sufficient to allow administrative sanctions to be taken. Furthermore, with a view to limiting the risk of evidence destruction, the suspect offender is not advised of the submission of the case to the CIF nor of the decision of the commission or subsequent referring of the case to the prosecutor.[49] The rights of defence are thus restricted, which has been admitted by criminal courts on the ground that the suspect will then have a fair trial.[50]

Although the penal system looks rather impressive, obstacles remain that may impair its effectiveness.

Obstacles to Repressive Effectiveness

Apart from the under endowment of police forces previously mentioned, three obstacles should be lifted to guarantee the effectiveness of the fight against economic and financial crimes in France.

On the one hand, according to Articles L188B and L228 TPB and 28-2 CCP, the Revenue administration enjoys an exclusive jurisdiction to register a complaint against suspected defrauders. Complaints for the enforcement of criminal sentences in tax offence cases may only be filled on prior approval by the CIF (so-called 'Bercy-locker'). Within the DGFiP, the tax inspection under-directorate (sous-direction du contrôle fiscal) is in charge of discretionarily selecting cases that will be referred to the CIF, which is made up of State Counsellors and Revenue Court magistrates and is in charge of allowing tax cases to be referred to the district prosecutor. On pain of inadmissibility, it is only once a case is thus referred to the district prosecutor that he/she is legally allowed, according to his/her discretionary power to assess the opportunity to start a prosecution, to decide either to close the case with no further action, to bring the offender before the correctional tribunal or, in most complex cases, to launch a preliminary inquiry or appoint an investigating judge. Prosecutions started by a district prosecutor on his/her own initiative shall be dismissed,[51] while the CIF owes no power to submit a case to the prosecutor on its own initiative. Despite criticisms, the legislator is not ready to amend this rule, as shown by the 2013 reform that slightly amended

---

[49] G Hézard, 'Présentation de la brigade nationale de répression de la délinquance fiscale' 65–66.
[50] Cass crim 2 mai 1984, Bull. crim No 151 et Cass crim 9 février 2011, No 10-86072.
[51] Cass crim, 27 juin 2001, No 01-81.865, Bull crim 2001, No 163.

but kept the requirement of such preliminary procedure as a prerequisite for initiating public prosecution.

Besides, in tax or customs cases, public authorities may decide not to refer the case to the public prosecution service with a view to trying first to search for an out-of-court settlement with the offender. Such settlements bar further prosecutions.

Furthermore, both the Revenue and the Customs are authorised by statute to initiate a prosecution concurrently with the public prosecutor. In such cases, investigations will be conducted directly by tax or customs officers under supervision of their hierarchy and may be brought to court by these authorities, leaving to public prosecutors only to request the enforcement of the law. Nonetheless, when in the course of such investigations, it appears necessary to resort to coercive measures outside the scope of the Ministry of Economy officers' powers, the case has to be referred to the public prosecutor as it is only on his/her request that the liberty and custody judge may issue a warrant allowing such a power to be enforced.

However, this obstacle should not be over-estimated. Criminal courts have allowed cases to be prosecuted on VAT fraud[52] or money laundering charges,[53] without prior approval by the CIF and complaint by the Revenue. Besides, decision rates reveal that, out of the about 1000 cases a year referred by the DGFiP, the CIF gives a 90 per cent agreement to lodge a complaint and 100 per cent agreement to launch complaint on suspicion procedures.[54]

On the other hand, following the ECHR decision of 4 March 2014, *Grande Stevens and others v Italy*, 18640/10, 18647/10, 18663/10, 18668/10 and 18698/10, the French *Conseil constitutionnel*, in decision 2014-453/454 QPC and 2015-462 QPC of 18 March 2015, has, on the ground of the *ne bis in idem* principle, decided that the consecutive pronouncement of administrative and criminal sentences to punish the same facts violates the Constitution. Now, nothing in the decision or in the legal provisions provides for priority to be given to criminal proceedings. Furthermore, both pragmatic and political reasons[55] have driven the French legislator to show a growing interest for out of criminal court settlements of business cases through sanctions passed by independent administrative authorities[56] while offenders and their lawyers are all in favour as the sentences are financial and felt as non infamous.[57]

---

[52] Cass crim, 19 oct. 1987, No 85-94.605, Bull crim 1987, No 353.

[53] Cass crim, 20 févr 2008, No 07-82.977, Bull crim 2008, No 43.

[54] O Debat, 'La Commission des infractions fiscales, les ressorts d'un désamour inépuisable '(2015/1) *REIDF* 80.

[55] Restrictions to the defence rights, celerity of the procedures, quicker recovery of fines but also challenging of criminal law and penal courts legitimacy to interfere with business activities.

[56] O Cahn, 'Le sentencing anglo-américain, avenir de l'administration des peines en France?' (36/2014) *APC* 250.

[57] B Fontaine, M Guyomar, F Pesin, S Baranger, 'Les procédures de contrôle sur place des régulateurs financiers: état des lieux et perspectives d'évolution', (2012) *Bulletin Joly Bourse et produits financiers* 378–388.

As a consequence, both the 'Bercy locker' and the intervention of independent administrative authorities are likely to restrain progressively the role of criminal courts in the fight against economic and financial crimes.

Finally, although Act of Parliament 2013-1117 has overruled Articles 435-6 and 435-11 CC—that used to reserve to the quasi-monopoly of public prosecutors the power to initiate investigations in foreign public agent corruption cases through conditioning victims' right to petition to become a civil party to a prior decision by the prosecutor to start proceedings—the legislator has maintained Articles 113-5 and 113-8 of the same code whereas these provisions insidiously protect French legal entities or individuals who commit acts of bribery abroad. Indeed, requirements stated in these provisions will hardly be satisfied when acts of corruption are perpetrated in countries where corruption is endemic. Furthermore, the combination of, on the one hand, Article 689-8 and Article 695-22 CCP and, on the other hand, the reluctance of French public prosecution services to prosecute serious corruption cases involving huge national companies, allows in practice the removal of nationals involved in corruption activities likely to infringe EU financial interests against whom a European arrest warrant has been issued by a foreign court. Besides, French legislation still does not properly guarantee the independence of the public prosecution services. Although the PRF gives evidence of her determination to break up with a tradition that long favoured the protection of French economic interests over the enforcement of economic and financial criminal law, there is no guarantee that her successors will perpetuate the legalistic policy she is implementing.

Part III

The Role of Administrative
Authorities in Investigating
Financial-Economic Crimes

4

The Investigation and Prosecution of Economic and Financial Crimes— Role and Function of Administrative Authorities in Germany

PROF DR MARTIN BÖSE[1]
Professor of Criminal Law, Criminal Procedure,
International and European Criminal Law
University of Bonn

Introduction

Criminal proceedings on economic and financial crime are often complex and require substantial resources and expertise. Therefore, it appears quite reasonable for a criminal justice system to create specialised institutions and to provide them with the resources, the expertise and the investigative powers that are necessary to effectively combat economic and financial crime. Even though the German legislator has adopted several measures to that end, the legal and institutional framework is still mainly orientated towards the traditional set of rules on criminal proceedings. In particular, there is no special procedural regime for the investigation and prosecution of economic and financial crime. Consequently, the corresponding proceedings are subject to the general rules of the Code of Criminal Procedure. Nevertheless, these rules are modified and supplemented by special provisions on the investigation and prosecution of financial and economic crimes.

Due to this legal framework of the German criminal justice system, this contribution will first give a brief overview of the general framework for the

[1] To a significant extent, the report is based upon two interviews conducted with officials of the revenue office for tax crimes and tax investigation (*Finanzamt für Steuerstrafsachen und Steuerfahndung*) and the public prosecutor's office (*Staatsanwaltschaft*) of Bonn in August 2015. The author would like to thank Mr Klaus-Dieter Hermann-Tenk (director of the revenue office for tax crimes and tax investigation) and his staff, and Mr Florian Geßler (public prosecutor) for their great willingness to provide information on operational aspects of criminal investigations in tax matters.

investigation and prosecution of financial and economic crimes. The second part will then highlight the role of administrative investigations and focus on the tasks and powers of the revenue authorities. Finally, the interplay between revenue authorities and the public prosecutor's office shall be examined.

The General Framework for the Investigation and Prosecution of Financial and Economic Crimes

Criminal investigations are usually conducted by the public prosecutor's office with the support of the police. The public prosecutor's office conducts the criminal investigation,[2] and the police has to comply with the public prosecutor's directions.[3] The police, however, shall investigate criminal offences and shall take all measures that may not be deferred, in order to prevent concealment of facts.[4] In practice, most of the investigative measures are carried out by the police. In that sense, the police enjoy de facto a certain degree of autonomy; in straightforward cases the police may even investigate the case on its own and transmit their findings to the public prosecutor's office for filing the indictment.[5] Nevertheless, the more complex a case is, the more coordination with the public prosecutor's office will be required. In any case, the police are subject to the public prosecutor's instructions[6] so that there is no autonomy in a strictly legal sense.

During the investigation, the public prosecutor may order any investigative measure available under the Code of Criminal Procedure.[7] As it has been mentioned before, German law does not provide for special measures for the investigation of financial and economic crimes. Correspondingly, there is no express legal basis for real time bank monitoring. However, this measure can be implemented by periodically issued production orders.[8] In the investigation of tax crimes, the most frequently used investigative measures are the examination of witnesses (eg, employees), search and seizure of business records and documents. With regard to the latter, searches are usually extended to the suspect's tax advisor in order to obtain the accounting documents.[9] By contrast, surveillance

---

[2] 1987 Code of Criminal Procedure (*Strafprozessordnung*), ss 160 and 161(1)1.

[3] 1987 Code of Criminal Procedure (*Strafprozessordnung*), s 161(1)2.

[4] 1987 Code of Criminal Procedure (*Strafprozessordnung*), s 163(1) CCP.

[5] Erb '§ 163' in Löwe, Rosenberg, *Strafprozessordnung*, vol. 5 (§§ 151–212b), XXVI edn (Berlin, De Gruyter, 2008), paras 24–26.

[6] 1987 Code of Criminal Procedure (*Strafprozessordnung*), s 161(1)2.

[7] 1987 Code of Criminal Procedure (*Strafprozessordnung*), ss 81a ff, 94 ff.

[8] See with regard to s 95 CCP and Art 3 of the Protocol to the EU convention on mutual legal assistance in criminal matters: explanatory memorandum of the federal government to the Protocol, Document of the Parliament (*Bundestags-Drucksache*) No 15/4230, 12.

[9] Information provided by the public prosecutor's office in Bonn. For the exemption of these documents from the legal professional privilege, see Menges '§ 97' in Löwe, Rosenberg, *Strafprozessordnung*, vol 3 (§§ 94–111p), para 111, with further references.

measures (eg, interception of telecommunications) become only relevant for a small number of (serious) cases (eg smuggling, organised crime).[10]

As economic and legal expertise is a key factor in effectively investigating financial and economic crime, German law allows for a local concentration of the competence to investigate and prosecute economic crimes.[11] For example, in the State of North Rhine-Westphalia, the public prosecutor's offices of Bielefeld, Bochum, Düsseldorf and Cologne contain special prosecution units (*Schwerpunkt-Staatsanwaltschaften*) which have been especially established to combat conomic and financial crime.[12] Notwithstanding the existence of these special units, the other public prosecutor's offices have also special departments for the investigation of these kind of crimes.[13]

Within the police, there is no unit specialised in combatting economic and financial crime. However, the District Police Headquarters (*Polizeipräsidium*) have special departments dealing with these crimes.[14] Furthermore, upon request of the public prosecutor's office, the State Office of Criminal Investigations (*Landeskriminalamt*) investigates complex economic and financial crimes with a transregional or transnational dimension.[15] Regardless of the special mandate of these offices, any criminal investigation is subject to the general rules.

The role of federal authorities in the investigation of financial and economic crime is rather limited. As a consequence of the federalist structure of the German State, law enforcement is generally not a federal but a state competence (*Länder*). Accordingly, the investigation, prosecution and adjudication of economic and financial crime falls within state competence. Investigative and prosecutorial powers of federal authorities, ie the Federal Criminal Police Office (*Bundeskriminalamt*) and the Federal Public Prosecutor (*Generalbundesanwalt*), have a rather limited scope (crimes against the State such as terrorism or core crimes of international criminal law) and do not extend to financial and economic crimes.[16] In general, the execution of administrative law falls within state competence, too.[17] Hence, administrative investigations are conducted by state authorities. In a number

[10] Information provided by the public prosecutor's office in Bonn.
[11] Courts Constitution Act, s 143(4).
[12] Circular of the Minister of Justice of the state *Nordrhein-Westfalen* of 30 March 1968 (4100—III A 172).
[13] Information provided by the public prosecutor's office in Bonn.
[14] See the information provided by the state office of criminal investigations (*Landeskriminalamt*), available at http://www.polizei.nrw.de/lka/artikel__9161.html (4 September 2015).
[15] See, eg, on the State North Rhine Westfalia: 2002 Police Organisation Act (*Polizeiorganisationsgesetz*), s 13(3) No 3; 2015 Regulation on the tasks of the state office of criminal investigations (*Verordnung über weitere polizeiliche Aufgaben des Landeskriminalamts bei der Gefahrenabwehr sowie der Erforschung und Verfolgung von Straftaten*), s 3(1) No 7.
[16] 1997 Act on the Federal Criminal Police Office (*Bundeskriminalamtgesetz*), s 4(1), and, as far as the federal public prosecutor ('Generalbundesanwalt') is concerned, 1975 Courts Constitution Act (*Gerichtsverfassungsgesetz*), ss 142a(1) and 120(1), (2).
[17] 1949 Basic Law (*Grundgesetz*), Art 83.

of areas of administrative law, however, federal authorities are involved in law enforcement and criminal investigations in particular, eg the Customs Criminal Investigation Office (*Zollkriminalamt*)[18] or the Federal Financial Supervisory Authority (*Bundesanstalt für Finanzdienstleistungsaufsicht*).[19] In particular, a federal agency (eg the Federal Central Tax Office—*Bundeszentralamt für Steuern*) can provide support to criminal investigations. Nevertheless, the majority of investigations are conducted not by federal but by state (*Länder*) authorities.

The Role of Specialised Administrative Authorities in the Investigation and Prosecution of Financial and Economic Crimes

Given the expertise of administrative authorities in their field of competence, it appears reasonable to extend their tasks to the investigation of criminal cases. The rationale behind this extended competence is not only to benefit from the legal and economic expertise of these authorities, but also from the information on single cases that is already available in administrative proceedings.[20] As a consequence, the role of the authority is no longer limited to administrative law enforcement, but covers also criminal investigations. This 'double hat model' allows for a more efficient handling of both administrative and criminal cases. Furthermore, the cumulation of investigative powers in the framework of administrative and criminal proceedings provides an added value for the investigation, in particular because the exercise of administrative powers (eg, inspections) does not require any suspicion. In that respect, administrative enquiries may become particularly relevant for criminal investigations where they reveal a crime and, thereby, trigger a criminal investigation.

As far as law enforcement by fines for regulatory offences is concerned, the double hat model has become a common pattern in the German system.[21] To a lesser extent, administrative authorities are also involved in criminal investigations, whether it be with an express mandate to investigate criminal cases (eg, revenue and customs authorities) or with the task of preliminary ('administrative')

---

[18] 2002 Act on the Customs Criminal Investigation Office and the Customs Investigations Offices (*Zollfahndungsdienstgesetz*), 3.

[19] 2002 Act on the Federal Financial Supervisory Authority (*Finanzdienstleistungsaufsichtsgesetz*).

[20] See with regard to the double function of tax authorities: explanatory memorandum on the Amendment of criminal law provisions of the Fiscal Code (*Gesetz zur Änderung strafrechtlicher Vorschriften der Reichsabgabenordnung*), document of the Parliament (*Bundestags-Drucksache*) 1967 No V/1812, p 21.

[21] M Böse, *Wirtschaftsaufsicht und Strafverfolgung* (Tubingen, Mohr Siebeck, 2005) 499.

investigations that may result in an initial suspicion (Federal Financial Supervisory Authority).[22]

The Double Function of Revenue Authorities

Revenue Authorities (*Finanzbehörden*)

First and foremost, the double hat model has been implemented in tax and customs law. Due to the different institutional framework of tax administration on the one hand and customs administration on the other, this contribution will focus on tax authorities; nevertheless, *cum grano salis*, investigations conducted by customs authorities follow the same rules.[23]

The primary task of the revenue authorities (*Finanzbehörden*) is to assess and levy taxes in a uniform manner and to ensure that taxes are not understated.[24] Tax proceedings have thus a purely fiscal objective and are not part of a criminal investigation. Accordingly, the investigative powers are limited to measures usually available in administrative proceedings which are necessary to ascertain the relevant facts for taxation.

For the purpose of the investigation, the revenue authority may require the person concerned to provide information,[25] to submit accounts, records, business papers or any other documents,[26] and to present valuable objects.[27] Furthermore, the revenue authorities may carry out inspections and enter properties, premises, ships, enclosed operating facilities and similar facilities. This power, however, must not be exercised outside regular business and working hours and does not apply to private homes.[28] In contrast to searches in the framework of a criminal investigation, the owner should be informed of the inspection in advance,[29] and

---

[22] See 1998 Securities Trading Act (*Wertpapierhandelsgesetz*), ss 4(5), 9, and the 2014 Annual Report of the Federal Financial Supervisory Authority, available at http://www.bafin.de/SharedDocs/Downloads/EN/Jahresbericht/dl_annualreport_2014.pdf?__blob=publicationFile (4 September 2015), p 211 *et seq*, 213.

[23] See in particular the competences of the main customs office (*Hauptzollamt*) and the customs investigation agency (*Zollfahndungsamt*) under 2002 Fiscal Code (*Abgabenordnung*), ss 386(1)2, 404.

[24] 2002 Fiscal Code (*Abgabenordnung*), s 85(1).

[25] 2002 Fiscal Code (*Abgabenordnung*), s 93.

[26] 2002 Fiscal Code (*Abgabenordnung*), s 97.

[27] 2002 Fiscal Code (*Abgabenordnung*), s 100.

[28] 2002 Fiscal Code (*Abgabenordnung*), ss 98, 99(1). The authority may enter private homes only where this is necessary to avert acute dangers to public security and order, and this requirement will hardly be met in tax proceedings, see Constitutional Court (*Bundesverfassungsgericht*) BVerfG NVwZ-RR 2010, 457 (458).

[29] 2002 Fiscal Code (*Abgabenordnung*), s 99(1)2.

the inspection must not be ordered for the purpose of searching for unknown objects.[30] On the other hand, the forementioned measures do not require facts indicating that a crime has been committed, but only (concrete) reasons to believe that the measure may reveal facts which are relevant for taxation purposes.[31]

The latter requirement does not apply where it is obvious that the measure will reveal relevant information, as in the case of external audits of business companies.[32] The revenue authority determines the scope of the external audit and shall disclose the audit order to the taxpayer in advance.[33] The taxpayer is obliged to cooperate in determining the facts that may be relevant for taxation; in particular, he or she shall furnish information, submit business records and other documents for inspection and provide the explanations necessary to understand the records.[34] The revenue authority may also use the taxpayer's data-processing system to examine electronically stored records, and may order the taxpayer to process the data to its specifications or to make them available on machine-readable data-storage devices.[35] An external audit is carried out on the business premises during normal business or working hours, and the auditors are entitled to enter and inspect sites and business premises.[36] In order to combat VAT-fraud and black market work, the revenue authorities have been vested with special powers to inspect business sites.[37] In contrast to an external audit, the revenue authority is not obliged to inform the business owner of the inspection in advance.[38]

As has been mentioned above, the mandate of the revenue authority is not limited to tax proceedings, but also extends to criminal proceedings for tax crimes, in particular tax evasion.[39] In that respect, the revenue authority conducts the criminal investigation independently where the act to be investigated is exclusively a tax crime or simultaneously contravenes other criminal laws concerning public-law levies linked to the taxation regime, unless an arrest warrant has been issued against the accused.[40] If these conditions are met, the revenue authority has the investigative and prosecutorial powers of the public prosecutor's office.[41]

---

[30] 2002 Fiscal Code (*Abgabenordnung*), s 99(2).

[31] Federal Fiscal Court (*Bundesfinanzhof*) BFH NJW 2002, 2340 (2343).

[32] 2002 Fiscal Code (*Abgabenordnung*), s 193(1); see by contrast for external audits with regard to other taxpayers ibid s 193(2) No 2.

[33] 2002 Fiscal Code (*Abgabenordnung*), ss 196, 197.

[34] 2002 Fiscal Code (*Abgabenordnung*), s 200 (1).

[35] 2002 Fiscal Code (*Abgabenordnung*), s 147(6).

[36] 2002 Fiscal Code (*Abgabenordnung*), s 200(2) and (3).

[37] 2005 Act on VAT (*Umsatzsteuergesetz*), s 27b; 2009 Act on income tax (*Einkommensteuergesetz*), s 42g.

[38] 2005 Act on VAT (*Umsatzsteuergesetz*), s 27b(1)1; 2009 Act on income tax (*Einkommensteuergesetz*), s 42g(2)2.

[39] 2002 Fiscal Code (*Abgabenordnung*), s 370. According to s 369(1), the term 'tax crimes' covers acts which are punishable under the tax laws, the illegal import, export or transit of goods, the forging of revenue stamps or acts preparatory thereto, aiding and abetting a person committing one of the forementioned crimes.

[40] 2002 Fiscal Code (*Abgabenordnung*), s 386(2) and (3).

[41] 2002 Fiscal Code (*Abgabenordnung*), s 399 (1).

The double function of revenue authorities notwithstanding, the competence to investigate and prosecute tax crimes can be transferred to one revenue authority for an area of several (other) revenue authorities.[42] In the State of North Rhine-Westphalia, the Minster of Finance has established ten Revenue Offices for Tax Crimes and Tax Investigation (*Finanzämter für Steuerstrafsachen und Steuerfahndung*).[43] This concentration of the competence to conduct criminal investigations does not affect the right and obligation of these revenue authorities to investigate the facts where a tax crime is suspected and to take non-deferrable investigative measures.[44]

In a criminal investigation, the 'tool-box' of the revenue authority contains the following measures: Search and seizure (with judicial authorisation),[45] examination of witnesses[46] and production orders.[47] Moreover, the revenue office for tax crimes and tax investigation may also collect information from other revenue authorities[48] or request a forensic investigation from the Customs Criminal Investigation Office (*Zollkriminalamt*) or the State Office of Criminal Investigations (*Landeskriminalamt*).[49] Furthermore, it has access to central databases (eg on VAT-fraud and risk profiles).[50] The investigative powers of the revenue authorities even include covert investigation measures,[51] but the revenue office for tax crimes does not exercise these powers; in practice, searches and witness examinations are the most important investigative measures.[52]

Whereas investigative measures can be taken by the revenue authorities, the decision whether or not to prosecute lies exclusively within the competence of the Revenue Office for Tax Crimes and Tax Investigation (*Finanzamt für Steuerstraf-sachen und Steuerfahndung*). It can close a case for a lack of sufficient evidence.[53] With the consent of the defendant and the court, the revenue office for tax crimes may impose conditions and instructions upon the defendant and dispense with

---

[42] 2002 Fiscal Code (*Abgabenordnung*), s 387(2).

[43] 2012 Regulation on the competence of revenue offices (*Finanzamtszuständigkeitsverordnung*), s 24. For instance, the revenue office for tax crimes and tax investigation in Bonn is competent for tax crimes related to the districts of six revenue offices (Bonn-Außenstadt, Bonn-Innenstadt, Euskirchen, Sankt Augustin, Schleiden, Siegburg).

[44] 2002 Fiscal Code (*Abgabenordnung*), s 399 (2).

[45] 1987 Code of Criminal Procedure (*Strafprozessordnung*), ss 94, 98, 102 ff.

[46] 1987 Code of Criminal Procedure (*Strafprozessordnung*), s 161a.

[47] 1987 Code of Criminal Procedure (*Strafprozessordnung*), s 95.

[48] Information provided by the revenue office for tax crimes and tax investigation Bonn; see 2002 Fiscal Code (*Abgabenordnung*), s 399 (2), and 1987 Code of Criminal Procedure (*Strafprozessordnung*), s 163(1)2.

[49] 2013 Directions for criminal proceedings and proceedings on regulatory offences in tax-related matters (*Anweisungen für das Straf- und Bußgeldverfahren [Steuer]*) ss 139(2), 141.

[50] The Federal Central Tax Office has created a central database for processing and analysing cases of VAT-fraud and developing risk-profiles (*Zentrale Datenbank zur Speicherung und Auswertung von Umsatzsteuerbetrugsfällen und Entwicklung von Risikoprofilen—ZAUBER*), see 2006 Fiscal Administration Act (*Finanzverwaltungsgesetz*), s 5(1) No 13.

[51] S Rolletschke, *Steuerstrafrecht* (München, Franz Vahlen, 2012) 328.

[52] Information provided by the revenue office for tax crimes and tax investigation Bonn.

[53] 1987 Code of Criminal Procedure (*Strafprozessordnung*), s 170(2).

prosecution.[54] Furthermore, the revenue office may terminate proceedings in minor cases or where the taxpayer has voluntarily disclosed and corrected his false declarations and paid the evaded taxes (and eventually a surcharge).[55] If the investigation provides sufficient grounds to bring a public charge, the revenue office for tax crimes may apply to the court for a written penal order.[56] Through a penal order, however, the court may only impose a fine or—if the accused has defence counsel—imprisonment not exceeding one year.[57] Thus, the revenue office for tax crimes shall not apply for a penal order if the expected sentence lies beyond this limit (eg, in particularly serious cases of tax evasion).[58] In such cases, the revenue authority is not competent to submit an indictment to the court and therefore has to send the file to the public prosecutor's office.[59]

If the criminal investigation is conducted by the public prosecutor, the revenue authorities still have the police investigative powers under the Code of Criminal Procedure.[60] These powers widely correspond to those of the tax investigation agencies.[61]

Tax Investigation (*Steuerfahndung*)

The public prosecutor and the revenue authorities are assisted by tax investigation offices (*Steuerfahndung*). The tax investigation office is usually incorporated into the revenue authority for tax crimes (*Finanzamt für Steuerstrafsachen und Steuerfahndung*), but nevertheless has different competences and powers. While the revenue office for tax crimes deals only with criminal cases, the tax investigation office has a 'double hat'. On the one hand, the tax investigation office is in charge of the investigation of tax crimes and tax-related regulatory offences.[62] For this purpose, tax investigators have received the same powers as the police

---

[54] 1987 Code of Criminal Procedure (*Strafprozessordnung*), s 153a. Although the court's consent is not required in minor cases (ss 153a(1)7, 153(1)2 CCP), the revenue office usually applies to the court to give its consent, information provided by the revenue office for tax crimes and tax investigation Bonn.

[55] 2002 Fiscal Code (*Abgabenordnung*), ss 398, 398a.

[56] 2002 Fiscal Code (*Abgabenordnung*), s 400; 1987 Code of Criminal Procedure (*Strafprozessordnung*), ss 407 ff.

[57] 1987 Code of Criminal Procedure (*Strafprozessordnung*), s 407(2)1 and 2.

[58] 2002 Fiscal Code (*Abgabenordnung*), s 400; see also 2013 Directions for criminal proceedings and proceedings on regulatory offences in tax-related matters (*Anweisungen für das Straf- und Bußgeldverfahren [Steuer]*) s 84(3)2, referring to particularly serious cases of tax evasion under s 370(3) Fiscal Code.

[59] 2002 Fiscal Code (*Abgabenordnung*), s 400; see Stefan Rolletschke, *Steuerstrafrecht*, 4th edn, (Franz Vahlen, 2012) 356.

[60] 2002 Fiscal Code (*Abgabenordnung*), ss 402, 399 (2)2.

[61] Stefan Rolletschke, *Steuerstrafrecht*, 4th edn (Franz Vahlen, 2012) 329, except the power to examine documents of the person affected by a search, *cf* 1987 Code of Criminal Procedure (*Strafprozessordnung*), s 110.

[62] 2002 Fiscal Code (*Abgabenordnung*), s 208(1)1 No 1.

authorities and officers according to the Code of Criminal Procedure.[63] These powers include the right to initiate a criminal investigation, to question suspects as well as to examine witnesses and experts, to secure objects relevant for the investigation.[64] In criminal proceedings, tax investigators act as investigators of the public prosecutor's office and, therefore, may take any investigative measure available to the public prosecutor's investigators,[65] such as search and seizure.[66] Furthermore, they have the power to examine the papers of the persons affected by a search.[67] As the term 'tax investigation' suggests, tax investigators do not dispose of prosecutorial powers (eg, to apply for a written penal order); the prosecution of tax crimes is a matter for the public prosecutor's office or the revenue office for tax crimes, but the decision whether or not to prosecute is taken on the basis of the tax investigator's final report. Thus, due to the scope of their investigative powers and their double function, tax investigators may roughly be called 'fiscal police' (which is, however, not a legal concept). Notwithstanding their function in tax proceedings, tax investigators mostly act in the framework of criminal proceedings.[68]

On the other hand, the tax investigation offices play also an important role in tax proceedings because they assess the facts relevant for taxation in cases subject to a criminal investigation.[69] Accordingly, the final report of the tax investigator has two parts, namely one part on the findings of the criminal investigation and a second part on the assessment of the evaded taxes.[70] The latter part is sent to the competent revenue authority that will then determine the taxes to be paid by the offender.

Furthermore, the tax investigation office is charged with detecting and investigating unknown tax cases.[71] The investigation does not require a suspicion that a tax crime has been committed and, therefore, is not considered to form part of a criminal investigation, but to pursue taxation purposes.[72] Accordingly, the investigative powers in tax proceedings apply,[73] regardless of whether there is a suspicion of a tax crime or not. Fishing expeditions or dragnet investigations, however, are not permitted. Any investigative measure must be based upon objective reasons

---

[63] 2002 Fiscal Code (*Abgabenordnung*), s 404 1.

[64] 1987 Code of Criminal Procedure (*Strafprozessordnung*), ss 163, 163a(4) and (5), 94; see also Rolletschke *Steuerstrafrecht*, 4th edn (Franz Vahlen, 2012) 329.

[65] 2002 Fiscal Code (*Abgabenordnung*), ss 404 2, 399(2)2.

[66] 1987 Code of Criminal Procedure (*Strafprozessordnung*), ss 94, 98, 102 ff; see also S Rolletschke. *Steuerstrafrecht*, 329–330.

[67] 2002 Fiscal Code (*Abgabenordnung*), s 404 2; 1987 Code of Criminal Procedure (*Strafprozessordnung*), s 110(1).

[68] Information provided by the revenue office for tax crimes and tax investigation Bonn.

[69] 2002 Fiscal Code (*Abgabenordnung*), s 208(1)1 No 2.

[70] 2013 Directions for criminal proceedings and proceedings on regulatory offences in tax-related matters (*Anweisungen für das Straf- und Bußgeldverfahren [Steuer]*) s 127.

[71] 2002 Fiscal Code (*Abgabenordnung*), s 208(1)1 No 3.

[72] 2013 Directions for criminal proceedings and proceedings on regulatory offences in tax-related matters (*Anweisungen für das Straf- und Bußgeldverfahren [Steuer]*) s 12(1)3; Federal Fiscal Court (*Bundesfinanzhof*) BFH NJW 2002, 2340 (2343).

[73] 2002 Fiscal Code (*Abgabenordnung*), s 208(1)3, ss 93 ff.

for the assumption that taxes have been understated.[74] This assumption may be based upon a common pattern of tax evasion that has been established in several cases and that might have been applied by other taxpayers or in other cases.[75] For instance, the tax investigation may require a pharmaceutical company to provide information on physicians who have been supplied with drugs where external audits of other physicians have revealed several cases of tax evasion with regard to the cash payment received for the application of the directly supplied drugs to their patients.[76] In such cases, the tax investigation office may issue collective information requests (*Sammelauskunftsersuchen*) against credit institutions in order to obtain information on unknown taxpayers that are considered relevant for taxation purposes.[77] Where the investigation on unknown tax cases results in the suspicion that a tax crime has been committed, the tax investigation office initiates a criminal investigation, and hereby triggers the applicability of the rules on criminal proceedings.[78]

Double Function, Parallel Proceedings and Defence Rights

The double hat model provides for several advantages. In particular, it allows for an efficient use of investigative powers, information and resources. Nevertheless, the cumulation of tasks and powers raises problems for the rights of the defendant who is confronted with a janus-faced authority with considerable powers under both the tax law and the criminal law regime. Correspondingly, the procedural status of the taxpayer and respectively, of the defendant, depends upon the applicable regime: Whereas tax law obliges the taxpayer to cooperate with revenue authorities (ie, to provide relevant information, to produce documents etc),[79] there is no such obligation for the defendant in the framework of criminal proceedings. Instead, the defendant has the right to remain silent and to refuse any active cooperation with the investigating authorities (*nemo tenetur se ipsum accusare*,

---

[74] Federal Fiscal Court (*Bundesfinanzhof*) BFH NJW 2007, 1308-1309; see also 2013 Directions for criminal proceedings and proceedings on regulatory offences in tax-related matters (*Anweisungen für das Straf- und Bußgeldverfahren [Steuer]*) s 12(1)1.

[75] Information provided by the revenue office for tax crimes and tax investigation Bonn.

[76] Federal Fiscal Court (*Bundesfinanzhof*) BFH NJW 2002, 2340 (2343); BFH NJW 2007, 1308 (1309).

[77] Federal Fiscal Court (*Bundesfinanzhof*) BFH NJW 2002, 2340 (2343-2344); see also 2002 Fiscal Code (*Abgabenordnung*), s 30a(5)2.

[78] 2013 Directions for criminal proceedings and proceedings on regulatory offences in tax-related matters (*Anweisungen für das Straf- und Bußgeldverfahren [Steuer]*) s 12(2).

[79] 2002 Fiscal Code (*Abgabenordnung*), s 208(1)3, ss 93, 97.

privilege against self-incrimination).[80] As the general rule is that tax proceedings shall be governed by tax law, and that criminal investigations in tax matters follow the rules of criminal proceedings,[81] the cumulation of investigative powers may seriously affect the procedural rights of the defendant in criminal proceedings.[82] In awareness of these concerns, the law provides for procedural safeguards for the rights of the defendant:

First of all, the privilege against self-incrimination must not be undermined by the obligation to cooperate in taxation procedures. Therefore, the exercise of coercive powers is not permitted where this would force a taxpayer to incriminate himself of a tax crime which he has committed.[83] This applies in any case where criminal proceedings have already been initiated against him.[84] The revenue authorities must not willfully delay the initiation of a criminal investigation in order to deprive the suspect of his defence rights. Therefore, criminal proceedings are deemed to have been initiated as soon as the revenue authority adopts a measure, the purpose of which is identifiably to institute criminal action against somebody for a tax crime.[85] This applies in particular to searches, seizures and examinations of suspects or witnesses.[86]

Furthermore, the revenue authority has to ensure transparency and clarity about the nature of proceedings, ie the operative 'hat'. In particular, the measure by which criminal proceedings are initiated must be entered in the records without undue delay, and the individual must be informed that he is under a criminal investigation at the latest when he is called upon to reveal facts or supply documents that are related to the investigation.[87] At the same time, the revenue authority shall inform the defendant of his rights to respond to the charges, or to remain silent, and the right to consult with defence counsel of his choice.[88] In particular, the defendant must be informed that, by the initiation of criminal proceedings, he must not be forced to provide information to the revenue authority for taxation purposes.[89] If the revenue authority does not properly advise the defendant of these rights, his statements must not be used as evidence in criminal

---

[80] 1987 Code of Criminal Procedure (*Strafprozessordnung*), s 136(1)2 (right to silence); with regard to the privilege against self-incrimination in the German criminal justice system see Gleß '§ 136' in Löwe-Rosenberg, *Strafprozessordnung*, vol 4 (§§ 112–150), 26th edn (de Gruyter, 2007), para 27, with further references.

[81] 2002 Fiscal Code (*Abgabenordnung*), s 393(1)1.

[82] M Böse, *Wirtschaftsaufsicht und Strafverfolgung*, 474–475.

[83] 2002 Fiscal Code (*Abgabenordnung*), s 393(1)2.

[84] 2002 Fiscal Code (*Abgabenordnung*), s 393(1)3.

[85] 2002 Fiscal Code (*Abgabenordnung*), s 208(1)3, s 397(1).

[86] 2013 Directions for criminal proceedings and proceedings on regulatory offences in tax-related matters (*Anweisungen für das Straf- und Bußgeldverfahren [Steuer]*) s 27(2).

[87] 2002 Fiscal Code (*Abgabenordnung*), s 208(1)3, s 397(3).

[88] 2002 Fiscal Code (*Abgabenordnung*), s 399(2), and 1987 Code of Criminal Procedure (*Strafprozessordnung*), ss 163a(4)2, 136(1)2; see also 2013 Directions for criminal proceedings and proceedings on regulatory offences in tax-related matters (*Anweisungen für das Straf- und Bußgeldverfahren [Steuer]*) ss 28(2) and 29.

[89] 2002 Fiscal Code (*Abgabenordnung*), s 393(1)4.

proceedings.[90] By contrast, as the privilege against self-incrimination does not apply to tax proceedings, the information may be used for taxation purposes.[91]

The Initiation of a Criminal Investigation and Cooperation with Other Revenue Authorities

A criminal investigation of tax crimes can be triggered by information provided by private persons (complaints, anonymous reports, voluntary disclosure by the offender)[92] or by public bodies. Under German law, courts and administrative authorities are obliged to notify the revenue authorities competent for criminal proceedings of facts that suggest that a tax crime has been committed.[93] Where the competent revenue authority cannot be informed directly, the information shall be transmitted to the Federal Central Tax Office (*Bundeszentralamt für Steuern*) that will pass the information to the competent authority.[94] However, the practical impact of this obligation appears to be rather limited as far as courts and administrative authorities not dealing with tax matters are concerned. Nevertheless, a considerable number of investigations result from suspicious transaction reports on money laundering that are forwarded by the money laundering clearing offices at the State Office of Criminal Investigations (*Landeskriminalamt*) or the public prosecutor's office.

In most cases, tax crimes are reported by the revenue authority competent for the assessment of the relevant taxes where the authority has reasons to believe that a tax crime has been committed.[95] For instance, the revenue authorities have to check carefully whether a newly registered enterprise is not a dummy company serving as a missing trader for VAT-fraud before they assign the tax identification number to the entrepreneur; if the assessment reveals a suspicion of VAT-fraud,

---

[90] Federal Court of Justice (*Bundesgerichtshof*), BGH NJW 1992, 1463 (1464); NJW 2002, 975 (976), with regard to the obligation under 1987 Code of Criminal Procedure (*Strafprozessordnung*), ss 163a(4)2, 136(1)2; see also S Rolletschke, *Steuerstrafrecht*, 373, with regard to 2002 Fiscal Code (*Abgabenordnung*), s 393(1)4.

[91] Federal Fiscal Court (*Bundesfinanzhof*) BFH NJW 2002, 2198 (2199).

[92] If certain conditions are met (voluntary and full disclosure, payment of the taxes evaded, eventually plus a surcharge of 10 to 20%), the offender shall not be criminally prosecuted, 2002 Fiscal Code (*Abgabenordnung*), ss 371, 398a.

[93] 2002 Fiscal Code (*Abgabenordnung*), s 116(1)1. With regard to expenditure, the Statutory Act against abuse of subsidies (*Subventionsgesetz*), s 6, establishes an obligation to report suspected cases of subsidy fraud, see Criminal Code (*Strafgesetzbuch*), s 264.

[94] 2002 Fiscal Code (*Abgabenordnung*), s 116(1)2.

[95] Information provided by the revenue office for tax crimes and tax investigation Bonn. The general obligation to report tax crimes also applies to the revenue authorities, see 2013 Directions for criminal proceedings and proceedings on regulatory offences in tax-related matters (*Anweisungen für das Straf- und Bußgeldverfahren [Steuer]*) s 130.

the case is reported to the revenue office for tax crimes and tax investigation (*Finanzamt für Steuerstrafsachen und Steuerfahndung*).[96]

In practice, the most important source for obtaining *notitiae criminis* is the external auditor whose findings might give rise to the suspicion that a tax crime has been committed. In this case, the auditor may initiate criminal proceedings by himself, thereby exercising the revenue authority's competence in criminal proceedings. The auditor must always inform the revenue office for tax crimes and tax investigation (Finanzamt für Steuerstrafsachen und Steuerfahndung) without undue delay where a suspicion of a tax crime or the mere possibility exists that criminal proceedings have to be initiated.[97] As follows from the latter alternative, the notification does not per se trigger a criminal investigation.[98] In any case, the auditor may not proceed with the auditing until the taxpayer has been informed that a criminal investigation has been initiated against him and that he cannot be forced to cooperate with the auditor and the revenue authority.[99] Thus, the assessment of the auditor whether there are grounds to believe that a tax crime has been committed is crucial for the initiation of criminal proceedings. In that respect, the auditor has a margin of appreciation, but must not wilfully delay the initiation of criminal proceedings (or the report to the revenue office for tax crimes).[100] For instance, a criminal investigation is deemed to be initiated when the auditor seeks to establish the taxpayer's intent to evade taxes.[101] Some authors, however, advocate for advising the taxpayers of his rights even before criminal proceedings are initiated in order to avoid the negative consequences of a delayed information (inadmissibility of evidence).[102] In any case, the revenue authority must provide the taxpayer with general information on his rights and obligations (including his rights if a criminal investigation has to be initiated) as an attachment to the audit order.[103]

After criminal proceedings have been initiated, the investigation is carried out by the revenue office for tax crimes and tax investigations. The tax investigator in charge may call in the auditor for the tax assessment.[104] In particular,

---

[96] Information provided by the revenue office for tax crimes and tax investigation in Bonn.

[97] 2000 Regulation on external audits (*Betriebsprüfungsordnung*), s 10(1)1 and 2.

[98] Jäger, § 397 in Franzen, Gast and Joecks (eds), *Steuerstrafrecht* (Munchen, CH Beck, 2009), para 66.

[99] 2000 Regulation on external audits (*Betriebsprüfungsordnung*), s 10(1)3 and 4.

[100] Madauß, 'Außenprüfung und Steuerstrafverfahren—Anmerkung aus der Praxis' (2014) *NZWiSt*, 296; for the initiation of criminal proceedings in general, see Federal Court of Justice (*Bundesgerichtshof*) NJW 1989, 96.

[101] Fiscal Court (*Finanzgericht*) of the state Schleswig-Holstein EFG 2005, 678; Buse 'Der strafrechtliche Verdacht des Außenprüfer' (2011) *Der Betrieb*, 1942.

[102] Jäger, § 397, para 50.

[103] 2000 Regulation on external audits (*Betriebsprüfungsordnung*), s 5(2)2; letter of the Federal Ministry of Finance (*Bundesfinanzministerium*) of 24 October 2013 BStBl 2013 I 1264. This general information, however, is not considered to be sufficient for properly advising the defendant of his rights in criminal proceedings.

[104] 2013 Directions for criminal proceedings and proceedings on regulatory offences in tax-related matters (*Anweisungen für das Straf- und Bußgeldverfahren [Steuer]*) s 125(1) and (2).

the examination of the relevant business records and documents is often carried out in close cooperation.[105] Accordingly, the final report on the assessment of the evaded taxes can be filed either by the tax investigator or by the auditor.[106]

On the other hand, the auditor can be assisted—respectively 'flanked'—by a tax investigator where a suspicion of a crime does not yet exist, but criminal proceedings might be initiated during the audit (*Flankenschutz*).[107] In this case, the tax investigator acting on behalf of the primarily competent authority can immediately initiate a criminal investigation and take the necessary measures to avoid obfuscation of the crime.

The Relationship between Administrative Authorities and Judicial Authorities in Criminal Investigations

As the revenue authority is vested with investigative and prosecutorial powers, it has to coordinate its investigations with other authorities charged with criminal investigations, first and foremost the public prosecutor's office. In this respect, issues of case allocation and potential conflicts of competences and rules and practices on cooperation are of particular relevance.

Case Allocation and the Governing Function of the Public Prosecutor's Office

As has been mentioned before, the revenue office for tax crimes and tax investigation (*Finanzamt für Steuerstrafsachen und Steuerfahndung*) has—at least in part—taken up the function of the public prosecutor's office. Insofar, as it may independently investigate and prosecute tax crimes, it is not subject to directions of the public prosecutor.

The competence of the revenue office, however, is limited to criminal conduct exclusively punishable as a tax offence. Furthermore, the revenue office is relieved of its autonomous competence as soon as an arrest warrant has been issued against the defendant or the findings of the investigation call for an indictment to be filed.[108] In these cases, especially where the defendant's conduct is punishable

---

[105] Meyer, 'Steuerstrafrechtliche Probleme bei Betriebsprüfungen' (2001) *DStR*, 461; Information provided by the revenue office for tax crimes and tax investigation in Bonn.
[106] 2013 Directions for criminal proceedings and proceedings on regulatory offences in tax-related matters (*Anweisungen für das Straf- und Bußgeldverfahren [Steuer]*) s 125(3).
[107] Information provided by the revenue office for tax crimes and tax investigation in Bonn.
[108] 2002 Fiscal Code (*Abgabenordnung*), ss 386(3), 400.

under both tax law and the Penal Code (eg, tax evasion and forgery), the public prosecutor's office is in charge of the criminal investigation, without prejudice to the revenue authorities' power to carry out investigations on behalf of the public prosecutor or to take undeferrable measures.

But even where the revenue office enjoys the autonomous competence to investigate and prosecute tax crimes, it may transfer the case to the public prosecutor's office at any time.[109] Vice versa, the public prosecutor's office may take over the case at any stage of the investigation.[110] As the exercise of this right depends upon proper information about ongoing investigations, the revenue office for tax crimes and tax investigations is obliged to notify the public prosecutor's office of any investigation that might appear appropriate to be conducted by the public prosecutor.[111] Therefore, generally the revenue office is not obliged to inform the public prosecutor's office of any investigation unless certain special conditions are fulfilled (eg, gravity and complexity of the case).[112] These conditions correspond to the criteria for transfer or adoption of proceedings that are laid down in internal guidelines.

The public prosecutor's office shall take over an investigation where this is required by special circumstances (important or complex cases, connection to not tax-related crimes, participation of officials of the revenue authority).[113] Under the same conditions, the revenue office for tax crimes shall hand over the case to the public prosecutor.[114] Furthermore, the investigation shall be transferred if an application for an arrest warrant or an order to intercept telecommunications shall be filed or the defendant enjoys privileges or immunities from criminal prosecution or special protection under the Youth Courts Law (Jugendgerichtsgesetz).[115] Due to the complexity of the system of mutual legal assistance in criminal matters, transnational investigations are conducted by the public prosecutor's office.[116] If the revenue office does not transfer the case, it shall inform the public prosecutor who then will decide whether the gravity or the complexity of the case, the public interest or the connection to other, not tax-related investigations require him to take over the investigation.[117] The same applies to voluntary self-disclosures that require a thorough examination whether the taxpayer is

---

[109] 2002 Fiscal Code (*Abgabenordnung*), s 386(4)1.

[110] 2002 Fiscal Code (*Abgabenordnung*), s 386(4)2.

[111] Federal Court of Justice (*Bundesgerichtshof*) NJW 2009, 2319.

[112] Federal Court of Justice (*Bundesgerichtshof*) NJW 2009, 2319.

[113] 1977 Guidelines for criminal proceedings and proceedings on regulatory offences (*Richtlinien für das Straf- und Bußgeldverfahren*), s 267(1).

[114] 2013 Directions for criminal proceedings and proceedings on regulatory offences in tax-related matters (*Anweisungen für das Straf- und Bußgeldverfahren [Steuer]*) s 22(1)3 no 3, 4, 5 and 7.

[115] 2013 Directions for criminal proceedings and proceedings on regulatory offences in tax-related matters (*Anweisungen für das Straf- und Bußgeldverfahren [Steuer]*) s 22(1)3 no 1, 2 and 6.

[116] Information provided by the public prosecutor's office in Bonn.

[117] 2013 Directions for criminal proceedings and proceedings on regulatory offences in tax-related matters (*Anweisungen für das Straf- und Bußgeldverfahren [Steuer]*) s 22(2)1.

exempted from punishment or not.[118] The aforementioned criteria are further elaborated in bilateral consultations. In Bonn, for instance, the public prosecutor shall be informed of cases where the evaded taxes amount to 200.000 Euro (or more).[119] Considerably serious or complex cases (eg VAT-fraud, organised crime) are referred to the special prosecution unit (*Schwerpunkt-Staatsanwaltschaft*) in Cologne.[120]

The information of the public prosecutor's office and the transfer of the case should occur at the earliest stage possible.[121] Especially in cases resulting in an indictment and a trial, the public prosecutor's involvement in the early investigation phase is considered crucial for an effective prosecution of tax crimes. If the case is transferred at a later stage of proceedings (eg, because the investigation revealed that the conduct is punishable under general criminal law), the public prosecutor has to become acquainted with the file before he can proceed with the investigation.[122]

A re-allocation of the case (ie, deferral to the revenue office for tax crimes) is permitted, but requires consensus of the public prosecutor's office and the revenue office.[123] Whereas this option is hardly used, the public prosecutor's office sometimes requests the revenue office to prosecute a minor tax crime.[124]

Even though the revenue office for tax crime has no right to take over an investigation, the public prosecutor's office shall inform the competent revenue office in order to avoid parallel investigations.[125]

Cooperation Between the Revenue Authority and the Public Prosecutor's Office

The practical scope of cooperation depends upon the role of the revenue authority. Acting as an independent investigative and prosecutorial body, the revenue office for tax crimes conducts the investigation on its own. Without prejudice to the

---

[118] 2013 Directions for criminal proceedings and proceedings on regulatory offences in tax-related matters (*Anweisungen für das Straf- und Bußgeldverfahren [Steuer]*) s 22(2)2. In that respect, the amount of the evaded taxes is also taken into consideration, Information provided by the revenue office for tax crimes and tax investigation in Bonn.

[119] Information provided by the revenue office for tax crimes and tax investigation in Bonn and the public prosecutor's office in Bonn. The threshold may vary considerably from region to region. For instance, in the district of Cologne, the relevant amount is 800.000 Euro.

[120] Information provided by the revenue office for tax crimes and tax investigation in Bonn and the public prosecutor's office in Bonn.

[121] Federal Court of Justice (*Bundesgerichtshof*) NJW 2009, 2319.

[122] Information provided by the public prosecutor's office in Bonn.

[123] 2002 Fiscal Code (*Abgabenordnung*), s 386(4)3.

[124] Information provided by the public prosecutor's office in Bonn.

[125] 1977 Guidelines for criminal proceedings and proceedings on regulatory offences (*Richtlinien für das Straf- und Bußgeldverfahren*), s 266(1).

general obligations to consult the public prosecutor's office where appropriate, cooperation is required in exceptional cases only. For instance, the revenue office shall coordinate its investigation with the public prosecutor's office where the tax crime under investigation is connected to another, not tax-related crime (eg, forgery) that is investigated by the public prosecutor's office.[126]

If a case is suited to treatment in summary proceedings, the revenue office applies to the judge to issue a written penal order.[127] In practice, the application is sent to the court via the public prosecutor's office, and the public prosecutor checks whether the application complies with the formal requirements, but does not examine the merits of the case.[128] If the defendant objects to the penal order, a trial will be held, and the public prosecutor will take up the position of the revenue office for tax crimes.[129] Nevertheless, the revenue office still has the right to attend the trial, to question witnesses and experts and to make statements.[130] The execution of the judgment (or the written penal order) is incumbent upon the public prosecutor's office.[131]

More complex cooperation issues arise where the public prosecutor's office conducts the investigation. In most cases, the investigation is initiated by the revenue authorities, but there are also investigations resulting from individual complaints or official reports to the public prosecutor's office, eg where a plaintiff in civil proceedings has stated that he agreed with the respondent party, a building contractor, on the construction works being not declared for tax purposes.[132]

In criminal proceedings conducted by the public prosecutor, the officials of the revenue authorities have the same position as police officers in criminal proceedings and, thereby, are obliged to comply with the request or order of the public prosecutor's office.[133] Insofar, tax investigators and other officials of the revenue office for tax crimes act as investigators of the public prosecutor's office.[134] Subject to the instructions of the public prosecutor's office, the tax investigator carries out the investigative measures (witness examination, search and seizure, analysis of records and data) and sends his report to the public prosecutor's office. Despite acting as an investigator of the public prosecutor's office, the tax investigator is still

---

[126] 2013 Directions for criminal proceedings and proceedings on regulatory offences in tax-related matters (*Anweisungen für das Straf- und Bußgeldverfahren [Steuer]*) s 140(3).

[127] 2002 Fiscal Code (*Abgabenordnung*), s 400.

[128] Information provided by the public prosecutor's office in Bonn.

[129] 2002 Fiscal Code (*Abgabenordnung*), s 406(1).

[130] 2002 Fiscal Code (*Abgabenordnung*), s 407(1).

[131] 1987 Code of Criminal Procedure (*Strafprozessordnung*), s 451(1); see also Rolletschke *Steuerstrafrecht*, 4th edn (Franz Vahlen, 2012) 315.

[132] Information provided by the public prosecutor's office Bonn; see also 1998 Instruction on reports in civil proceedings (*Anordnung über die Mitteilungen in Zivilsachen*), Part II, Chapter 1 II.5. and 7.

[133] 2002 Fiscal Code (*Abgabenordnung*), s 402(1); 1987 Code of Criminal Procedure (*Strafprozessordnung*), s 163(1)2.

[134] 2002 Fiscal Code (*Abgabenordnung*), ss 402(1), 399(2)2 and 404 sent. 2; see also 1975 Courts Constitution Act (*Gerichtsverfassungsgesetz*), s 152 (1).

influenced by the double function of the revenue authorities whose main interests lie in the additional taxes to be recovered from the offender. Accordingly, tax investigators tend to prioritise cases according to the additional tax income expected to result from the investigation.[135] In court proceedings, the revenue office for tax crimes has the right to participate in the trial and, thereby, to assist the public prosecutor's office in its tasks.[136]

In order to foster cooperation, the revenue office for tax crimes and the public prosecutor's office shall held regular meetings to exchange information on current investigations and general issues of cooperation.[137] In these meetings, the revenue office and the public prosecutor's office consult on the cases to be reported to the public prosecutor's offices (eg, evaded taxes of 200.000 Euros or more) and the sentencing tariffs where the revenue office applies to the court to issue a penal order.[138] The meetings usually do not touch upon operational issues of current investigations; accordingly, one or two meetings per year are considered sufficient.[139]

Conclusions

The role of tax authorities in criminal investigations highlights the eminent importance of administrative investigations for combatting financial crime. The cumulation of tasks and powers, however, require procedural safeguards for the rights of the defendant. Furthermore, the 'double hat model' might give fiscal reasons a considerable weight in choosing the cases to be investigated and prosecuted.[140] On the other hand, the establishment of tax authorities for tax crimes and tax investigation illustrates the need for specialised units for criminal proceedings that act as intermediary between tax authorities *stricto sensu* and judicial authorities (ie, the public prosecutor's office).

---

[135] Information provided by the revenue office for tax crimes and tax investigation in Bonn. In Bonn, a tax investigator is expected to generate an amount of 1 million Euros additional tax income per year.

[136] 2002 Fiscal Code (*Abgabenordnung*), s 407(1); for a corresponding obligation of the revenue office, see 2013 Directions for criminal proceedings and proceedings on regulatory offences in tax-related matters (*Anweisungen für das Straf- und Bußgeldverfahren [Steuer]*) s 94.

[137] 2013 Directions for criminal proceedings and proceedings on regulatory offences in tax-related matters (*Anweisungen für das Straf- und Bußgeldverfahren [Steuer]*) s 140(1).

[138] Information provided by the revenue office for tax crimes and tax investigation Bonn and the public prosecutor's office in Bonn. See also 2013 Directions for criminal proceedings and proceedings on regulatory offences in tax-related matters (*Anweisungen für das Straf- und Bußgeldverfahren [Steuer]*) s 140(1).

[139] Information provided by the revenue office for tax crimes and tax investigation in Bonn.

[140] See the concerns raised by Theile, 'Zur Ermittlungs- und Abschlusskompetenz in Steuerstrafsachen—Anmerkung zu BGH, Beschl v 30.4.2009—1 StR 90/09' (2009) *Zeitschrift für internationale Strafrechtsdogmatik*, 446.

5

The Role of Fiscal Administrative Authorities in Poland

PROF DR HAB CELINA NOWAK
Professor of Criminal Law at the Kozminski University

Introduction

The pre-trial, investigative, stage of criminal proceedings in Poland for all types of crimes, including economic and financial ones, is in principle governed by the Code of Criminal Procedure (CCP) of 1997,[1] which entered into force on 1 September 1998 and has been amended over 60 times. The Code refers to two phases of the proceedings: the pre-trial proceeding (investigation) and the judicial proceeding (before the trial court). However, some elements of pre-trial proceedings related to economic and financial crimes are also regulated under the Fiscal Criminal Code of 1999.[2] Therefore, it seems worthwhile to first examine the general framework of criminal investigation in Polish law and then conduct a more detailed analysis of institutional and other issues related to investigations carried out in cases of economic and fiscal crimes, in order, finally, to address the role of special financial pre-trial authorities of an administrative character.

Main Features of Criminal Investigation in Poland

In Poland a criminal investigation may be carried out by three types of bodies: the Public Prosecutor's Office, the Police, and specialised bodies.[3]

---

[1] Code of Criminal Procedure of 6 June 1998, published in OJ No 89, item 555 as amended.
[2] Fiscal Criminal Code of 10 September 1999, consolidated text published in OJ of 2013, item 186 as amended.
[3] C Nowak and S Steinborn, 'Poland' in K Ligeti (ed), *Toward a Prosecutor for the European Union. A Comparative Analysis*, vol I, (Oxford, Hart 2013) 499–500.

In principle, pre-trial (preparatory) proceedings may be carried out in two different forms: investigation and inquiry. Investigation is a more formalised type of pre-trial proceeding, reserved for more complex matters and more serious offences (Article 309 CCP).[4] Inquiry, on the other hand, is less formalised and carried out in the case of less serious offences.[5] Moreover, in principle, it is always a public prosecutor who is responsible for the pre-trial proceedings—as the authority who either conducts or supervises the proceedings (Article 298 CCP).

An investigation is conducted by a public prosecutor, who may, however, order the police to conduct the entire investigation or to carry out some actions within the scope of the investigation (Article 311 § 1 CCP), except with regard to some cases he must handle personally (Article 311 § 2–3 CCP).

An inquiry is conducted by the police or other authorised bodies, unless it is carried out directly by the prosecutor.

An investigation may be conducted by the police or other authorised bodies, including: the Border Guards, the Internal Security Agency, the Customs Service, the Central Anti-Corruption Bureau (Article 312 CCP), as well as—among others—the Military Gendarmerie, Trade Inspection agencies, the Forest Guard, Tax Office and Fiscal Control inspectors and the Customs Office. Their competence is however limited to the matters which lie within their jurisdiction.

Concerning the relationship between the public prosecutor and the police, they cooperate closely when it comes to investigation. When the proceedings are conducted by the prosecutor, he may carry out some investigative actions on his own. However, he often orders the police to carry out some (or all) investigative activities. In this situation the police are in a subordinate position vis-à-vis the prosecutor and do not enjoy any autonomy. When the police conduct the pre-trial proceedings on their own, they do have some autonomy, but it should be

---

[4] Pursuant to Art 309 CCP, investigation is conducted in cases: (1) which fall under the jurisdiction of the district court; (2) of misdemeanours, if the suspect is a judge, a public prosecutor, an official of the Police, the Agency of Internal Security or the Intelligence Agency, the Military Intelligence Agencies, the Customs Service, or the Central Anti-Corruption Bureau; (3) of misdemeanours, if the suspect is an official of the Border Guard, Military Police, financial inquiry agencies or a supervising authority with oversight over the financial inquiry agencies, with respect to cases within the scope of competence of these authorities or misdemeanours committed by these officials in connection with the performance of their duties; (4) of misdemeanours in which an investigation is not conducted; and (5) of misdemeanours in which an investigations is conducted, if the public prosecutor so decides because of the seriousness or complexity of the case.

[5] An inquiry is conducted in the case of offences subject to the jurisdiction of a regional court: (1) offences carrying a penalty not exceeding 5 years of deprivation of liberty, and offences against property only if the value of the objects of the offence or the damage caused or intended does not exceed 100,000 PLN; (2) the offences set forth in Art 159, 254a and in Art 262 § 2 of the Penal Code; and (3) some offences against property, if the value of the objects of the offence or the damage caused or intended does not exceed 100,000 PLN. An inquiry is not conducted for some more serious offences, including offences against economic trade and money. In addition, an investigation is not be conducted: (1) with respect to an accused deprived of liberty in the case concerned or another case, unless custody or preliminary detention was applied to a perpetrator caught in the act or immediately afterwards; and (2) if the circumstances referred to in Article 79 § 1 on mandatory defence apply.

mentioned that all pre-trial proceedings conducted by the police are in any case supervised by the prosecutor,[6] who is obligated to ensure that the entire proceedings are conducted correctly and efficiently. His scope of authority in this regard is rather large; he is entitled to: (1) obtain information as to the intentions of the person conducting the preparatory proceedings, oversee the course of the proceedings, and issue rulings in respect thereof; (2) request that materials collected in the course of preparatory proceedings be presented to him; (3) participate in actions carried out by the person conducting the proceedings, carry them out in person, or personally take over the case and proceed with it himself; and (4) issue orders, rulings or instructions, and amend and reverse orders and rulings issued by the person conducting the preparatory proceedings.

Sadly, the provisions on criminal proceedings in Poland have recently been subject to rather radical changes and their future shape still remains uncertain. As of 1 July 2015, the model of criminal proceedings in Poland has changed towards a more adversarial one. This has brought about a revolution in both the investigative and judicial stages of the proceedings. At the trial stage, the judge has become a passive figure and is involved in the gathering and presenting of evidence only in exceptional cases. The adversarial system, with a passive judge and active parties, implies much more work and responsibility for the prosecution. Prosecutors are expected to focus more attention on serious cases, whereas other authorities have greater autonomy in conducting the pre-trial proceedings. In particular, since the reform entered into force, most of the procedural decisions taken by the police within the framework of an inquiry have not required the prosecutor's approval (the exceptions being decisions to discontinue proceedings concerning an individual and decisions to suspend the proceedings). And although the prosecutor's authority to supervise proceedings he does not conduct himself, as per the above-mentioned Article 326 CCP, has not changed, the scope of supervision has been diminished, since the obligation of the police to obtain the prosecutor's approval in connection to some procedural decisions has been reduced.

The 2015 reform has been criticised by many, including pre-trial authorities, for it increased their workload and responsibility, as well as overall bureaucracy, and was not accompanied by appropriate changes in their internal organisational structure; nor did they receive more funding. Interestingly, at the beginning of 2016, the new government that was sworn in in November 2015 announced a return to the former inquisitorial model. A new bill based on the provisions in force before 1 July 2015 has already been drafted and is awaiting legislative debate. It may come into force as early as April 2016.

---

[6] Art 326 § 1 CCP: 'The public prosecutor shall supervise the preparatory proceedings to the extent that he is not personally conducting the same'.

Investigation into Common Economic
and Financial Offences

In Polish law, economic and financial offences are divided into two categories: common offences and fiscal offences. Common offences, ie, offences against property and economic trade, are regulated under the Penal Code, whereas fiscal offences are considered to be specifically detrimental to Polish public financial interests and are regulated under special legislation, ie, the Fiscal Criminal Code, which is discussed at length below.

Investigation into Common Economic Offences

Concerning the institutional framework of investigations, it should be mentioned at the outset that the proceedings related to common financial and economic offences are usually conducted by investigative bodies vested with general competence over the investigation and prosecution of crime, such as the public prosecutor's offices and the police, while fiscal offences are mainly prosecuted by specialised authorities with limited jurisdiction.

As regards the institutional framework of the prosecution of financial and economic offences of a general nature by prosecutorial services, there are no general rules for the establishment of units specialised in economic and financial crimes within the public prosecutor's office. Pursuant to Article 17-17 of the Act on the Public Prosecutor's Office,[7] departments and bureaus may be established in the General Public Prosecutor's Office, units and subunits may be established in appellate and district public prosecutor's offices and units and sections in regional public prosecutor's offices. This means that decision-making regarding the establishment of specialised units for investigating economic and financial crimes has been decentralised and depends upon the initiative of a competent public prosecutor.

In the General Public Prosecutor's Office and in the appellate public prosecutor's offices there are special departments for organised crime and corruption, which—to some extent—specialise in economic crimes. Moreover, at lower levels of the public prosecutor's office, in some district and regional offices there are special units for economic crimes. Their establishment depends on a decision of the superior prosecutor. When such a unit is created, it usually employs prosecutors with the best expertise and best results in prosecuting economic crime.

---

[7] Act of 20 June 1985 on the Public Prosecutor's Office, consolidated text published in OJ No 270 of 2011, item 1599 as amended.

For example, in the district public prosecutor's office in Warsaw there is a special unit for economic crime. It is in charge of conducting and supervising proceedings (investigations) in cases of serious crime against economic trade (this refers to the name of the chapter in the Penal Code in which most typical economic offences are defined) and other economic offences. The scope of competence is therefore broadly defined and practical arrangements between different units within the public prosecutor's offices seem decisive as to which unit runs which proceedings.

As for the internal organisational structure of the police, it should be noted that there are specialised units (departments) at different levels in charge of investigating economic and financial crimes. First, within the Police Headquarters there is a special unit for combating economic crime. Its most important tasks include monitoring, analysing and assessing the threat of economic crime and planning and implementing actions to combat economic crime; providing support to police organisational units which combat economic crime; and supervising, coordinating police operational and investigative activities with regard to economic crime. Similar units charged with combating economic crime also exist on lower levels of the police structure.

In addition, it should be noted that there exists a special agency—the Central Anti-Corruption Bureau, which—to some extent—is likewise responsible for fighting economic crime. It is clearly expressed in Article 1-1 of the Act on the Central Anti-Corruption Bureau,[8] which provides that the Bureau is established as a special agency in charge of combating corruption in public and economic life, in particular in state and territorial self-government institutions, as well as of combating actions aimed at the state's economic interests. The Bureau is independent and separate from the police, but its tasks in many respects duplicate those of the police.

Investigative Means

Regarding the investigative means employed in criminal investigations into economic and financial offences of a common nature, it may be observed that they are the same as the means applied in investigations into other types of offences. There are no special investigative means available to the investigating authorities in respect of economic crime: for instance, real-time monitoring of bank accounts is not possible. In order to get information on bank accounts, pursuant to Article 105 of the Banking Act,[9] the prosecutor must request the bank to waive

---

[8] Act of 9 June 2006 on the Central Anti-Corruption Bureau, consolidated text: OJ of 2014, item 1411 as amended.
[9] Act of 29 August 1997, consolidated text: OJ of 2015, item 128, as amended.

banking secrecy (and other agencies conducting investigations in economic matters must ask the prosecutor to make such a request).[10]

The only specificity of criminal proceedings concerning common economic and financial offences is that an expert witness[11] in the field of economics (accountancy, etc) is usually appointed. Prosecutors do not feel sufficiently competent when it comes to establishing the economic features of crime (for instance the amount of damage). Therefore, they most often decide to refer the case to an expert in the field. This makes proceedings involving economic and financial offences longer, more expensive and more complicated than proceedings relating to non-economic offences. Furthermore, the quality of expert witnesses' opinions is sometimes contested by the courts—regrettably, due to financial constraints, public prosecutor's offices cannot avail themselves of the most qualified people in the market. In some famous trials, the prosecution failed to prove its case before the court when the expert witnesses turned out to be incompetent.

Special Legislation: The Polish Fiscal Criminal Code

Fiscal Offences and Financial Authorities

The offences covered by the Fiscal Criminal Code (FCC) are called fiscal offences. They affect State Treasury or local government interests (Article 53 § 26 FCC) or the financial interests of the European Union (Article 53 § 26a FCC). The category of fiscal offences encompasses four groups of criminal acts: tax offences, customs offences, offences related to currency trade, and offences against the organisation of gambling games (games of chance). The FCC also covers four types of contraventions (prohibited acts of lesser social consequences), of a similar nature.[12]

Since the material scope of the FCC is limited and very particular, the legislator decided to entrust the conduct of proceedings relating to these specific matters primarily to administrative authorities specialised in the field of fiscal law, namely, tax offices, fiscal control inspectors and customs offices. In the FCC these authorities, which are a part of the State's fiscal administration—ie, a special division of the public administration—are referred to as 'financial authorities overseeing pre-trial proceedings'. The superior financial authorities include: the customs chambers, tax chambers, General Inspector of Tax Control, and Minister of Finance (Article 53 § 39 FCC).

---

[10] *cf* C Nowak and S Steinborn, 'Poland', 521.
[11] ibid, 521–522.
[12] L Wilk and J Zagrodnik, *Prawo karne skarbowe* (Warsaw, CH Beck, 2009) 4ff and in detail: 193.

The financial authorities conduct pre-trial proceedings with regard to the fiscal offences and fiscal contraventions set forth in the FCC. Their criminal jurisdiction varies depending on their primary administrative field of expertise. Customs offices have jurisdiction over customs frauds (mainly affecting excise duty) and other customs offences (affecting, for instance, currency trade) and fiscal control inspectors deal with fiscal offences that they have detected while conducting their regular inspection activities, whereas tax offices are responsible for proceedings involving all the remaining fiscal offences (Article 133 § 1 FCC). The abovementioned authorities may also open criminal proceedings for fiscal offences not covered by their jurisdiction—for instance, if detected in the course of their regular activities—but once they establish which authority is competent in a given case, they are bound to transfer the proceedings to that authority (Article 133 § 2 FCC). The territorial jurisdiction of financial authorities in criminal matters depends on their territorial jurisdiction in administrative cases.

Criminal proceedings are conducted by officials working in special units of the respective offices, structurally and organisationally separated from other units which deal with administrative proceedings. In practice, the biggest workload is borne by the tax offices, which conduct the most proceedings related to fiscal offences.

Regarding the general scope of their competence in criminal matters, the financial authorities are entitled to carry out investigative activities at the pre-trial stage and to submit and support a bill of indictment before the court (Article 122 FCC).

Opening of Proceedings

The financial authorities engaged in pre-trial proceedings are notified about a suspicion of a fiscal offence either internally or through outside sources. An internal notification usually comes from other units of the tax offices or customs offices, or fiscal control offices, which—most frequently in the course of their regular inspection activities—detect suspicious behaviour, or an inconsistency in fiscal disclosures. Such information, in the form of an official note or a record of actions taken so far in the case, is transferred to a special unit within a given office which is responsible for prosecuting fiscal offences. Upon receiving such notification, this unit must take a decision as to whether to open pre-trial proceedings or not. If they decide that the information provides grounds for suspecting that a fiscal offence was committed, they issue a formal decision to open the proceedings. However, after verifying the aforesaid information, they may also decide that there is not sufficient evidence to open proceedings or that the behaviour had minimal social consequences or was the result of a taxpayer error, and in such a case they will not open proceedings.

An external notification comes mainly from two sources: other public institutions or individuals. Any administrative agency that receives information that an offence might have been committed has a formal obligation to notify the appropriate investigative authorities (Article 304 § 2 CCP), including financial authorities.

In the event that the financial authorities receive such notification, they usually open proceedings and immediately afterwards suspend them in order to verify the initial information through financial administrative proceedings. This is due to that fact that the amount of detriment to public financial interests (such as, for example, the amount of taxes due), if any, may only be formally established within the framework of administrative proceedings. For instance, a formal administrative decision is required to establish that the taxes which were not paid by the taxpayer should have been paid. The administrative procedure has several stages: first there is an analytical part and then proceedings in two instances; therefore, the process as a whole may take a relatively long time, up to as much as a year. Only after the final conclusion of administrative proceedings may fiscal criminal proceedings be taken up again.

Investigative Powers

The financial authorities responsible for conducting pre-trial proceedings theoretically have investigative powers just like the police (Article 150 § 1 FCC). Yet in practice they find that their powers are limited. When necessary, they may request assistance from the police in relation to an investigative measure (Article 150 § 2 FCC), but that does not actually happen in practice. As far as evidence is concerned, the investigative authorities receive information from the notifying agencies or request it formally in the course of the proceedings. The autonomy of financial authorities conducting the pre-trial proceedings is limited, however, as they are required to ask the prosecutor to carry out some actions in the course of the proceedings (for instance, to exempt witnesses from their obligation to maintain professional secrecy or confidentiality in the exercise of their profession or function, to issue warrants to search premises or persons, to file motions for temporary detention, to waive banking secrecy, or to issue a freezing order over property—Article 122 § 2 FCC).

Again regarding evidence, it should be noted that there is no preferential source to which administrative investigative bodies should turn in order to obtain proof regarding offences against economic and financial interests. However, they typically have recourse to three categories of evidence: documents, testimony of witnesses and explanations from the suspect. At times they also appoint expert witnesses—usually in order to have them examine handwritten documents or the suspect's state of mental health (expert psychiatrists). They choose the experts from the lists available in district courts. The financial authorities do not have access to any electronic means of gathering evidence, such as monitoring of bank accounts, either because a given type of evidence is not allowed under Polish law, or because they have to request the prosecutor to conduct the evidence gathering activities, even though they would like to be able to seek evidence on their own.

In addition, they emphasise that the level of cooperation of both suspects and witnesses is limited. It seems that citizens are rarely aware that financial authorities also conduct criminal proceedings and, for instance, may not follow the official summons they receive from administrative bodies, even though they have the same force as those sent by the police. The administrative authorities (unlike the police) have no means to force people to comply with their obligation to appear and they find it rather frustrating.

The financial authorities seem to regret that they cannot use all the evidence that they have collected in the course of the administrative proceedings within the framework of criminal proceedings.[13] It would certainly contribute considerably to decreasing their burden of work and would speed up criminal proceedings. However, since the collection of evidence within administrative proceedings does not guarantee the necessary procedural safeguards for the suspect, the evidence gathering activities must be repeated in criminal proceedings.

The financial authorities also raise a controversial point regarding the evidence they present to the court. The pre-trial proceedings they conduct are based, to a large extent, on the findings of the financial administrative investigation (conducted prior to the criminal proceedings or while they were suspended). As mentioned above, one of the crucial formal elements on which criminal proceedings are based is a final decision taken at the end of administrative proceedings. However, the courts conducting trials in cases of fiscal offences sometimes refuse to recognise the binding force of administrative decisions and consider them simply as part of the body of evidence. That means that the courts judge themselves to be entitled to assess the accuracy of a decision taken by a competent authority within a separate formal procedure. Such an approach is worthy of criticism.

Forms and Supervision of Proceedings

The proceedings regarding fiscal offences are conducted in the form of an investigation or inquiry.[14] An investigation is opened when aggravating circumstances are present (eg, commission of a fiscal offence by members of an organised crime group), the suspect is a judge, prosecutor, police officer, or an officer of another law enforcement body, the suspect is an official of the financial authorities overseeing

---

[13] Interestingly, the same argument is raised by OLAF officials with regard to the transfer of evidence they collect in their administrative proceedings to the national authorities for use in criminal proceedings. For more on this subject, see C Nowak (ed), *Evidence in EU Fraud Cases* (Warsaw, Wolters Kluwer, 2012).

[14] *cf* V Konarska-Wrzosek, T Oczkowski and J Skorupka, *Prawo i postępowanie karne skarbowe* (Warsaw, Wolters Kluwer, 2010) 381.

the pre-trial proceedings or superior financial authorities, or a prosecutor or financial authority orders one (Article 151a § 2 FCC).[15] However, in practice, most of the proceedings are conducted as less formalised inquiries.

When the pre-trial proceedings are conducted in the form of a more formalised investigation, they are mandatorily supervised by a public prosecutor (Article 151c § 1 FCC). The autonomy of financial authorities is far greater when the proceedings are conducted in the form of an inquiry. An inquiry is supervised by a prosecutor only when the circumstances referred to in Article 79 § 1 on mandatory defence occur or when there is a doubt regarding the suspect's mental health and expert psychiatrists were also appointed while the suspect was detained. A prosecutor may also supervise a case of particular significance or complexity (Article 151c § 1 FCC).

Otherwise, the proceedings conducted in a form of an inquiry are supervised by superior financial authorities.

Even though there is a general obligation of supervision stemming from the Code of Criminal Procedure,[16] to the extent that the prosecutor may personally take over and proceed with the case,[17] in reality the scope of the supervision, whether by a prosecutor or by superior financial authorities, is limited by Article 325e § 2 CCP, pursuant to which the most important procedural decisions taken by the authority conducting the pre-trial proceedings, namely, decisions regarding the institution of proceedings, refusal to open proceedings, discontinuance of an inquiry and entry of the case into the register of offences—and with the exception of the decision to discontinue and suspend an investigation—do not have to be approved by the supervising prosecutor or a superior financial authority. This means that in actual fact the prosecutor is in many cases not aware that pre-trial proceedings involving fiscal cases have been opened and are being conducted by financial authorities.[18]

Pre-trial proceedings regarding fiscal offences should in principle be concluded within three months. However, they may be prolonged by a supervising prosecutor or a superior financial authority. The authority to prolong the proceedings does not, however, mean that the prosecutor will supervise or control them after taking that decision.

The lack of supervision by a public prosecutor may seem like a good solution, as it gives a good deal of autonomy to the financial authorities in conducting

---

[15] ibid, 381–382.

[16] Pursuant to Art 113 FCC, the Code of Criminal Procedure applies for fiscal criminal proceedings, unless the provisions of the FCC provide otherwise. The CCP provides in Art 298 that the preparatory pre-trial proceedings must be conducted or supervised by a prosecutor. In addition, Art 326 states that the pre-trial proceedings must be supervised by a prosecutor (or superior financial authorities) to the extent that he is not personally conducting the same. See A Światłowski in P Hofmański (ed), *System prawa karnego procesowego. Tom I cz. 2. Zagadnienia ogólne* (Warsaw, LexisNexis 2013) 768.

[17] *cf* Art 326 § 3, p 3 CCP. This right does not apply to superior financial authorities—pursuant to Art 122 § 1, p 2 FCC.

[18] L Wilk and J Zagrodnik, *Prawo karne skarbowe* (Warsaw, CH Beck, 2009) 507.

pre-trial proceedings. However, in practice the lack of supervision leaves the financial authorities without valuable assistance from the prosecutorial service, which is the authority with the best expertise in the field of pre-trial proceedings. There is, of course, some cooperation between the financial authorities and the public prosecutor's office, but it seems to be mainly based on personal relations between officials of the financial authorities and prosecutors themselves, and to depend—due to the absence of any applicable legal provisions—on the individual willingness of prosecutors to assist the financial authorities.

Notwithstanding the form of pre-trial proceedings in fiscal cases, the actions undertaken by the financial authority (as well as any non-financial authority conducting the proceedings) follow a typical order applied in common proceedings.[19]

Conclusion of Proceedings

With respect to the conclusion of pre-trial proceedings, it should be noted that the criminal proceedings in fiscal cases may be brought to an end in several ways. First, they may be closed when the case does not give rise to any formal accusation. However, the initial suspicion about the commission of a fiscal offence is confirmed more frequently than not. In such a case, pursuant to the FCC, the financial authorities have a variety of available procedural options, bearing in mind that in fiscal cases the objective of repression is less of a priority than the main objective of the proceedings, which is to recover the funds due to the State Treasury or local government (Article 114 § 1 FCC).[20]

The option most rarely adopted in practice is conditional discontinuance of the proceedings, applied when the case is of lesser significance. The authorities may also negotiate a penalty with a suspect who voluntarily submits to liability for a fiscal offence (Article 142 FCC *et seq*). If a settlement can be reached, which happens rather frequently, the financial authorities will file a motion to the court requesting that permission be granted accordingly instead of filing a bill of indictment.[21]

Finally, the financial authorities may also file a traditional bill of indictment with the court.[22] If an investigation or inquiry has been supervised by a prosecutor, within 14 days after the conclusion of the proceedings the financial authorities will send a bill of indictment, together with all necessary documents, to the prosecutor, who will approve it and submit to the court (Article 155 FCC).

---

[19] *cf* V Konarska-Wrzosek, T Oczkowski and J Skorupka, *Prawo i postępowanie karne skarbowe* (Warsaw, Wolters Kluwer, 2010) 384.

[20] L Wilk and J Zagrodnik, *Prawo karne skarbowe* (Warsaw, CH Beck, 2009) 12–13.

[21] For more on this subject, see S Baniak, *Prawo karne skarbowe* (Warsaw, Wolters Kluwer, 2009) 106.

[22] *cf* L Wilk and J Zagrodnik, *Prawo karne skarbowe*, 512.

In such a case the financial authorities enjoy the same rights as the public prosecutor. However, when the proceedings have been conducted in a form of an inquiry that is not supervised by a prosecutor, the financial authorities will submit the bill of indictment directly to the court. The prosecutor is only informed of their decision. Before the trial court they act directly as prosecutors.

Overlapping Competences

Notwithstanding the competence of fiscal authorities engaged in pre-trial proceedings, in the case of fiscal offences proceedings may also be carried out by other bodies, for instance, the prosecutor (Article 151b FCC) or the police, should they detect a fiscal offence in the course of their activities (Article 134 FCC).

In an event of a conflict of competence between a financial and non-financial authority,[23] the general rule is that the proceedings are to be conducted by a financial authority (except in the case of proceedings conducted by the Military Gendarmerie). However, the decision as to which authority is competent belongs to the prosecutor with jurisdiction over the territory in which the non-financial authority is located (Article 135 § 3 FCC).

In this respect, it seems regrettable that neither Polish criminal law nor Polish fiscal criminal law establishes any mechanism of control and coordination of the activities of the different bodies involved in investigations concerning economic and financial crime. Each authority involved in investigating economic crime acts independently. This overlapping of competences and lack of a coordinating mechanism warrants criticism, as it implies some level of competition between different agencies interested in conducting proceedings in fiscal cases and may give rise to conflicts of competence, for instance, between the fiscal authorities and the police in cases of fiscal offences. In practice, though, it must be said, most proceedings are conducted by financial authorities, as non-financial ones have shown themselves to be unwilling to deal with the fiscal cases.

Conclusions

The Polish model of proceedings in fiscal cases is rather unique. The criminal proceedings for fiscal offences are conducted mainly by special units of financial administrative authorities which are vested with competence in criminal cases. They have the most expertise on fiscal issues and are able to detect fiscal crimes in the course of their regular activities. The proceedings they conduct must be in line

---

[23] *cf* L Wilk and J Zagrodnik, *Prawo karne skarbowe*, 328–329.

with all the requirements of criminal procedural law—in particular when it comes to safeguards for the suspect—otherwise their findings would not be accepted by the courts. The judicial evaluation of evidence is the ultimate guarantee of the quality of the proceedings conducted by financial authorities.

The observance of the *ne bis in idem* principle is not an issue, as the Tax Act[24] does not provide for any sanctions for non-payment of taxes. If a taxpayer fails to pay taxes, the administrative proceedings may only result in a decision obliging him to pay the taxes due plus statutory interest. There is no additional penalty. Such sanctions may only be pronounced during criminal proceedings.

The Polish model is not perfect. First, the scope and quality of supervision by the prosecutor is susceptible of improvement. Secondly, even though in practice the financial authorities conduct most of the proceedings, there are too many bodies with overlapping jurisdiction over fiscal cases. Some time ago there was an idea of establishing one financial authority to deal with all types of fiscal offences: a sort of fiscal administrative police. Such a task was to be confined to fiscal control offices. It could have been an opportunity to introduce clear rules on jurisdiction in fiscal cases and ensure that fully specialised staff would deal with these cases. Regrettably, the idea has been abandoned and today all financial authorities have to cope with this additional burden.

---

[24] The Tax Act of 29 August 1997, consolidated text: OJ of 2015, item 613, as amended.

Part IV

Prosecuting Financial-Economic Offences Outside the Roman Legal System

6

The Dynamics of Investigating and Prosecuting Financial and Economic Crimes in the UK

PROF DR VALSAMIS MITSILEGAS
Professor of European Criminal Law, Queen Mary University of London

DR THEODORA A CHRISTOU
Transnational Law and Governance Convenor, Queen Mary
University of London

Introduction

The following chapter provides an overview of operational models deployed by a selection of the numerous agencies and bodies in the UK, with a mandate to investigate and prosecute economic and financial crimes. In addition to the police and the Crown Prosecution Service, we will consider the National Crime Agency, the Serious Fraud Office and the Financial Conduct Authority.

As noted by the European Commission, the range of crimes at national level under which the 'protection of the financial interests of the European Union' could fall are broad and varied across the Member States.[1] According to section 6(3) of the Financial Services and Markets Act 2000, in the UK a financial crime is said 'to include any offence involving (a) fraud or dishonesty; (b) misconduct in, or misuse of information relating to, a financial market; or (c) handling the proceeds of crime'. The term 'to include' means that 'financial crime' can be interpreted widely

---

[1] Communication From The Commission to The European Parliament, The Council, The European Economic And Social Committee and The Committee of The Regions On the protection of the financial interests of the European Union by criminal law and by administrative investigations An integrated policy to safeguard taxpayers' money, Brussels, 26.5.2011, COM(2011) 293 final, available at: http://eur-lex.europa.eu/LexUriServ/LexUriServ.do?uri=COM:2011:0293:FIN:EN:PDF.

to include a range of offences. These include but not limited to: fraud,[2] bribery and corruption,[3] insider dealing and market abuse,[4] and money laundering.[5]

---

[2] Section 1 of the Fraud Act 2002 sets out the offence of fraud which can be committed in one of three ways: fraud by false representation (s 2); fraud by failing to disclose information where under a duty to do so (s 3); and fraud by abuse of position which a person or company is expected to safeguard, or not to act against, the financial interests of another person (s 4). In practice most fraud offences fall under the s 2 offence. See: D Ormerod and K Laird, *Smith and Hogan's Text, Cases, and Materials on Criminal Law*, XIth edn (Oxford, Oxford University Press, 2014) ch 25.

[3] The offences are now provided for under the Bribery Act 2010 which is applicable only for conduct which occurred after its entry into force, 1 July 2011. Conduct which took place before this date is subject to the pre-existing law, namely: Common law offences of bribery and accepting a bribe; Public Bodies Corrupt Practices Act 1889; Prevention of Corruption Act 1906. Available at: www.legislation. gov.uk/ukpga/2010/23/contents. The offences include: payment of a fine (s 1); receiving a bribe (s 2); bribery of a foreign public official (s 6). The Act has been subject to some criticism because of the extremely low level of prosecutions. However, because a company could be prosecuted unless it could establish that it had adequate procedures in place, the Act did have a practical impact in that companies re-evaluated their anti-bribery controls. See: M Taddia, *Economic crime: corruption conundrum*, *Law Society Gazette*, 27 October 2014 http://www.lawgazette.co.uk/law/economic-crime-corruption-conundrum/5044646.fullarticle. See also, J Mukwiri, 'British law on corporate bribery' (2015) 22(1) *Journal of Financial Crime* 16–27. See also P Aldridge, 'The UK Bribery Act: The Caffeinated Younger Sibling of the FCPA' (2012) 73 *Ohio State Law Journal* 1181–1216.

[4] Section 52 of the Criminal Justice Act 1993 sets out the three offences of insider dealing: Dealing; Encouraging; and Disclosure. Part 7 of the Financial Services Act 2012 creates new offences including the offences of making false or misleading statements (s 89) or creating false or misleading impressions (s 90). There are seven types of behaviour constituting market abuse which are set out in s 118 of the Financial Services and Markets Act 2000. These are: (a) where an insider deals, or attempts to deal, in a qualifying investment or related investment on the basis of inside information relating to the investment in question, (b) where an insider discloses inside information to another person otherwise than in the proper course of the exercise of his employment, profession or duties, (c) where the behaviour (not falling within subsection (2) or (3)) is: (a) based on information which is not generally available to those using the market but which, if available to a regular user of the market, would be, or would be likely to be, regarded by him as relevant when deciding the terms on which transactions in qualifying investments should be effected; and (b) likely to be regarded by a regular user of the market as a failure on the part of the person concerned to observe the standard of behaviour reasonably expected of a person in his position in relation to the market, (d) where the behaviour consists of effecting transactions or orders to trade (otherwise than for legitimate reasons and in conformity with accepted market practices on the relevant market) which: (a) give, or are likely to give, a false or misleading impression as to the supply of, or demand for, or as to the price of, one or more qualifying investments; or (b) secure the price of one or more such investments at an abnormal or artificial level, (e) where the behaviour consists of effecting transactions or orders to trade which employ fictitious devices or any other form of deception or contrivance, (f) where the behaviour consists of the dissemination of information by any means which gives, or is likely to give, a false or misleading impression as to a qualifying investment by a person who knew or could reasonably be expected to have known that the information was false or misleading, (g) where the behaviour (not falling within subsection (5), (6) or (7)): (a) likely to give a regular user of the market a false or misleading impression as to the supply of, demand for or price or value of, qualifying investments; or (b) would be, or would be likely to be, regarded by a regular user of the market as behaviour that would distort, or would be likely to distort, the market in such an investment, and the behaviour is likely to be regarded by a regular user of the market as a failure on the part of the person concerned to observe the standard of behaviour reasonably expected of a person in his position in relation to the market.

[5] The terrorism funding nexus of any of these crimes will not be considered. Proceeds of Crime Act 2002 (POCA) applies to activities after 23 February 2003. The Act has three principal offences: 'Concealing, disguising, converting or transferring criminal property or removing criminal property from the UK' (s 327); 'Entering into, or becoming concerned in, an arrangement knowing or suspecting that it facilitates the acquisition, retention, use or control of criminal property by or on behalf of

General Criminal Investigation and Prosecution

Police

The majority of investigations into crimes are conducted by the police. There are 43 police forces[6] across England and Wales responsible for the investigation of crime, collection of evidence and the arrest or detention of suspected offenders. If the crime involved is classified as minor the police have the power to give a caution or warning; a police fine, called a penalty notice; or a community resolution. In the case of more serious offences the police send the case papers to the Crown Prosecution Service to decide upon prosecution.

When it comes to economic and financial crimes, the practice is not standardised across the UK, some police forces have specialist Economic Crime Units (such as Leicestershire Police Force) whilst others do not, meaning that they are investigated by the entire force and not a specific unit.

The City of London

The City of London Police Economic Crime Directorate (ECD) is recognised as the national policing lead for fraud and economic crimes. Sitting within the ECD are a number of other bodies, these include Action Fraud which is the UK's national reporting unit. There is also the National Fraud Intelligence Bureau (NFIB) whose Know Fraud system is one of the most advanced police intelligence systems in the world with the ability to process vast amounts of data to pinpoint patterns and linkages in offending. Where the NFIB identifies clear evidence of fraud this is sent to the relevant law enforcement agency, which could be the CPS or another body.

---

another person' (s 328); 'Acquiring, using or possessing criminal property' (s 329). See: P Aldridge, 'Two Key Areas in Proceeds of Crime Law' (2014) *Criminal Law Review*, 170–188.

The 'secondary' offences are: failure by a person in the 'regulated sector' to disclose, if he knows or has reasonable grounds to know or suspect, that an individual is engaged in money laundering (s 330); and failure by a 'nominated officer' to disclose knowledge or suspicion of money laundering to the National Crime Agency (ss 331–332).

The Money Laundering Regulations 2007 (SI 2007/2157) transposed the requirements of the Third Money Laundering Directive (2005/60/EC), into UK law. The Regulations require firms to take specified steps to detect and prevent both money laundering and terrorist financing. The Money Laundering Regulations 2007 designate a number of authorities as supervisory authorities, their powers are set out under Part 5 of the Regulations. These include: The power to require information from, and attendance of, relevant and connected persons (s 37); Search and seizure powers with or without a warrant (ss 38 and 39); Power to impose civil penalties (s 42); Prosecution of offences (s 46). The text of the Money Laundering Regulations 2007 can be accessed here: www.legislation.gov.uk/uksi/2007/2157/contents/made. See M Anderson and TA Anderson, 'Anti-money laundering: history and current developments' (2015) *JIBLR*, 30(10), 521–531.

[6] The official website of the Police Force can be found here: http://www.police.uk/.

The Crown Prosecution Service

The Attorney-General is the chief legal adviser to the government and super-intends the principal prosecuting authorities within England and Wales. These are the Crown Prosecution Service and the Serious Fraud Office. The Attorney-General also has overall responsibility for the Treasury Solicitor's Department, the National Fraud Authority and Her Majesty's Crown Prosecution Service Inspectorate.

The Crown Prosecution Service (CPS)[7] is the principal prosecuting authority for England and Wales, acting independently in criminal cases investigated by the police and others from whom it receives reports. Before considering its modern day role it is worth looking at the evolution of prosecutions in the UK. Before the Prosecution of Offences Act 1879 individuals had to either present their own cases or instruct a lawyer to do so on their own behalf. With the establishment of police forces from 1829 this began to change. The first Director of Public Prosecutions (DPP) was appointed in 1880, however he formed part of the Home Office, only handled limited cases which were either important or complex and once a decision to prosecute was made, the actual prosecution was dealt with by the Treasury Solicitor. In 1884 the two roles were merged until 1908 when the Prosecution of Offences Act 1908 separated the roles of the DPP and the Treasury Solicitor.

Prosecution of the remaining cases was conducted by the police who contin-ued to hold this responsibility until 1986. In 1962 a Royal Commission report held that it was not acceptable for the same police officers to both investigate and prosecute cases. Its recommendation was that police forces set up their own pros-ecuting solicitor's departments. This recommendation was followed by some but not all forces, others took advice on prosecution from local solicitor firms. In 1981 another report by a Royal Commission on Criminal Procedure was critical of the criminal justice system. It found that in the interests of fairness the police should not both investigate and decide whether to prosecute cases; that the standards used to decide upon prosecution varied across police forces; and that too many weak cases were being prosecuted leading to a high number of acquittals. The recom-mendation was for the establishment of an independent prosecution authority.[8]

The Crown Prosecution Service (CPS) that we have now, was set up in 1986 by the Prosecution of Offences Act 1985, headed up by the DPP and included the existing Police Prosecuting Solicitor's Departments which had been established by some police forces. The CPS and police continue to work in partnership. In minor cases the police will take the decision to either caution, take no further action,

---

[7] The official website of the Crown Prosecution Service can be accessed here: www.cps.gov.uk.
[8] The Report itself is not available online, it is held at the National Archives: http://discovery.nation-alarchives.gov.uk/details/r/C3028. However, the parliamentary debate on the report is interesting Criminal Procedure (Philips Report), HC Deb 20 November 1981 vol 13 cc 527–98. It can be accessed here: http://hansard.millbanksystems.com/commons/1981/nov/20/criminal-procedure-philips-report.

issue a fixed penalty notice or refer to the CPS for a conditional caution. In serious cases, the police will send the file to the CPS who will decide upon prosecution.

The CPS has four primary roles, namely to decide which cases should be prosecuted; to determine the appropriate charges in more serious or complex cases by advising the police during the early stages of investigations; to prepare cases and present them at court—using a range of in-house advocates, self-employed advocates or agents in court; and to provide information, assistance and support to victims and prosecution witnesses.

The Code for Crown Prosecutors[9] is a public document, issued by the Director of Public Prosecutions that sets out the general principles Crown Prosecutors should follow when they make decisions on cases. The Code is followed by other bodies who have prosecutorial powers. As will be seen, in addition to the police and the CPS there are a number of designated bodies who have investigatory and prosecutorial powers over financial and economic crimes.

The CPS has a Specialist Fraud Division (SFD)[10] for serious and complex frauds. The criteria applied to determine whether the SFD runs the prosecution include, for police-investigated cases: cases with a minimum provable loss of £1m; difficult corruption and bribery cases, especially concerning public (including foreign public) bodies or officials (other than the police, which are referred to the Special Crime division); cases where local concern makes it appropriate to refer the case outside the area; frauds on government departments or the governments of other countries; cases where widespread concern makes it appropriate for the SFD to coordinate and set standards; difficult cases requiring specialist knowledge such as Stock Exchange practices, regulatory bodies, complex banking issues, shipping law etc; complex and high value 'boiler room' and 'Ponzi' frauds; and money laundering connected with fraudulent activity.

The CPS has no involvement in the cases which the SFO has selected for investigation, even where that investigation is being supported or supplemented by police or National Crime Agency (NCA) investigators.

A key difference with Civil Law jurisdictions is the non-involvement of the judiciary in either the investigation or the decision to prosecute. In addition to the CPS and the SFO, those other agencies with prosecutorial powers exercise their decision to prosecute unfettered by the police, CPS and courts.

Specialised Bodies with Powers of Investigation and Prosecution

In addition to the police and CPS, there are several bodies when it comes to investigating economic and financial crimes.

---

[9] The Code for Crown Prosecutors can be accessed here: http://www.cps.gov.uk/publications/code_for_crown_prosecutors/index.html.
[10] Further details about the Specialist Fraud Division can be found here: http://www.cps.gov.uk/your_cps/our_organisation/sfd.html.

These are some of the other bodies involved in counter fraud work: Serious Fraud Office; Department of Business, Innovation and Skills; Financial Conduct Authority; Her Majesty's Revenue and Customs; The Home Office; The Insolvency Service; National Fraud Authority; National Crime Agency; Department of Work and Pensions.

The powers of investigation and prosecution of select bodies will be considered in turn below. Bodies such as the Fraud Advisory Panel,[11] which acts as an independent voice and supporter of the counter fraud community will not be considered since their role is only advisory.

It is worth noting that there are a number of others who are also part of the anti-money laundering system such as the Joint Money Laundering Steering Group[12] composed of 17 UK trade associations from the financial industry. Once again, the work of such bodies will not be considered since they do not possess powers of investigation or to prosecute; their roles tend to be more advisory in issuing guidelines for best practice.

Agencies and Regulatory Authorities

The specific powers and operational models[13] of the National Crime Agency, the Financial Conduct Authority and the Serious Fraud Agency to investigate and prosecute economic and financial crimes will be considered in turn.

National Crime Agency

The National Crime Agency (NCA)[14] is a non-ministerial government department whose Director General has independent operational direction and control over activities but is accountable to the Home Secretary for the agency's performance. It became operational in October 2013, replacing the Serious Organised Crime Agency.[15] The role of the NCA's Economic Crime Command is to fight economic

---

[11] Further details about their work can be found on their official website which can be accessed here: www.fraudadvisorypanel.org/.

[12] Further details about their work can be found on their official website which can be accessed here: http://www.jmlsg.org.uk/.

[13] These are found in the legislation, further described in official documents if the respective agencies and further clarified by individuals interviewed by Dr Theodora A Christou under Chatham House Rules.

[14] The official website of the National Crime Agency can be found here: www.nationalcrimeagency. gov.uk.

[15] See: M Roberts and A Hohl, 'The new NCA: what does it mean for the SFO?' (2013) 24(10) *Practical Law Companies* 11–12. This comments on the NCA's lead in coordinating the response to serious and organised crime across regional and international borders, the implications for the SFO and the relationship between the NCA and SFO.

crime, specifically fraud (against both private and public actors), bribery and corruption, and money laundering.

The NCA's UK Financial Intelligence Unit (UKFIU) receives, analyses and distributes financial intelligence gathered from Suspicious Activity Reports (SARs). A SAR is information which alerts law enforcement of potential money laundering. Out of 350,000 SARs receive yearly, the UKFIU identifies the most sensitive and sends them to the appropriate organisations for investigation.

The powers and functions of the NCA are set out in Part 1 of the Crime and Courts Act 2013 (CCA 2013).[16] The NCA has a dual function; first the 'crime-reduction function'; and secondly the 'criminal intelligence function' gathering, storing, processing, analysing, and disseminating information. It can discharge its functions in one of three ways.

First, by the NCA itself which includes '(a) preventing and detecting organised crime and serious crime, (b) investigating offences relating to organised crime or serious crime, and (c) otherwise carrying out activities to combat organised crime and serious crime, including by instituting criminal proceedings in England and Wales and Northern Ireland.' Notably it does not have the power to prosecute offences itself.

According to section 10 of the CCA 2013, the Director General may designate any NCA officer as a person having one or more of the following: '(a) the powers and privileges of a constable; (b) the powers of an officer of Revenue and Customs; (c) the powers of an immigration officer.' This would include criminal investigation tools such as gaining entry to property, search and seizure powers, detaining and arresting suspects and executing warrants.

The second is to secure 'activities to combat organised crime or serious crime are carried out by persons other than the NCA.' The third way is by the NCA securing improvements '(a) in co-operation between persons who carry out activities to combat organised crime or serious crime, and (b) in coordination of activities to combat organised crime or serious crime.'[17]

Serious Fraud Office[18]

The Serious Fraud Office (SFO) was established in April 1988 by the Criminal Justice Act 1987 (as amended). The Act was a result of recommendations in

---

[16] The text of the Crime and Courts Act 2013 can be accessed here: http://www.legislation.gov.uk/ukpga/2013/22/part/1/enacted.

[17] Comments on the reforms introduced by the Serious Crime Act 2015 Pt 1 to improve the efficiency of the restraint and compliance regime for proceeds of crime such as changes relating to assets held by third parties, the payment of confiscation orders, victim surcharge and restraint orders, absconding defendants, default sentences, civil liability exemptions for money laundering disclosures, are discussed in, J Fisher, 'The Part 1 of the Serious Crime Act 2015: strengthening the restraint and confiscation regime' (2015) 10 *Crim LR* 754–765.

[18] The official website of the Serious Fraud Office can be found here: www.sfo.gov.uk.

The Roskill Report,[19] which recommended the establishment of a new organisation for the investigation and prosecution of serious fraud crimes.[20]

The Serious Fraud Office (SFO) is an independent governmental department set up under Part 1 of the Criminal Justice Act 1987 (CJA 1987) with both investigative and prosecutorial powers.[21] It has a mandate over serious or complex fraud, bribery and corruption cases. It is composed of seven operational divisions: three dealing with fraud; two with bribery and corruption cases; one with proceeds of crime and one provides and coordinates international assistance. It operates under the superintendence of the Attorney-General.[22]

The SFO has a dedicated Intelligence Unit which receives and analyses information to assess whether a case should be recommended for acceptance by the Director of the Serious Fraud Office. Prior to formal acceptance by the Director of the Serious Fraud Office, cases are known as operations rather than investigations. An SFO investigation only begins when the Director formally accepts the case for investigation.

The SFO powers are set out under section 2 of the CJA 1987, these include the power to search property;[23] and to compel persons, other than suspects, to answer questions or furnish information at a specified time and place; and produce documents either immediately or at a specified and time. These powers are compulsory powers which means that non-compliance is a criminal offence and sanctions can be imposed against individuals. A notice is served on the person stating a particular action which must be fulfilled and a date and time by which

---

[19] Fraud Trials Committee Report 1986.

[20] For a Review of the SFO 20 years after the Roskill Report, see: R Wright, 'Fraud after Roskill: A View from the Serious Fraud' (2003) 11(1) *Office Journal of Financial Crime* 10–16; M Raphael, 'Fraud on Trial—Reviewing the Roskill Legacy' (2003) 11(1) *Journal of Financial Crime* 8–9; and M Levi, 'The Roskill Fraud Commission Revisited: An Assessment' (2003) 11(1) *Journal of Financial Crime* 38–44.

[21] For a historical view of its powers, see: S Savla, 'Serious Fraud Office powers under section 2 of the Criminal Justice Act 1987 and Police and Criminal Evidence Act 1984' (1997) 4(3) *Journal of Financial Crime* 223–231.

[22] For an examination of the SFO and the creation of corporate liability for the crime of fraud see S Gentle and E Proudlock, 'The problems of creating criminal corporate liability in the investigation of fraud: establishing criminal responsibility at board level' (2011) *SFO, Serious Economic Crime: A boardroom guide to prevention and compliance* 233–38, available at: https://www.kingsleynapley.co.uk/assets/files/KIngsley%20Napley%20chapter%20Serious%20Economic%20Crime.pdf. For a critical view of the work of the SFO and the FCA following the bank crisis and in particular the lack of prosecutions see: JS Rakoff, 'The financial crisis: Why have no high-level executives been prosecuted?' 9 January 2014 *New York Review of Books*; R Quigley, 'The impulse towards individual criminal punishment after the financial crisis' (2015) 22 *Virginia Journal of Social Policy & the Law* 103. See M Thompson and M Hunting, *Two steps forward, one step back: the SFO, Fraud Intelligence* 2015, Apr/May, 18–19 for consideration of the UK's National Anti-Corruption Plan and the future of the Serious Fraud Office (SFO). This also discusses two recent cases illustrating the SFO's mixed performance suggesting that SFO investigators may move to the National Crime Agency and SFO prosecutors may become part of the Crown Prosecution Service or a new specialist financial crime agency. See also: C Thomson and H Garfield, 'SFO enforcement: has the tanker turned?' (2015) *Practical Law Companies* 26.

[23] Under s 2(4) the SFO must apply to the courts for a search warrant.

it must occur. If there are reasonable grounds for believing that serving a notice would seriously prejudice the evidence, the SFO may apply to the court for a warrant to search and seize documents. Section 2 powers can be used before the opening of an investigation but only in cases of foreign bribery. The amendments in 2008 mean that now under section 2A of the CJA 1987, these powers can now be used at the pre-investigatory stage in cases involving allegations of bribery and corruption.

It should be further noted that they can be normally only be used against witnesses but not suspects. A key safeguard is that answers given by those being questioned following a Notice under section 2(2) cannot be used as evidence against them save in very limited circumstances. Suspects must be questioned in accordance with the Police and Criminal Evidence Act 1984 (PACE).

Additional powers are found in other legislation including: Fraud Act 2006, Serious Crime Act 2007, Proceeds of Crime Act 2002, and RIPA.

The formal decision to open an investigation is taken by the Director of the SFO. Having considered the evidence, a panel will have made a recommendation to the Director, however he has full discretion as to whether to prosecute or not and exercises this based upon the SFO case selection criteria. The extent of the Director's discretion is set out in the CJA. The case selection criteria are set out on the SFO website. This is in contrast to the CPS who must take a case referred to them by the police, even if they decide to discontinue it.

The decision as to whether to prosecute also takes into account the Code for Crown Prosecutors. The two stages of the decision are first whether it satisfies the evidential test, and secondly if it is in the public interest.

When deciding whether it should take the lead in prosecuting the SFO has established a statement of principles to evaluate the seriousness and complexity of the fraud, bribery or corruption to be taken into account: cases which undermine UK commercial/financial PLC in general and the City of London in particular; cases where the actual or potential loss involved is high; cases where actual or potential harm is significant; cases where there is a very significant public interest element; and new species of fraud.

The Director will also take into account whether the case calls for the multidisciplinary approach and the unique statutory powers available to the SFO.

The case team who works on cases can consist of accountants, lawyers, IT experts, specialist investigators and other support staff. The case team will also work closely with the relevant police or NCA team as appropriate. Each team is headed by a case controller and will be composed of lawyers, investigators, and often accountants, with other expertise being brought in as required.

Memorandum of Understandings (MoUs) are in place between the SFO and other competent bodies. In addition to these, MoUs are negotiated on a case by case basis as and when required. MoUs are written agreements between agencies on a matter of mutual interest. The can cover a range of matters, normally how information is to be shared and how each agency will act on a particular issue.

The MoU between the SFO and the Solicitors Regulatory Authority and that with the Competition and Markets Authority[24] are similar in that they both cover exchange of information between agencies. A common feature of both is the nominated single point of contact, normally within the SFO Intelligence Unit.

Another common feature is the gateway for disclosure of information to others by the SFO. This is set out under section 3(5) of the CJA 1984. It permits information gathered by the SFO to be disclosed to: (a) any government department, Northern Ireland department, other authority, body discharging its functions on behalf of the Crown; (b) any competent authority; (c) for the purposes of any criminal investigation or criminal proceedings, whether in the United Kingdom or elsewhere; or (d) to assist an authority to discharge a designated function specified in an order made by the Secretary of State.

The section also deals at section 3(1) of the CJA 1987 with information which is disclosed by Her Majesty's Revenue & Customs under section 18(2) of the Commissioners for Revenue and Customs Act to any SFO member for the purposes of any prosecution of an offence relating to a former Inland Revenue matter. That information may be disclosed by any SFO member: (a) for the purposes of any prosecution conducted by the SFO; (b) to the CPS for the purposes of any prosecution of [an offence relating to a former Inland Revenue matter; (c) to the DPP for Northern Ireland for the purposes of any prosecution of [an offence relating to a former Inland Revenue matter; or (d) in order to comply with a requirement imposed under paragraph 7 of the Schedule to the Crown Prosecution Service Inspectorate Act 2000.

However under section 3(3) of the CJA 1987 where such information does not fall under the Taxes Management Act 1970, any information disclosed may only be done by a SFO member who is designated by the Director for the purposes of any prosecution and only for the purposes prescribed in Section 3(3).

The focus of the MoU between the SFO and the Crown Office Procurator Fiscal Service is on agreeing primacy over prosecution of an individual which could be brought by either organisation. A set of criteria is set out for identifying the 'responsible organisation'. The MOU also contains provision for the exchange information and intelligence.

Finally the MoU on Tackling Foreign Bribery governs the procedure, with personal consent being required from either the Director of Public Prosecutions or the SFO Director, as required under Article 10 of the Bribery Act 2010.[25]

Where overlapping prosecution competence exists, the competent bodies will discuss the case and agree between them who is to take the lead. They will also

---

[24] The MoU between the SFO and the Competition and Markets Authority can be accessed here: https://www.gov.uk/government/uploads/system/uploads/attachment_data/file/307038/MoU_CMAandSFO.PDF.

[25] The MOU is between a number of organisations, namely, the SFO, FCA, NCA, City of London Police, Crown Office Procurator Fiscal Service and the Ministry of Defence Police.

work together to exchange evidence. Cooperation channels also exist in the form of other statutory powers.

Schedule 17 of the Crimes and Courts Act 2013 introduced deferred prosecution agreements (DPA). The SFO and CPS issued a Deferred Prosecution Agreements Code of Practice. The Code sets out the procedure and states that a DPA is a discretionary tool which a defendant has no right to expect. It is an alternative to prosecution. In considering whether a DPA is appropriate, the prosecutor must apply the two stage full Code test set out above. Once these have been satisfied a further list of factors to be taken into account is listed in the Code. When the decision is made to offer a DPA, a formal letter is sent marking the start of the negotiation period. Under section 7(1) of Schedule 17 of the 2013 Act, after commencement of negotiations but before the terms of the DPA are agreed, the prosecutor must apply to the Crown Court for a declaration that entering into a DPA is likely to be in the interests of justice, and the proposed terms of the DPA are fair, reasonable and proportionate. Once the terms are agreed the prosecutor must apply to the court for approval, a declaration under Section 8 of Schedule 17. Whilst the negotiations and initial submission to the court are confidential, once approved, a declaration is made in open court along with reasons. Once the declaration is made the SFO will publish the DPA and relevant declarations on its website.

The United Kingdom Central Authority (UKCA) is the designated authority in the UK for the purposes of Mutual Legal Assistance requests from other jurisdictions. Where the matter under investigation involves serious or complex crime, the UKCA can refer the request to the SFO under section 15(2) of the Crime (International Co-operation) Act 2003.[26]

Financial Conduct Authority (FCA)[27]

Regulation of the financial services industry began with the Banking Act 1979 and gradually evolved over time.[28] The Financial Services and Markets Act 2000 (FSMA), replaced the multi-agency structure by an innovative single agency, the Financial Services Authority.[29] The FSA's powers were strengthened by the Financial Services Act 2010 amending FSMA. A change of government saw a change in regulatory ideas and the role of the Bank of England.[30] Reform of the

---

[26] Most of the original legislation has been superseded by the Crime (International Co-operation) Act 2003. The International Assistance team of the SFO was established under s 164(2) of the Criminal Justice Act 1994 amending the Criminal Justice Act 1987.

[27] The official website of the Financial Conduct Authority can be accessed here: www.fca.gov.uk.

[28] For discussion of the history since 1988 see: A Samuel, 'Two kings to rule them all' (2013) *Compliance Monitor* Apr 1–6.

[29] See: E Ferran, 'Examining the UK Experience in Adopting the Single Financial Regulator Model' (2003) 28 *Brooklyn Journal of International Law* 257–307.

[30] See: E Ferran, 'The Break-Up of the Financial Services Authority', *University of Cambridge Faculty of Law Research Paper Series No. 10/04* (October 11, 2010, who considers this cycle of reform and the FSA).

financial regulatory system was initiated by the Chancellor of the Exchequer[31] and followed by two consulation papers from the Treasury.[32] The reform of the financial regulatory authorities culminated in the Financial Services Act 2012 which created two separate authorities: the Financial Conduct Authority (FCA) and Prudential Regulation Authority.[33] For the purposes of this chapter only the FCA is relevant. The FCA took over the responsibility of the abolished Financial Services Authority and retained its powers of investigation and prosecution.[34]

The level of reforms that took place following the banking crisis in 2007–2009 are unprecedented. There are volumes of consultations, reports and proposals from government and the agencies themselves. However, the focus of almost all the reforms have been on the regulation of the banking sector, consumer protection and competition, none of particular relevance to the topic of this chapter.[35]

The FCA is a private company limited by guarantee. Its status, independence and accountability are set out under section 1A FSMA 2000 as amended by the Financial Services Act 2012 (FSMA 2000).[36] It has institutional, regulatory, supervisory, and budgetary independence.[37]

---

[31] In his Mansion Speech. For further information on this see P Rawlings, 'Bank Reform in the UK: Part II: Return to the Dark Ages?' (2011) 8 *Int CR* 55.

[32] See Consultation Papers: A new approach to financial regulation: the blueprint for reform, June 2011 Cm 8083 and *A new approach to financial regulation: building a stronger system*, February 2011, Cm 8012. A discussion of which can be found in J Mayfield, 'A blueprint for reform' (2011) 161(7472) *NLJ* 914.

[33] The PRA received the transferred prudential regulation responsibilities from the FSA. For proposals see: Chancellor of the Exchequer, *White Paper, A new approach to financial regulation: the blueprint for reform*, June 2011 Cm 8083 a discussion of which can be found in J Mayfield, 'A blueprint for reform' (2011) 161(7472) *NLJ* 914; P Yeoh, 'Reform of financial regulations in the UK: contents and implications' (2011) 32(10) *Bus LR* 244–250; E Ferran, 'The Reorganisation of Financial Services Supervision in the UK: An Interim Progress Report' (49/2011) *University of Cambridge Faculty of Law Research Paper*.

[34] Professor Haynes, refers to it as a change of name. A Haynes, 'Financial services: all change or new cosmetics?' (2014) *Comp Law* 129–131. For some of the differences see: M Taddia, 'Regime change' (2015) 112(18) *LSG* 11–13.

[35] Further discussion of the proposals can be found in: M Killick, 'Twin peak—a new series or a new chimera? An analysis of the proposed new regulatory structure in the UK' (2012) 33(12) *Comp Law* 366–382; J Hill and E Ligere, 'The UK's new financial services regulatory structure—the shape of things to come' (2013) 28(4) *Journal of International Banking Law and Regulation* 156–159. For an overview of the key changes see: A Kokkinis, '*The Financial Services Act 2012: the recent overhaul of the UK's financial regulatory structure*' (2013) 24(9) *ICCLR* 325–328.

[36] To be read in conjunction with sections 1A-1T and 3A-3T and Sch 1ZA FSMA 2000. FSMA 2000 as amended. It can be found here: http://www.legislation.gov.uk/ukpga/2000/8/contents.

[37] The evolution of the FCA and peculiarities in its structure and of its reform are beyond the scope of this chapter. Those interested in finding out more can refer to the following: M Taylor, 'Road From Twin Peaks' (2009) 16(1) *Connecticut Insurance Law Journal*, who in this article describes the debate in the UK prior to the creation of one unified regulatory agency, the Financial Services Authority (FSA). Next, it explores justifications for a single regulator, such as the FSA, followed by a discussion of the rejection of the 'Twin Peaks' approach in the UK. The 'Twin Peaks' approach, is to structure regulation around two agencies, one responsible for the safety and soundness of all financial firms and the other for regulating their sales practices. For a detailed explanation of Financial Services Law refer to G Walker, R Purves and M Blair QC, *Financial Services Law*, 3rd edn (Oxford, Oxford University Press, 2014).

The powers of the FCA include: making Rules (sections 137A (1)(b), 137D (1) and Schedule 1ZA, para 11 FSMA 2000); supervision and monitoring (section 1L(1) FSMA 2000);[38] civil and criminal; and enforcement powers[39] to exercise official listing function. The powers of enforcement are extensive and detailed in the FCA Enforcement Guide.[40] What follows is a summary of the key tools and powers.

The FCA prosecutes in line with its regulatory objectives which according to section 2 of FSMA 2000 are: market confidence; financial stability; public awareness; the protection of consumers; and the reduction of financial crime.

There are specific offences set out FSMA 2000, but the FCA can also prosecute other offences as long as it is in line with its regulatory objectives. Those specified in FSMA 2000 cover all financial crimes which are defined under section 6(3) FSMA 2000 to include: (a) fraud or dishonesty; (b) misconduct in, or misuse of information relating to, a financial market; or (c) handling the proceeds of crime. This is a broad category to encompass all the report's relevant offences, including market abuse and insider dealing defined in section 118 FSMA 2000. It should be further noted that according to the Supreme Court, 'it is unlikely that Parliament would have intended to restrict the power of the FSA to the prosecution of the offences mentioned in sections 401 and 402.'[41]

The FCA has a number of powers of investigation and enforcement. It has the power to require information and documents from firms (section 165 FSMA 2000); to appoint a 'skilled person' to produce a report on the firm (section 166 FSMA 2000); to conduct investigations (section 167 FSMA 2000); to appoint investigators (section 168 FSMA 2000); to get assistance from overseas regulators (section 169 FSMA 2000); to provide investigators with additional powers (section 172 FSMA 2000); and to impose a financial penalty (section 206(1) FSMA 2000).

The FCA does not on its own possess the power of search and seizure. It can apply to a justice of the peace for a warrant to enter premises where documents or information is held (section 176 FSMA 2000). The warrant authorises a police constable or an FCA investigator in the company, and under the supervision of, a police constable, to amongst other things, enter and search the specified premises, and take possession of any documents or information. A detailed account of the investigation an enforcement procedure is set out in Parts 4–6 of the FCA Enforcement Guide.

---

[38] See: G Baber, 'The Financial Conduct Authority and financial conduct: hand in glove?' (2015) 36(9) *Comp Law* 263–274 and E Ferran, 'Institutional Design for Financial Market Supervision: The Choice for National Systems' (2014) *University of Cambridge Faculty of Law Research Paper No. 28/2014*, for a consideration of the FCA's supervisory model.

[39] See: T Woodcock, 'How the FCA makes enforcement decisions' (2014) 119(Sep) *Compliance Officer Bulletin*, 1–25 for consideration of the administrative procedures of the FCA enforcement mechanism.

[40] The FCA Enforcement Guide can be accessed here: http://media.fshandbook.info/Handbook/EG_FCA_20141212.pdf.

[41] *R v Rollins* [2010] UKSC 39, §19.

In addition the FCA has prosecuting powers under sections 401 and 402 FSMA 2000 to prosecute any crimes where to do so would be consistent with meeting any of its statutory objectives. When deciding whether to prosecute it will apply the basic principles set out in the Code for Crown Prosecutors.[42]

In addition to FSMA 2000 a number of other acts grant or govern the FCA's powers. These include:[43] methods of surveillance and information gathering under the Regulation of Investigatory Powers Act 2000 (RIPA); powers to enforce breaches of consumer protection law under the Enterprise Act 2002; and for confiscation of the proceeds of their crime under the Proceeds of Crime Act 2002.

In relation to money laundering, the Money Laundering Regulations 2007 grant to the FCA investigative and sanctioning powers in relation to both criminal and civil breaches of the Regulations. The FCA is responsible for monitoring and enforcing compliance with the power to prosecute, take regulatory action or impose civil penalties. The Regulations also provide investigation powers for use by the FCA when investigating whether breaches of the Regulations have taken place. These powers include: the power to require information from, and attendance of, relevant and connected persons (regulation 37); and powers of entry and inspection without or under warrant (regulations 38 and 39).

Annex 2 of the FCA Enforcement Guide sets out Guidelines for determining which authority will take the lead on an investigation. The guidelines concern the following authorities: the Financial Conduct Authority (the FCA); the Serious Fraud Office (the SFO); the Department for Business, Innovation and Skills (BIS); the Crown Prosecution Service (the CPS); the Association of Chief Police Officers in England, Wales and Northern Ireland (ACPO); the Crown Office and Procurator Fiscal Service (COPFS); the Public Prosecution Service for Northern Ireland (the PPS); and the Association of Chief Police Officers in Scotland (ACPO).

The criteria are set out in Annex 2 which will cause the decision to lean towards FCA action. These relate to the subject matter, the specific primacy mandate of the FCA, the nexus of the alleged offender to the FCA, and the relevance of the FCA's particular powers.[44]

---

[42] The full list of considerations the FCA takes into account when deciding whether to prosecute crimes relating to money laundering or market abuse are set out in Pt 12 of the FCA Guide.

[43] The full list is set out in Pt 19 of the FCA Enforcement Guide.

[44] The Annex 2 criteria are:

- Where the suspected conduct in question gives rise to concerns regarding market confidence or protection of consumers of services regulated by the FCA.
- Where the suspected conduct in question would be best dealt with by:
  - criminal prosecution of offences which the FCA has powers to prosecute by virtue of the Financial Services and Markets Act 2000 ('the 2000 Act') (See Appendix, para 1.4) and other incidental offences;
  - civil proceedings under the 2000 Act (including applications for injunctions, restitution and to wind up firms carrying on regulated activities);
  - regulatory action which can be referred to the Tribunal (including proceedings for market abuse); and
  - proceedings for breaches of Part VI of the Act, of Part 6 rules or the Prospectus Rules or a provision otherwise made in accordance with the Prospectus Directive.

The FCA also uses MoUs with relevant agencies and bodies in order to establish clear competences and powers. The purpose of these vary, we will consider a few examples.

The first concerns the arrangements for cooperation and coordination between the Financial Reporting Council (FRC) and the FCA in carrying out their respective regulatory responsibilities. It covers arrangements for exchange of information.[45]

The second is between the FCA and the Financial Ombudsman, in addition to containing a provision on information sharing the focus is on coordinating their independent and separate roles.[46] For example it is stated that the 'FCA discharges its objectives by setting standards that regulated firms must meet and taking action where such firms may be breaching those standards. The FCA does not investigate individuals' complaints against the firms it regulates and cannot deal with a complaint on behalf of individual consumers. This is the role of the Financial Ombudsman Service (ombudsman service).' The MoU goes on to provide that the two bodies agree to seek to dispel confusions and misunderstandings about their different roles; achieve a complementary and consistent approach; meet and communicate regularly to discuss matters of mutual interest; and consult and share for comment documents that affect the other's functions.

Finally the MoU[47] between the FCA and HMRC[48] deals with exchange of information which may be disclosed by the FCA to HMRC only with a view to a

— Where the likely defendants are authorised persons or approved persons.
— Where the likely defendants are issuers or sponsors of a security admitted to the official list or in relation to which an application for listing has been made.
— Where there is likely to be a case for the use of FCA powers which may take immediate effect (eg, powers to vary the permission of an authorised firm or to suspend listing of securities).
— Where it is likely that the investigator will be seeking assistance from overseas regulatory authorities with functions equivalent to those of the FCA.
— Where any possible criminal offences are technical or in a grey area whereas regulatory contraventions are clearly indicated.
— Where the balance of public interest is in achieving reparation for victims and prosecution is likely to damage the prospects of this.
— Where there are distinct parts of the case which are best investigated with regulatory expertise.

[45] The Memorandum of Understanding between the Financial Reporting Council (FRC) and the Financial Conduct Authority (FCA) can be accessed here: http://www.fca.org.uk/static/documents/mou/mou-frc.pdf.

[46] The Memorandum of Understanding between the FCA and Financial Ombudsman Service (FOS) can be accessed here: http://www.fca.org.uk/static/fca/documents/mou/mou-fos.pdf.

[47] The Memorandum of Understanding between the FCA and HMRC (Inland Revenue) can be accessed here: http://www.fca.org.uk/static/fca/documents/mou/mou-hmrc.pdf.

[48] HM Revenue and Customs is a designated authority with supervisory responsibilities under the Money Laundering Regulations 2007. The VAT Fraud Team of HMRC also has overall policy responsibility for all civil litigation of VAT fraud in HMRC and is the client of the Solicitor's Office. HMRC has investigatory powers but not prosecutorial powers. All criminal tax, excise and strategic export cases, are prosecuted by the CPS. Further information can be found on the official website of Her Majesty's Revenue and Customs can be accessed here: www.hmrc.gov.uk/index.htm.

criminal investigation by HMRC. With respect to the FCA obtaining information from HMRC, the gateway has been widened by the Financial Services Act 2012 to allow the FCA to obtain and use HMRC information for any of the FCA's statutory functions.

Conclusions

What would have become evident to the reader is that unlike the Civil Law systems where judicial involvement in investigations is extensive, in the common law system, judicial interference in the investigatory stages is almost non-existent, save to authorise warrants when required. The authorities mandated with investigatory and prosecutorial powers are also granted extensive enforcement powers ranging from the ability to summon witnesses for questioning to coercive powers such as search and seizure.

The police force is at the forefront of investigating crimes, however when it comes to economic and financial crimes, in particular those of a very high level of seriousness or complexity, this competence is shared with a number of specialised bodies. Besides the City of London Police Economic Crime Directorate, other key bodies include the Financial Intelligence Unit of the NCA, the FCA and in the case of the most serious crimes the SFO. In the same way, whilst the Crown Prosecution Service is the principal prosecution body, when it comes to economic and financial crimes this competency is also shared with a number of specialist agencies. As identified, key amongst these are the SFO and the FCA.

What is of particular value for the EPPO project is how the interaction and management of shared competences between the different bodies with investigation and prosecution powers is achieved through cooperation but also through the existence of extensive factors used to identify competence, for example those set out in Annex 2 of the FCA Enforcement Handbook or the SFOs criteria. In addition to these clear detailed competency factors, the second important tool for managing shared competences, is the use of Memorandums of Understandings. As set out above, these range from longstanding ones between numerous bodies and ad hoc ones entered into for a particular case between only two bodies. These set out the scope of each party's mandate, the evidence exchange rules, as well as providing a clear line of communication through the nomination of a contact point in each of the bodies. Amongst others, these two methods could be utilised to coordinate the activities of the EPPO, the European Delegated Prosecutors and other bodies spread out across the European Union.

Part V

Final Cross-sectional Essays

7

Data Protection Issues in Transnational Financial-Economic Investigations

Dr FRANCESCO MORELLI
Researcher, University of Ferrara

Data Protection and Data Sharing on the European and Domestic Level

The flow of information between OLAF and national judicial authorities is a crucial instrument in fighting offences against the EU budget. The information has to be channelled in a two-way flow: from EU institutions to national administrative or judicial authorities and vice versa.

Moreover, an efficient management of information about investigative proceedings is a necessary condition for the establishment of the future EPPO, because the new European Public Prosecutor will need a huge flow of information from all the Member States in order to find crimes that damage EU economic interests.

The sharing of information is key to building an integrated system of investigation, because on one hand it allows EU institutions to protect EU interests throughout Europe, and on the other hand it allows the national authorities to conduct investigations successfully even when they involve more than one Member State.

In such a system, information sharing is the ultimate target of the European institutions that are charged with fighting economic offences.

All the many rules that govern the gathering, processing and storage of the personal data needed for the purpose of an investigation aim to protect the privacy of the defendant, witnesses and any third parties involved in the investigation itself. However, in the same system there are many exceptions to data protection rules because of the interest pursued by the investigation: the fight against crimes that harm the EU budget.

Therefore, it is necessary and unavoidable that there be a huge flow of information between OLAF—and, in the future, the EPPO—and the administrative and judicial authorities, and also with non-member states or institutions, such information including the personal data of individuals involved in the investigation.

Although European privacy rules are set forth in great detail, it seems that the system is geared mainly toward facilitating investigation activities. In all European data protection legislation, the priority of fighting this kind of crime is always seen as a good reason to derogate from many of the provisions intended to protect the privacy of individuals.

The indiscriminate dissemination of personal data is what the rules aim to avoid, but fast and efficient sharing of information between European and national institutions is always guaranteed.

In this context, the proposal for a Regulation on the establishment of the EPPO seeks to create an internal system of checks on the data collected: it provides for time limits for the storage of data, and a right of access, rectification and erasure for the persons involved and third parties. Furthermore, the regulation on personal data protection (Regulation EU 45/2001) will continue to be fully applicable under the proposal. However, the same regulation rules out or limits all these rights in activities involving criminal proceedings.

Moreover, Article 20 of the proposal establishes that the EPPO 'shall be able to obtain any relevant information stored in national criminal investigation and law enforcement databases, as well as other relevant registers of public authorities, or have access to such information through European Delegated Prosecutors'. It is a necessary provision that has to have wide application, because information feeds transnational investigations. Moreover, the information has to be shared in a fast and efficient way, if the objective is to combat financial offences. Accordingly, every EU provision designed to protect individual privacy must not represent an obstacle to achieving this specific objective and the information flow between European and national authorities has to be facilitated. As a result, many of the instruments available to an individual seeking to protect his or her personal data can be limited or denied altogether: the right to access and the right to have data rectified, blocked or erased can in fact be restricted or excluded in this area of action of the integrated system of investigation,[1] insofar as the detection of a crime or protection of European financial interests is concerned. Ultimately, all personal data and information stored in databanks regarding the activity of a suspect can be processed for the purpose of the investigation and an efficient fight against offences that harm the European economic system cannot be conducted without their collection and a huge flow of personal data and information between the domestic and European authorities.

However, even when it comes to uncovering frauds committed against the European Union, the safeguarding of the right to privacy must be guaranteed.

---

[1] Art 20, Reg (EC) 45/2001.

Paradoxically, the whole EU system cannot rely just on European privacy rules, because by the time they are enforced it could be too late, after a data breach has already occurred in processing and transmission from domestic bodies to European authorities or vice versa, or else they might not apply at all because of the derogations provided for under the same EU regulations.

In these investigations, the European authorities are often not the first to collect the information; rather, they may acquire data stored in national databanks or obtain evidence from a national judicial authority. This information is already stored and processed in the Member State. OLAF presently obtains information from administrative and judicial authorities in the same manner.

This means that the data protection system lies on two levels.

The first level of protection is entrusted to European institutions—today OLAF but in the near future the EPPO—even if their functions and powers differ. The second is entrusted to the national authorities charged with territorial investigations in the member state or designated by the EPPO or OLAF to collect data for different purposes (like revenue or tax agencies).[2]

The data protection that is put in place on a national level is probably the most important for the protection of individual rights in the integrated system of combating crimes that harm EU financial interests.

Therefore, it is essential to have a high level of personal data protection in every Member State, because when a European institution gathers the data, the national investigation and/or domestic proceeding has already started, and in criminal matters it is very difficult to select which evidence should be transferred to the EU authorities: in order to achieve meaningful results they need to be able to process all the available data. In fact, an individual's rights of access, rectification and erasure can be restricted or denied according to EU data protection provisions and the information would thus seem to be under the EU investigative body's control once it is obtained from the police or a judicial authority of a Member State.

If a national investigation authority violates an individual's rights (such as the right to privacy) while gathering evidence, the possibility of a violation or data breach can quickly increase, because such information is collected solely in order to be shared. Moreover, we have to consider that the authorities can acquire data that may usually not be collected (data about race or ethnic origins, political opinions) for the purpose of a criminal investigation, so it is important to consider the necessity of the data processing right from the moment it is collected.

This is the most important step in data protection. When data have been gathered for the first time in the course of a criminal investigation they will probably have to be shared throughout the European area. And if the data were collected unlawfully, it will be very difficult to stop them from being processed and shared,

---

[2] See S Allegrezza, 'Verso una Procura Europea per tutelare gli interessi finanziari dell'Unione' *www.penalecontemporaneo.it* 6.

because neither the suspected person nor any third parties involved in the investigation can have any contact with the authorities in the earliest stage of the proceeding. Therefore, they often cannot prevent the circulation of data gathered by the police or a public prosecutor or included in national databases in violation of their right to privacy.

For this reason, the key to ensuring effective data protection in criminal matters seems to lie in the principles and rules applied by national judicial authorities when the information is first collected.

OLAF has, and the EPPO will probably have in the future, many tools for checking and verifying that information is collected and processed in a manner that is consistent with EU law.[3] Articles 13, 14 and 16 of Directive EU 2016/680 (and, formerly, Article 4 of Council Framework Decision 2008/977/JHA) are a good example of these tools, which are aimed at ensuring that personal data shared for the purpose of crime detection are always processed lawfully. However, under the same Directive, when data that should not have been collected are shared, the right to obtain their rectification or erasure may be denied, and even if such rights are enforceable, they do not guarantee, in every case, that an individual's right to privacy will be respected, because every single step of unlawful processing of information implies a specific violation, and the same applies in the case of data transmission and sharing. Moreover, the exercise of the rights referred to in Articles 13, 14 and 16 of the aforesaid Directive can be governed by national law when the personal data are contained in a file being processed in a criminal investigation, and in such cases every domestic system will probably choose this option, since in the early phases the secrecy of the operations is necessary to achieve the aim of the investigation itself.[4]

For this reason, every action that EU authorities are obliged to take in respect of data unlawfully obtained by a national body represents just a late remedy to a privacy violation. The system as a whole could probably not prevent personal data from being transferred to all the authorities that are involved in an investigation, even when they have been collected in violation of individual rights. Even if this breach of privacy could be partially mended during the proceeding, illicit data

---

[3] By way of example, see Directive (EU) 2016/680 repealing Council Framework Decision 2008/977/JHA.

[4] See Case C-293/12, *Digital Rights Ireland v Minister of Communications, Marine and Natural Resources and Others*, Case C-594/12, *Kärntner Landesregierung and Others*. In these cases, the European Court of Justice ruled that Directive 2006/24/EC is invalid, among other reasons, because the Directive 'therefore applies even to persons for whom there is no evidence capable of suggesting that their conduct might have a link, even an indirect or remote one, with serious crime' (para 58), and because, 'whilst seeking to contribute to the fight against serious crime, Directive 2006/24 does not require any relationship between the data whose retention is provided for and a threat to public security' (para 59). But when a criminal proceeding is involved, no EU regulation obstructs data collection and sharing, if consistent with the principle of proportionality under Art 52 of the Charter of Fundamental Rights of the European Union. On this point see, A Balsamo, 'Il contenuto dei diritti fondamentali, in Manuale di procedura penale Europea' in R Kostoris, *Manuale di procedura penale europea* (Milano, Giuffrè, 2015) 89.

processing will have already taken place during the transmission of the information from the national authority to the European one or vice versa.

The Relevance of the Data Collected

The first and most important step seems to be to correctly select which personal data will need to be gathered right from the outset.

Existing data protection provisions cannot be sufficient to safeguard an individual's right to privacy, as the most important restrictions to gathering and processing personal data are lifted when such data become relevant in a criminal investigation. Moreover, all the remedies provided for under European or domestic law can only be implemented after a breach of privacy has taken place due to unlawful transmission of information to the European authorities by domestic bodies or vice versa.

Consequently, the condition that the data collected be relevant now seems to be the first and the most important restriction on investigation activities.[5] Only where this condition is met in the evidence-gathering process will it be possible to avoid the most significant violations of individual rights in the management of personal data. Personal data are relevant insofar as relate to the investigation or criminal proceeding, and their processing and exchange are thus justified by the need to protect EU interests. Moreover, if the condition of 'relevance' is fulfilled, any breach resulting from the processing and exchange of this information will not involve data that should not have been entered in the data-sharing network between EU institutions and domestic authorities, and will thus seem less of a violation of the right to privacy.[6]

In all EU regulations concerning privacy, one of the most important conditions to be met in order for the gathering of personal data to be considered lawful is their relevance for the purpose of achieving the objective of the data processing itself. Under Article 4 of Regulation (EC) 45/2001 the data must be 'adequate, relevant and not excessive in relation to the purposes for which they are collected and/or further processed'. And Directive EU 680/2016 (which repeals Council Framework Decision 2008/977/JHA) contains a similar provision in regard to data processing

---

[5] See L Laudati, 'Data Protection at OLAF' (2013) 1 *EU crim* 15: 'The data quality requirements specify that any personal data gathered must be adequate, relevant, and not excessive in relation to the purpose of the processing concerned, which must be analyzed on a case-by-case basis'.

[6] V Mitsilegas, 'The External Dimension of Mutual Trust: the Case of Transatlantic Counter-terrorism Cooperation' in C Grandi (ed) *Justice and Trust in the European Legal Order* (Napoli, Jovene, 2016) 172, stresses that no adequacy can be guaranteed in 'generalised, mass and unlimited surveillance' that is contrary, therefore, to privacy and data protection. And the first obstacle against an indiscriminate collection of personal data seems to be their relevance in the first gathering: it could select all the functioning data, and leave the others to the own privacy of the individual.

and data sharing in police and judicial cooperation. However, as we have just seen, information is often collected by domestic authorities and then transmitted to European bodies. Under EU law, an evaluation of the data's relevance takes place only after they have been processed and transmitted and this means that the personal data of the people involved in a proceeding are not adequately protected. From the perspective of the EU authorities, unfortunately, it is very hard to verify the relevance of the data collected at the very outset of an investigation, especially when the information is obtained from databases, administrative agencies, banks or agencies engaging in investigation activities like interception or surveillance, because they are not the first data collectors.

The entire system of data protection in the European Union must rely on the first authority that gathers the evidence, also when it is stored in databanks or included among personal data which are not all important in the financial or criminal investigation.

Even in a future scenario, it seems that the police and judicial bodies of the EU Member States would bear the main responsibility for ensuring that data is lawfully collected in a financial investigation.

In fact, relevance seems to be a fundamental requirement for obtaining information for the purposes of an investigation under Article 20 of the EPPO proposal, and this could be the best safeguard that EU law and domestic regulations can provide to protect individual rights in criminal investigations. This provision would allow the EPPO to obtain any relevant information from national databases and stored in national criminal investigation and law enforcement databases, as well as other relevant registers of public authorities, or have access to such information through European Delegated Prosecutors. And such information could be requested from Europol and Eurojust too. The data are gathered by national authorities or by the national public prosecutor.

Some investigation measures are listed in Article 26 of the proposal for a regulation on the establishment of the EPPO. All of them relate to personal data and hence imply an evaluation of their relevance: when the European Public Prosecutor Office orders or requests such investigation measures, the national police and judicial authorities will be able, for example, to search any premises, land, means of transport, private homes, clothes and any other personal property or computer system; request the production of any relevant object or document, or of stored computer data, including traffic data and banking account data, encrypted or decrypted, either in original or in some other specified form; intercept telecommunications, including emails; undertake real-time surveillance of telecommunications by ordering instant transmission of telecommunications traffic data; monitor financial transactions, by ordering any financial or credit institution to inform the European Public Prosecutor's Office in real time of any financial transaction carried out through any specific account held or controlled by the suspected person or any other accounts which are reasonably believed to be used in connection with the offence; undertake surveillance measures in non-public places, by ordering the covert video and audio surveillance of non-public places, excluded video surveillance of private homes, and the recording of its results; undertake identification measures, by ordering the taking of photos, visual recording of persons and the recording of a person's biometric features; undertake measures to track and control persons, in order to establish the whereabouts of a person; track and trace any object by technical means, including controlled deliveries of goods and controlled financial transactions; and obtain access to national or European public registers and registers kept by private entities in a public interest.

Everyone of these measures involves personal data and has the specific aim of collecting information that must then be shared between domestic and European investigation bodies.

However, every measure is regulated by national law. If the latter does not always provide for a fast selection of relevant information and the removal of non-relevant information, the transmission of personal data in violation of the right to privacy will not be avoidable, because the sharing of all the information gathered will not be proportionate and necessary for the purpose of fighting fraud against the EU.[7]

The individual or body charged with selecting the data is likewise important, because in the first steps of an investigation the public prosecutor might be more interested in the future progress of the investigation, while an impartial judge might pay more attention to evaluating the relevance of the materials collected, in consideration of the right to privacy of the defendant or third parties. In the EPPO proposal, when a judge's authorisation is requested, it is in order to be able to adopt intrusive means; such authorisation does not regard the selection of the data collected as evidence.[8]

Moreover, the EPPO could ask a national judicial authority for any relevant information. But in national proceedings all non-relevant information remains a part of the file even after the relevant data have been selected. Or, in other cases, the EPPO could simply ask for and obtain information stored in databases or gathered through interception or surveillance before any selection of the relevant data is made. Therefore, the EPPO would be able to obtain any item of information contained in the national files of a criminal proceeding and share that information with other EU institutions or with the judicial authorities of another Member State.

From the perspective of simply obtaining these data, without necessarily deciding anything about a criminal proceeding, it might be assumed that the EPPO will not evaluate the relevance of any single element of an individual's file; however, the EPPO will probably consider the entire file of a national criminal proceeding concerning an offence against EU budget to be relevant.

---

[7] As is required under Arts 4–5, Reg 45/2001 and Art 4, Directive EU 680/2016.

[8] S Allegrezza, 'Verso una Procura Europea per tutelare gli interessi finanziari dell'Unione' *www. penalecontemporaneo.it* 7 ff.

Many data could thus be processed even if they are not relevant to the proceeding.

The EPPO or the delegated prosecutor will also be able obtain information stored in national criminal investigation and law enforcement databases, as well as other relevant registers of public authorities. This information must be relevant. But, at this first stage, nobody except the EPPO itself can evaluate its relevance and nobody has to verify the nexus with the criminal investigation except the same EPPO.

Probably only a suspected person, or a witness, will be able to verify that the EPPO has stored and maybe transmitted non-relevant personal data. But by the time they find out about the existence of a proceeding that involves them, the data processing will have already reached an advanced stage, even if the EPPO will then be obliged to erase or rectify the data.

The key to ensuring real data protection lies in first stage of data collection by the authorities of a Member State or, in the future, the EPPO or a delegated prosecutor, as the relevant information should be selected from the very outset.

All measures of protection implemented after this time might not be sufficient in criminal proceedings: if many instruments of protection may be set aside in order to obtain an efficient flow of information, basic guarantees must be efficient when the data first come into the proceeding; this will ensure that the sharing of personal data between European and national authorities, as well as their processing will be justified by the detection of a crime that harms European financial interests, without any unlawful breach of the right to privacy.

Only in the case of a few measures (search and seizure for instance) must the relevance of the information needed as evidence be a condition for the collection of legal evidence. As regards many other investigation measures, the relevance can only be evaluated after a huge number of data have been gathered: interception of communications, surveillance, GPS tracking, the monitoring of financial transactions, and all the instruments of live digital forensics. A suspected person and third parties cannot be protected against a breach of privacy unless the information is duly selected by the first investigation body that gathers the evidence: in other words, even if the EPPO will soon be operative, the police and judicial national authorities.

Any additional European rule concerning data protection cannot protect an individual from an unlawful personal data breach; moreover, such rules would risk being a huge obstacle to EU anti-fraud efforts. The real guarantee must lie in a sharing only of relevant information for which a limitation of the right to privacy is justified for the purpose of detecting crime or protecting European financial interests.

Therefore, in order to fulfil the proportionality requirement under Article 52 of the Charter of Fundamental Rights of the European Union, and respect the proportionality principle that is also enshrined in Article 8 of the ECHR, what is needed, perhaps, is not more European regulations intended to safeguard the right to privacy, but rather a harmonisation of national legislation to ensure that relevant evidence is separated from non-relevant information at the moment that the information is obtained by the police or national judicial authority.[9] In this way, only data that is relevant to the investigation or proceeding would be shared without any unlawful prejudice to the individual's position.

Is there a Concept of Relevance in Directive EU 680/2016?

The new directive introduces many rules about processing personal data. However, some of these rules require that the data be relevant: according to Article 4 letter (c) Directive EU 2016/680, the data collected must be 'adequate, relevant and not excessive in relation to the purposes for which they are processed'. From this perspective, the relevance of the data seems to refer to the purpose of their collection, which is 'prevention, investigation, detection or prosecution of criminal offences or the execution of criminal penalties, including the safeguarding against and the prevention of threats to public security' (Article 1 Directive (EU) 2016/680). The purpose of the data collection is the factor that enables a balance to be struck between the individual's right to privacy and the public interest to prosecute EU frauds. This aim gives significance to the principle of proportionality and tries to keep the data processing within well-defined borders.[10] But this is not enough: whenever the balance between 'interests' is at stake, the borders can never be exactly drawn. In this case and especially when the purpose is to fight illicit behaviour and the opposed interest is an individual's right not concerning personal freedom, proportionality in data processing is very hard to guarantee, both during the course of the proceedings and after the data themselves have been handled by multiple authorities.

Any provision that the Directive could introduce in order to ensure respect for the right to privacy cannot prevent a disproportionate processing of data at all times during the proceedings: after the data have been transmitted to other authorities or agencies conducting the investigation, just the fact that the data have been gathered in a national criminal or administrative investigation means they are being processed for an adequate purpose. It would be very difficult for the individual to demonstrate the irrelevance of the data. It would be difficult for the individual even to locate that data, because they are stored so as to be easily shared: 'the Directive's expressed aim for the "free movement of such data", as after

---

[9] S Recchione, 'European Public Prosecutor Office. Anche gli entusiasti diventano scettici?' *www.penalecontemporaneo.it* 21.

[10] P De Hert and V Papakonstantiou, 'The new police and criminal justice data protection directive' (2016) 7 *New Journal of European Criminal Law* 11. The importance of the principle of proportionality is underlined, in matter of transatlantic counter-terrorism cooperation by V Mitsilegas, 'The External Dimension of Mutual Trust: the Case of Transatlantic Counter-terrorism Cooperation' in C Grandi (ed) *Justice and Trust in the European Legal Order* (Napoli, Jovene, 2016) 169.

all included in its title, ought never to escape our attention. The Directive's intention is not to restrict the flow of information among the agencies involved in law enforcement-related personal data processing within the same or even among different Member States. In fact, quite the opposite is true: by introducing a comprehensive data protection legal framework on how to execute such processing and exchange such personal data, the Directive aims at institutionalizing and streamlining such data flows'.[11]

The real protection of personal data starts—and often ends—with an accurate description of the illicit behaviour that has triggered the investigation, and with the gathering of the data that are strictly related to the subject of the investigation.[12]

In this perspective, the balance between opposite interests is not enough: proportionality has to be assured through clear provisions.[13] And these provisions, enacted by Member States, have to relate to the investigation tool that, as a first step, allows data to be found and gathered.

We have to consider that, for the purposes of the criminal investigation, these data are, actually, evidence. And, as evidence, they have to be related to the reason the investigation was undertaken to begin with.

In the Italian system, every investigation tool aimed at obtaining relevant data can be activated if the measure is related to the fact which is the subject of the investigation. According to Article 253 of the Italian Code of Criminal Procedure, the judicial authority can seize the items 'necessary for ascertaining the facts of the case'. Even the seizure of correspondence has to concern the communications 'related to the offence' (Article 254 of the Italian Code of Criminal Procedure). The same applies for inspections, searches, wiretapping, and so on.

The issue to be addressed is what 'relevance' means in light of the proportionality and pertinence required by the Directive.

In investigations concerning offences that may harm European economic interests, the investigative tools used often entail collecting a number of data that cannot be managed immediately. In reality, this is the case for every investigative tool used which avails itself of the current level of technological development: seizure of bank data, wiretapping, video recording, seizure of accounting documents, seizure of hardware and entire hard disks containing a large number of potentially relevant files and searches of virtual archives.

In order to ensure a protection of personal data that guarantees the individual's position and an effective flow of information between the entities charged with

---

[11] P De Hert and V Papakonstantiou, 'The new police and criminal justice data protection directive' (2016) 7 *New Journal of European Criminal Law* 11.

[12] In Italy, such considerations have been set forth by several authors, including M Nobili, 'Diritti per la fase che "non conta e non pesa"' in *Scenari e trasformazioni del processo penale*, (Padova, Cedam, 1998) 40.

[13] M Caianiello, 'Il principio di proporzionalità nel procedimento penale' (2016) 3–4 *Dir. Pen. Cont.* 162; the author includes the relevance of the data gathered or seized in the general duty to respect the principle of proportionality.

countering fraud in Europe, it is essential for there to be a precise definition of the fact being alleged.

Providing this basis means ensuring the correct functioning of every guarantee imposed by the Directive and all other applicable European legislation.

An evaluation of the fact that has determined the collection of relevant data is also essential to identify the type of processing it should undergo. It is fundamental, for example, for there to be a fact meeting one of the conditions specified in Article 6 of Directive EU 2016/680. Here the Directive calls on Member States to require the data controller, to the extent possible, to distinguish between the data belonging to different categories of data subjects, in relation to the offence: a person undergoing investigation, a convicted person, a victim or potential victims, witnesses, persons informed about the facts, or contacts of one of the persons described previously.

Each of these distinctions is not only useful for managing the data once collected, but also serves to justify the decision to collect them, and manifests the wish of the European legislator that careful attention be paid to the data's relevance: it is not enough that they have a general bearing on the context of the investigation, but rather it will be necessary to explain why the individual item of data is important in relation to that person. This procedure will assure the collection of pertinent data with a specific function from an investigative standpoint.

It is important that the relevance of the data—that is, their connection with the subject of the proceedings that justified their collection—always be specified in the measure leading to their acquisition.

Only in this manner will it be possible to verify, also at later stages of the proceedings, that the requirement of relevance, ie, that the data be necessary for the purpose of the investigation, is always complied with.

8

Best Practices and Operational Models in Financial-Economic Investigations in Europe in View of the EPPO

PROF DR DANIELE NEGRI
Professor of Criminal Procedure, University of Ferrara

A Preliminary Overview of the 'State of the Art' in Regard to the Establishment of a European Public Prosecutor

To an outside observer, the most recent work undertaken toward the establishment of a European Public Prosecutor Office dedicated to combating crimes affecting the Union's financial interests suggests the image of a 'house of cards' resting precariously on a tottering table.[1] If this impression is accurate, we are very far from the fanciful metaphors that have long accompanied the portrayals of yet another much awaited figure on the European scene, allegories that are sometimes reassuring, sometimes threatening, but in any case seek to outline a future for the supranational actor: 'two-headed Janus', 'extended arm', 'two-headed dragon'. In short, the present situation does not bode well for the future of a body whose creation was prepared at length and with zeal by the expert jurists called upon to tackle the issue,[2] until it was eventually consecrated after Lisbon thanks to the legal

---

[1] We are alluding to the situation, at the time of writing, in the negotiations held up to the beginning of December 2016, during the Slovak presidency of the EU Council. Reference is being made to the text of 2 December 2016 (*Report on the States of Play*, 15200/16, transmitted by the EU Council Presidency), which represents the consolidated version of the draft regulation.

[2] We are mainly referring to M Delmas-Marty, *Corpus juris portant dispositions pénales pour la protection des intérêts financiers de l'Union européenne* (Paris, Economica, 1997); M Delmas-Marty and JAE Vervaele, *The Implementation of the Corpus Juris in the Member States: Penal Provisions for the Protection of European Finances* (Antwerpen-Groningen-Oxford, Intersentia, 2000); M Wade, 'Euro NEEDs. Evaluating the need for and the needs of a European Criminal Justice System', in *Max-Planck-Institut für ausländisches und internationales Strafrecht, Preliminary Report/January 2011*; K Ligeti (ed), *Toward a Prosecutor for the European Union. A Comparative Analysis*, vol I, (Oxford, Hart, 2013).

basis provided by Article 86 TFEU and the Commission's subsequent exercise of the option of implementation through its proposal for a regulation on the establishment of the European Public Prosecutor's Office, issued on 17 July 2013, COM (2013) 534. Since then, the reference legal text has fallen prey to a multitude of amendments that follow one another incessantly with rotations in the presidency of the European Council: like a constantly unravelled 'Penelope's shroud', wholly altered from its original form and continually rewoven, with no end in sight. Therefore, although no *requiem* has yet been sung for the ambitious project, we think that this is because there is still the fallback of enhanced cooperation among at least nine EU Member States should unanimity not be reached—as appears inevitable.[3] A special procedure is envisaged by Article 86 TFEU, which would provide an opportunity to test, on a reduced scale, the potential of an instrument that has no precedents and has thus aroused understandable concerns, given how much is at stake. The hope would be to subsequently win over the more reluctant Member States.

The building foundations are thus wobbly—as we said at the beginning—since, alongside countries that are leaving the EU, like the United Kingdom, others (Ireland, Denmark) have decided to remain outside the area of freedom, security and justice in which the EPPO would be called on to act. Choices like this are in themselves apt to undermine a design which would be all the more effective the broader the transnational scope of the powers entrusted to the European Public Prosecutor, in consideration of the fact that the crimes committed to the detriment of EU finances are spread equally among a number of sovereign territories and need to be more effectively repressed than is presently the case. It should be added, moreover, that the governments taking part in the ongoing negotiations in the EU Council have largely conflicting—if not diametrically opposed—views concerning the organisational and operational model to be adopted in the design of the supranational prosecuting body.

In consideration of the foregoing, we can presently envisage a dual outcome: on the one hand, a step backwards by some Member States would lead to a fragmentation of the continental area in which the EPPO could exercise its jurisdiction, forcing it to seek the cooperation of the judicial authorities of individual non-participating countries, just as is currently the case for national criminal prosecution authorities. For this purpose, a central role would continue to be played by Eurojust, which would be called on to cooperate and provide judicial assistance not only in cases involving third countries, but also and above all in internal

---

[3] This point has been recently addressed by M Fidelbo, 'La cooperazione rafforzata come modalità d'istituzione della Procura europea. Scenari futuri di un dibattito ancora in evoluzione', www.penalecontemporaneo.it, 21 November 2016. But a view that the solution of enhanced cooperation was 'inevitable' had already been expressed by L Salazar, 'Il negoziato sulla Procura europea nell'agenda della presidenza italiana dell'Unione Europea 2014' in G Grasso, G Illuminati, R Sicurella and S Allegrezza (eds), *Le sfide dell'attuazione di una Procura europea: definizione di regole comuni e loro impatto sugli ordinamenti interni* (Milano, Giuffrè, 2013) 698.

investigations which, despite being within the boundary of the European Union, embrace countries that are outside the EPPO system. An essential role in this regard will be played by the 'working arrangements' established between the states concerned and the European Public Prosecutor's Office, to which reference is made in Article 59a of the latest published version of the draft regulation; such arrangements are to be made on the basis of the principle of sincere cross-border cooperation enshrined in Article 4(3) TEU.[4] On the other hand, once the ambitious idea of considering the territories of participating Member States as a 'single legal area'[5] has faded, investigations that go beyond a national scope within that circumscribed geographic area will also necessarily take on a cross-border nature and thus require forms—albeit simplified ones—of international judicial cooperation; at present, the envisaged strategy is for the European Delegated Prosecutor handling the case to 'assign' an investigative measure to his counterpart in the Member State from which assistance is requested. However, due to the lack of harmonisation of national legislation on criminal proceedings, if there is no provision for a similar measure in the legal system of the state in which it is to implemented, it will be necessary to rely on the ordinary legal instruments of mutual recognition and cooperation available within the framework of the European Union: the present Article 26(5a) of the draft regulation clearly implies the use of means such as—in the cases that most closely concern us here—the European Investigation Order in criminal matters.

The overall impression one derives, also based on what we will say shortly, is that European institutions are building a cumbersome entity, whose functioning is highly complicated at both a central and decentralised level, so much so as to raise some doubts about its actual ability to improve the performance of Member States when it comes to prosecuting and repressing crimes affecting the financial interests of the Union. Fitting into this general context—which is a cause for pessimism about the success of the initiative—are more specific considerations concerning certain aspects of the phenomenon that are called into question because of the involvement, in the stages leading up to a criminal investigation or in the activities directly related to it, of agencies of a heterogeneous nature and functions. These vary from state to state, but are all liable to establish relations—which are likewise of a highly diverse nature—with magistrates and police authorities having

---

[4] Art 57 and Recital 102a of the proposal for a regulation. Concerning the impact of the competence of the EPPO on the role of Eurojust, with regard in particular to the relations of mutual judicial assistance with states not belonging to the EPPO area, see C Deboyser, 'European Prosecutor's Office and Eurojust: "Love Match or Arranged Marriage?"' in LH Erkelens, AWH Meij and P Pawlik (eds), *The European Public Prosecutor's Office. An extended arm or a Two-Headed dragon?* (The Hague, TMC Asser Press, 2015) 90 ff. See also V Mitsilegas, 'The European Public Prosecutor's Office facing national legal diversity' in C Nowak (ed), *The European Public Prosecutor's Office and National Authorities* (Padova, Cedam, 2016) 30 ff.

[5] It was the fundamental principle enshrined in Art 25 of the original proposal. On this subject see S Allegrezza, 'Verso una Procura europea per tutelare gli interessi finanziari dell'Unione. Idee di ieri, chances di oggi, prospettive di domani', *www.penalecontemporaneo.it* 31 October 2013.

primary competence to exercise investigative functions. Such relations are often scarcely formalised from a legislative viewpoint, or else governed by convoluted, stratified and tangled regulations; as a result, positive law gives way to operational procedures evolving from practice, sometimes laid down in protocols concluded between the authorities in question, other times left up to unwritten instructions.

We therefore wonder what kind of situation would arise should the European Public Prosecutor actually become operational: in other words, it needs to be verified whether, given the specific characteristics of investigations regarding economic-financial crimes, and especially the disparate array of actors potentially present at the national level, we should welcome the arrival on the scene of yet another protagonist, the European Public Prosecutor, whose own features, in turn, have become increasingly complicated compared to those envisaged in the original proposal for a regulation presented in 2013.

Introduction on the Architecture of the EPPO System: The Scant Attention Paid to the Initial Acquisition of Information Relating to a Criminal Offence

Albeit in a legislative framework dominated by political uncertainty, we shall seek to propose an initial strategy for bridging national experiences and the future establishment of the EPPO, focusing, obviously, on the subject matter of the research conducted here, namely, the operational models of the law enforcement bodies and administrative authorities of the individual Member States involved in combating financial-economic crimes.

It is worth beginning with an observation that may become clearer over the course of the discussion. The development of the system pertaining to the EPPO has so far mainly focused attention on the top, examining, in other words, the structure of the supranational public prosecutor's office and the rules governing its criminal prosecution activities from the moment an investigation is launched.

With respect to the first aspect—as we pointed out earlier—the design of the European Public Prosecutor's Office has undergone an evolution that risks undermining its efficiency as a result of the compromises among the different stances emerging in the Council during the negotiations. As was predictable, Member States have been reluctant to consent to the attribution of extensive powers of investigation for the purpose of criminal prosecution to an entity whose composition is not representative of all the participating nations. The entity outlined in the Commission's original proposal was presented as a result: at the central level, the office was headed by the European Public Prosecutor, with only Deputies to assist him; the European Delegated Prosecutors, located in the various Member States, would act under his direction, in a hierarchical relationship, and according to the 'double hat' principle, ie, as an integral part of the supranational structure while simultaneously maintaining the investigative and prosecutorial functions typical of the respective national legal systems. A much more complex and cumbersome configuration emerges from the latest drafts of the resolution currently in the process of approval. First of all, the formulation of strategies and general supervision over the activities of the European Public Prosecutor's Office are now entrusted to a collegiate body, which includes a Prosecutor for each Member State. The 'umbilical cord' which connects the central office with the individual States is not limited, however, to this aspect, but rather penetrates deep into the dynamics of the body's functioning through the essential supervisory role played by the 'central' European Prosecutors vis-à-vis the individual European Delegated Prosecutors responsible for handling the cases within the national territory:[6] it should be noted that, despite the explicit opposition of the Commission, there is a pairing here between the two figures, in the sense that both—the supervisor and the supervised—must be from the same Member State.[7] This privileged relationship is tempered by the inclusion of a further central body, of which the European Prosecutors constitute the link with the decentralised level of the structure: the Permanent Chambers, having a plural composition and endowed with the power to direct the conduct of investigations and impart instructions in relation to individual cases in the hands of a European Delegated Prosecutor. These bodies are entrusted with many crucial decisions, which have accordingly been removed from the sole competence of the European Public Prosecutor. Among them we should mention, because of their importance, the choice whether to bring a case to judgment or dismiss it, to impart instructions to initiate an investigation where none has been initiated and to exercise the right of evocation of an investigation falling within the competence of the European Public Prosecutor's Office when proceedings have been initiated by the national authorities.[8] Once the functions have been distributed in this manner, we can see that the Chief Prosecutor, despite preserving the power to organise and direct the office he heads and although he presides over all the collegiate bodies making up the central structure, has fewer prerogatives than were attributed to him in the original design of the Commission, which placed him firmly at the head of the institution.

As for the second aspect, concerning the powers of investigation, we see a considerable reduction in the types of measures that the regulation places directly at the European Public Prosecutor's disposal and which, therefore, the Member States would be bound to introduce into their respective legal systems should they not already be envisaged therein. In the most recent version, the long list contained in the original proposal loses a series of essential instruments, such as, in particular, the power to question suspected persons or witnesses, to undertake covert

---

[6] A few observations in this regard may be found in A Met-Domestici, 'The EPPO at the European level: institutional layout and consequences on the links with the national level' in C Nowak (ed), *The European Public Prosecutor's Office*, 49 ff.

[7] Art 11.

[8] Art 9.

surveillance measures, also using electronic and video and audio equipment, to monitor and freeze financial transactions and to order covert infiltration activities. Similar measures have at least in part been transferred under the aegis of the European Investigation Order, which, however, is governed by a Directive (2014/41/EU), and as such needs to be transposed into national legislations. Above all it establishes a mode of cooperation among Member States, facilitated by the principle of mutual recognition of their respective measures. However, the draft regulation for the establishment of the EPPO still includes, for the time being, searches of premises, the production of stored data, freezing of assets subject to confiscation, interception of electronic communications, and the tracking and tracing of an object by technical means, including controlled deliveries of goods, provided that the offence being prosecuted is punishable by a penalty of at least four years of imprisonment.[9]

And yet, while so much effort has been devoted to the organisational architecture and investigative means of the European Prosecutor's Office, less attention has been paid, so to speak, to the lower part of the framework, the bottom, where the criminal investigation has the opportunity to gain momentum thanks to the search and retrieval of information concerning the possible offence.

Indeed, Article 86 (2) TFEU, which provides for the establishment of the EPPO, gives the office the power to investigate, prosecute and bring to judgment anyone who has committed a crime against the financial interests of the Union, as identified by the specific regulation establishing the EPPO. In turn, regulation proposal COM(2013)534 of 17 July 2013, specifically adopted to this end, leaves the task of defining the crimes in question to a particular Directive (Article 12 of the original text; Article 17 of the version drafted during the ongoing negotiations within the EU Council).

This legislation, which is subject to withdrawal, is currently at the proposal level for Directive COM(2012)363, which aims to replace and supersede the so-called PIF Convention of 1995 and its protocols, creating a higher approximation of the Member State's criminal laws on Community fraud.[10] By and large—and leaving aside the thorniest issue regarding the inclusion of VAT-related fraud, for which negotiations are still dragging on[11]—the provisions are intended to harmonise the definitions of criminal conducts such as obtaining European funds by deception

---

[9] Art 25.

[10] On the complicated legislative process taking place in European institutions in relation to the so-called proposal for the 'PIF Directive', see A Venegoni, 'Il difficile cammino della proposta di direttiva per la protezione degli interessi finanziari dell'Unione europea attraverso la legge penale (c.d. direttiva PIF): il problema della base legale' (2015) *Cassazione penale* 2442 ff. In general terms, in regard to the jurisdiction *ratione materiae* of the EPPO, see A Klip, 'The Substantive Criminal Law Jurisdiction of the European Public Prosecutor's Office' (2012) 20 *European Journal of Crime, Criminal Law and Criminal Justice* 367 ff.

[11] With an opinion destined for the Committee on Economic and Monetary Affairs, on the subject 'Towards a definitive VAT system and fighting VAT fraud' [2016/2033(INI)], the LIBE Committee (Committee on Civil Liberties, Justice and Home Affairs) of the EU Parliament formally requested European institutions to amend the new proposal for a directive on the fight against fraud to the

or omission as the violation of an obligation, misappropriation of funds for purposes other than those for which they were initially granted, fraud in public procurement, embezzlement, abuse of office and corruption and money laundering.[12]

So it is easy to see that the criminal offences outlined by the Directive are rooted mainly in the economic and financial sectors, frequently at the point of contact with public administration actions, so that the crimes in question present a dual peculiarity from the point of view of criminal procedure.

First, these types of crimes, also because of their frequently transnational dimension, reside within a complicated legal framework, give rise to sophisticated accounting issues, involve professionally qualified perpetrators and entail the analysis of a huge number of documents, particularly as regards intricate transaction chains. Accordingly, all these characteristics demand a high level of specialisation from the investigative bodies if we are to combat Community fraud successfully and, therefore, protect the Union's financial interests in a truly effective way.[13]

Secondly, criminal phenomena of this kind rarely exhibit, so to speak, *in rerum natura*, the stigma of criminality. Reports of such offences are not chanced upon by law enforcement bodies out of the blue, nor, in more important cases, do they appear to offer any comprehensive information, right from the start, regarding the constituent elements of the offence, as if ready to be substantiated. Rather, information emerges gradually from a long and complex reconstruction put into focus by experts in the analysis and cross-referencing of data which appear to be neutral if taken in isolation, but reveal the criminal aspect of the facts under examination when specialists vastly experienced in crime detection put it under the spotlight. If a report concerning the suspected commission of a crime is the *prémis* of criminal proceedings, it is commonly accepted that this starting point is actually the final product of a preliminary activity located within the administrative inquiry. It could be said that without this preparatory activity the criminal investigation would be destined, in most cases, never to be launched due to lack of impetus.

Not coincidentally, national legislations frequently call upon the administrative authorities to pursue criminal investigations into the same facts that led to

Union's financial interests by means of criminal law (so-called PIF Directive), which, as highlighted by the LIBE Committee, did not include VAT within the scope of application of the directive. In the Justice and Home Affairs Council meeting of 13–14 October 2016, the majority of Member States declared themselves to be in favour of prosecuting serious cross-border VAT fraud at the EU level on the basis of the PIF directive. On 8 December 2016 the Council reached an agreement on the directive regarding the protection of EU financial interests, which paves the way for a formal adoption of the text. Consequently, Article 20(3)(b) of the Proposal for the Regulation of the Establishment of the EPPO was adapted to ensure that the supranational investigating body had the right to exercise its competence in respect of offences related to EU funds and certain cases of major cross-border VAT fraud, even if the damage to the EU budget is less than that to the national budget.

[12] A Venegoni, 'La definizione del reato di frode nella legislazione dell'Unione dalla convenzione PIF alla proposta di direttiva PIF', *www.penalecontemporaneo.it* 16 October 2016.

[13] Similar considerations may be found in L Bachmaier Winter, 'The Potential Contribution of a European Public Prosecutor in Light of the Proposal for a Regulation of 17 July 2013' (2013) 23 *European Journal of Crime, Criminal Law and Criminal Justice* 126 ff.

their own inquiry once information about a possible crime has emerged in the course of the latter. The aim is to prevent the initially collected information from getting lost, be able to rely on specialist analyses and assure, thanks to operational continuity, an effective activity of combating the crimes concerned, which would otherwise risk being suspended or even interrupted if jurisdiction were to pass over exclusively to criminal justice agencies, usually engaged in general crime detection. The dual function approach characterises—for example—the German tax authorities, which are authorised to conduct criminal investigations autonomously right to the very end, at least in the case of less serious offences.[14] Similarly, the Polish system has seen a considerable expansion in the areas of operation of such authorities, to the extent that the public prosecutor has been relegated to the role of a mere supervisor of the investigation.[15] The Italian model, in turn, can exploit the amphibious position of a strategically decisive agency such as the Guardia di Finanza (tax police).[16] In Spain, on the contrary, the leading role is played by the public prosecutor, investigating judge and judicial police, to which the administrative authorities—with a few exceptions—are mostly called on to provide mere support.[17] Different still is the approach chosen by French legislators, who have established multiple judicial police offices, dividing among them the competences related to the activity of combating economic crime in the various sectors in which it manifests itself.

Two Conspicuous Shortcomings: The Failure to Provide for the Establishment of a European Police Force and Disregard for the Part of the Administrative Inquiry Preparatory to the Criminal Investigation

Once the choice had been made to circumscribe the competence of the European Public Prosecutor to crimes affecting the financial interests of the Union, one would have expected supranational legislators to focus their attention on both of the above-mentioned aspects, which are closely connected. On the one hand, it would have been wise to emphasise clearly that, in this area, a criminal investigation is almost inevitably a continuation of activities originally undertaken in the administrative realm. The judicial proceedings should thus be viewed in relation to the latter in order to exploit the results with respect both to the complex analyses based on the valuable investigative work carried out and the acquisition of the *notitia criminis*

---

[14] See M Böse in Part III, Chapter 4.
[15] See C Nowak in Part III, ch 5.
[16] See F Nicolicchia in Part I, ch 1.
[17] See JJ González López and A Nieto Martin in Part I, ch 2.

in the strict sense. Two segments of a phenomenon to be considered unitary on an operational level, despite the different nature of the actions ascribable to each, should have been incorporated into the draft regulation, especially for the purpose of defining the essential link between them. On the other hand, and as a consequence, an effort should have been made to solve the problem of how to enable communication between the centralised structure of the EPPO and the plethora of administrative agencies present in the different Member States, custodians of the documentation collected on the unlawful activity that has come to light. Sometimes, as we have seen, they are also endowed with veritable powers of criminal investigation. Such communication would serve to avoid perpetuating the *status quo* in the dynamics of the fight against Community frauds: if every initiative were to remain in the hands of national magistrates, they would be likely to maintain the same relations as today with the national administrative authorities, even if officially acting in a capacity as delegates of the European investigating body. The existing relations have shown to be—it should not be forgotten—a root cause of ineffectiveness of the repressive action. This, after all, is the reason that led to the proposal to introduce the EPPO, based on the principle of subsidiariety enshrined in Article 5(3) of the EU Treaty.[18]

Neither of these two crucial aspects is covered by the proposal for a regulation establishing the EPPO currently under discussion.

As regards the first aspect, it must be reiterated that the projects under discussion continue to be afflicted, for various economic and political reasons, by a general weakness, in other words, the lack of a European criminal investigation police force. Article 18 of the 2013 proposal (currently Article 23) establishes that the designated European Delegated Prosecutor should directly conduct the investigation or hand it over to the competent authorities of the Member State where he is based. It is easy to foresee that, given their limited number, the European Delegated Prosecutors will hand over inquiries, almost exclusively, to national police forces and will limit themselves to giving impetus to and coordinating investigations which are substantially carried out by others.[19] This prognosis, in relation to the original draft of the regulation proposal, will undoubtedly be confirmed in the text of the ongoing negotiations, which disempowers the EPPO's central office by removing its investigative duties, thereby limiting the role of the Chief Prosecutor to one of mere supervision of his deputies.[20]

---

[18] In this regard, see generally HBF Madsen Sørensene and T Elholm, 'The EPPO and the Principle of Subsidiarity', in P Asp (ed), *The European Public Prosecutor's Office—Legal and Criminal Policy Perspectives* (Stockholm, Stiftelsen skrifter utgivna av Juridiska fakulteten vid Stockholms universitet, 2015) 31 ff.

[19] On this subject see M Caianiello, 'The Proposal for a Regulation on the Establishment of an European Public prosecutor's Office: Everything Changes, or Nothing Changes?' (2013) 21 *European Journal of Crime, Criminal Law and Criminal Justice* 120, as well as RE Kostoris, 'Pubblico Ministero europeo e indagini "nazionalizzate" (2013)', *Cassazione penale* 2744 ff.

[20] This point has been recently addressed by L Camaldo, 'La nuova fisionomia della Procura europea all'esito del semestre di presidenza italiana del Consiglio europeo' (2015) *Cassazione penale* 807 ff. The problem is addressed in general terms by S White, 'Towards a Decentralised European Public Prosecutor's Office?' (2013) 4(1–2) *New Journal of European Criminal Law* 22 ff.

If this is true in general terms, in the area of economic and financial crime this means that European Delegated Prosecutors, who may be two or more in number for each Member State (as provided for in Article 12(2) of the latest draft of the proposal; according to Article 6 of the original text, there could also be only one) and are isolated and distant due to territorial distribution, will have to deal with a highly fragmented base of criminal investigators charged with acquiring *notitiae criminis*, as well as the problem of their distribution at the decentralised level. This aspect has been highlighted by the national reports included in this volume.[21] The difficulty would increase exponentially in the handling of transnational cases, which involve a vast array of actors in the 'underbrush' of administrative inquiries.

One might wonder, therefore, which police forces would be at the service of the European Delegated Prosecutor, seeing that the supranational draft legislation has not yet addressed the issue. It simply and optimistically places trust in the 'double hat' formula, in the assumption that magistrates, when they act in their capacity as European prosecutors, will have at their disposal the same police units as when they are engaging in ordinary investigative activity.

It is worth observing that the draft regulation leaves the Member States free to assign European Delegated Prosecutors simultaneous functions as national public prosecutors. Admittedly, the possibility of cumulating the two tasks—domestic and European—is subject to the condition that this will not prevent the designated magistrates from 'fulfilling their obligations' on the supranational level (Article 12(3)). It is however likely that, especially in countries where public prosecutors' offices suffer from chronic understaffing and are burdened by an enormous over-load of criminal proceedings, the European Delegated Prosecutors would end up in practice being diverted from their duties to protect the interests of the Union in order to deal with the preponderant domestic criminal affairs. And we might well expect the same behaviour on the part of police forces, all the more so given that they are not formally vested with any direct European role.

As regards the relationship between the criminal investigation phase and the administrative inquiry which normally precedes it in the case of financial-economic crimes, the draft regulation omits it entirely, or at least fails to address it explicitly. But, as was said earlier, the smooth running of all these activities and the optimal shift from one area of investigation to the next are crucial to ensure the transfer of information about suspected criminal conduct to the competent judicial authority, which in the future will be—either exclusively or as a matter of priority, depending on the chosen solution—the EPPO.

In truth, a number of border rules are envisaged which give rise to the possibility of a closer connection between the administrative and the criminal fields, rather than just regulating the interaction between these two spheres.

Essentially, what is at issue here are Articles 15, 16, 21 and 58 of the original text of the Proposal for a Regulation for the Establishment of the EPPO.

---

[21] See above, Part I, ch 1, Part I, ch 2, Part II, ch 3, Part III, ch 5 and Part IV, ch 6.

The first provision concerns the sources through which the EPPO is informed of a crime already detected by others. The rule says nothing about the priority stage regarding the modalities for the initial issuing of a *notitia criminis*, which will be addressed later. It was envisaged, in particular, that all the 'national authorities' of the Member States would be obliged to 'immediately' inform the EPPO of any behaviour which might constitute an offence within its competence. It is unclear whether the first statement, which has remained unchanged in the articles of the negotiated drafts of the proposal, alludes only to judicial authorities (magistrates and, at most, criminal investigation police) or, more generally, all law enforcement authorities, including, for example, tax agencies and customs officials which, in this case, would establish a direct relationship with the EPPO. This second interpretation certainly appears preferable in the context of better safeguarding the financial interests of the Union, as it connects the EPPO with the national bodies that receive the *notitiae criminis* and is therefore a solution capable of increasing the flow of reports towards the EPPO charged with dealing with them more effectively.[22]

Nevertheless, the updated version of this rule (currently Article 19) contains some significant changes. First, no longer are 'all' the authorities of the Member States responsible for informing the EPPO, but only those that are competent according to applicable national law. Therefore, the European rule does not remove the differentiation among sources of reports on criminal conduct by introducing a general obligation to inform not covered by individual laws, but rather acknowledges the existence of many national rules which establish whether or not a particular authority is required to hand over the information in its possession to the person in charge of the criminal proceedings. It is therefore essential, from the point of view of the EPPO, to map the above bodies which are already obliged to transmit information to the judicial authorities of Member States, since the EPPO is destined to take over their role as the final collector of reports and information on criminal conduct. What is more, the direct channel to the EPPO envisaged in Article 12 of the original proposal is made doubtful by leaving it up to individual Member States to decide whether to set up a 'direct' or a 'centralised' reporting system at a national level.

The reporting times indicated also help us to understand how much space the EPPO regulation proposal gives to the administrative inquiry; although they are never expressly mentioned, administrative investigations can be identified implicitly among the activities which give impetus to the criminal investigation. While Article 15 initially imposed an immediate reporting of offences, implying

---

[22] This topic is thoroughly addressed by J Vervaele, 'La relazione tra OLAF, il futuro EPPO, altri organi europei e le autorità giudiziarie nazionali', in V Bazzocchi (ed), *La protezione dei diritti fondamentali e procedurali dalle esperienze investigative dell'OLAF all'istituzione della procura europea* (Roma, Fondazione Lelio e Lisli Basso Issoco, 2014) 121.

an instant passage from the administrative to the criminal department, the corresponding Article 19 now states that the process must take place 'without undue
delay'. A more elastic formula which appears to give national authorities more
leeway in carrying out their activities once a crime has emerged during administrative investigations, before handing it over to the EPPO.

On the one hand, the clause in question is better suited to the purpose of
verifying whether the crime comes under the jurisdiction of the EPPO, something
now made more complex by the envisaged setting of thresholds for the level of
damage done to the financial interests of the Union, below which jurisdiction
might remain with national judicial authorities if there are no other elements
involved which themselves are hard to evaluate, such as possible repercussions at
an EU level. On the other hand, extended times means that the report will not be
limited to giving the bare bones of a possible crime, but will be able to provide an
appropriate description of its intended injurious effect on the subjective position
of the individual involved—in other words, the start of a criminal investigation—
and supply the EPPO with enough information with which to evaluate the
integrity of the report itself. According to the current draft of the proposal the
report must contain 'as a minimum'—meaning it could go into further depth—'a
description of the facts, including an assessment of the damage caused or likely
to be caused, the possible legal qualification and any available information about
potential victims, suspects and any other involved persons'.

In fact, the quality of the report is decisive for the launch of a criminal investigation, as identified in the 'reasonable grounds to believe that an offence within
the competence of the European Public Prosecutor's Office is being or has been
committed'. Thus stated Article 16 of the draft regulation of 2013, with the intention of leaving it up to the EPPO to evaluate what degree of likelihood is required
to launch criminal proceedings, making the criteria uniform at a supranational
level. However, this aspect has also undergone a rethink following the negotiations, given that the corresponding Article 22 of the updated text specifies that
the assessment of 'reasonable grounds' is made 'in accordance with applicable
national law'.

This has led to the problem, still unresolved, of the different criteria each
national legal system applies, respectively, when establishing the grounds for initiating an administrative inquiry into a possible tax violation or episode of corruption, on the one hand, and the report of a crime originating from the same source,
on the other. No clear stance is taken—with a view to harmonisation—concerning
the degree of overlap between the relevant constituent elements of criminal
offences in the two realms (administrative and criminal, precisely), or between the
respective criteria for determining the likelihood of an offence having been committed (*fumus delicti*), in order to assess whether it might be feasible to proceed
with investigations in a unitary fashion and thereby reduce the current juridical
and time lag in investigative activities. Thus an essential aspect has not been clarified: whether the joining of efforts in the administrative and criminal realms for
the purpose of combating criminal conducts affecting the financial interests of the

EU encounters structural obstacles of an endemic character, or the problems are rather tied to specific features only of certain national legal systems.

The Persistent Coexistence of the Administrative Inquiry and Criminal Investigation

The considerations set forth so far, in light of the evolving regulation, suggest a design for the relationship between the EPPO investigation, on the one hand, and the preliminary activities of national administrative authorities, as well as OLAF, on the other, that is far from that initially envisaged as one of the aims of the establishment of the EPPO: the removal of a two-tier protection of Community finances, in favour of an immediate investiture of the EPPO as the body charged with criminal investigation. The web of national particularities and the numerous autonomous financial-economic crime verification centres, appear, however, to have decidedly come to the fore. If this fragmentation[23] is not tackled with rules harmonising the prerequisites and time limits for reporting criminal conducts, there will be no efficient channel of communication between the individual authorities of the Member States and the EPPO, and its valuable role as a source of information will be lost.[24]

It has been widely stressed that that OLAF's reports and those of the equivalent national agencies must be transferred to the EPPO in good time, even during the administrative inquiry or sidestepping it altogether: in other words, as soon as a possible crime is identified and without waiting for the conclusion of an often laborious phase which might better be immediately replaced by criminal proceedings.[25] This requirement is all the more important in consideration of those legal systems for which the future EPPO might pursue a criminal action, where the period of time after the offence is committed leads to its time restriction regardless of criminal proceedings having been launched in the meantime and thus risks rendering ineffective the duty of care imposed on the Union and the Member States by Article 325 TFEU.[26]

Articles 21(2) and 58(3), of the 2013 draft regulation, respectively dealing with the provision to the EPPO of required information by the national authorities and the cooperation of the EPPO with OLAF, were intended to avoid administrative

---

[23] The topic is addressed also by P Asp, 'Jeopardy on European Level—What is the Question to which the Answer is the EPPO?' in P Asp (ed), *The European Public Prosecutor's Office* 59.

[24] See P Csonka, 'Istituzione dell'Ufficio del Procuratore europeo' in V Bazzocchi (ed), *La protezione* 93.

[25] On this point, A Venegoni, 'Protezione degli interessi finanziari dell'UE: ripartizione di ruoli tra OLAF e futuro Procuratore europeo' in V Bazzocchi (ed), *La protezione* 105 ff.

[26] As also shown by the recent ruling of the EU Court of Justice of 8 September 2015, Case C-105/14 *Taricco and others*.

inquiries running parallel to, or overlapping with, a criminal investigation.[27] The *ne bis in idem* principle reveals the difficult relationship between the two channels of sanctions—the administrative and the criminal—according to the canons of the European Court of Human Rights and the EU Court of Justice.[28] In fact, the draft regulation seeks to resolve the problem by expressly forbidding OLAF to open any administrative investigations parallel to the criminal ones, where they are related to the same facts (Article 57a (2) of the current text). At the same time, when the European Public Prosecutor's Office has decided not to start an investigation or to dismiss a case, it may (Article 57a (4)) provide information to OLAF so that the latter may assess whether to undertake administrative action accordingly. This provision is related to what is set forth in Article 33(4): 'The dismissed cases may also be referred to OLAF or to competent national administrative or judicial authorities for recovery or other administrative follow-up'.

Undoubtedly, the result of not overlapping the two types of investigation shows a clear reconciliation given the clear definition of the EPPO's exclusive competence, in view of the general obligation to immediately provide information relating to the suspected offence, which is a deterrent to the drafting of reports rich in information and, therefore, inevitably drawn up at the end of a long preparatory period, and given the centralised and uniform substantiation of the crime report necessary to launch the criminal investigation.

The moment each of these controls is loosened and opens itself up to a high degree of discretion, the objective becomes lost. But we must also consider that the need for a speedy administrative inquiry—as has been clarified by European case law—'though legitimate when the facts are clear and likely to be accepted, cannot, nevertheless, justify a partial or selective examination of the possible responsibilities'.[29] It should not be forgotten, in fact, that although the decision to launch criminal investigations against a certain individual does not imply restrictions on personal freedom in a strict sense, it can hardly be excluded from the category of acts which directly and individually regard the accused person and have the effect of modifying his subjective legal situation. Therefore—in our opinion—the

---

[27] cf among others, A Damaskou, 'The European Public Prosecutor's Office. A Ground-Breaking New Institution of the EU Legal Order' (2015) 6(1) *New Journal of European Criminal Law* 149 ff.

[28] *Grande Stevens and others v Italy*, App nos 18640/10, 18647/10, 18663/10, 18668/10 and 18698/104/3/2014 (ECHR 4 March 2014); *Nykänen v Finland*, App no 11828/11 (ECHR 20 May 2014); EU Court of Justice judgment of 26 February 2013, *Åkeberg Fransson*, Case C-617/10. However, see the more recent judgment in the case *A and B v Norway*, App nos 24130/11, 29758/11 (ECHR, Grand Chamber, 15 November 2016), according to which criminal prosecution and the imposition of a criminal penalty against a party already sanctioned by the tax authorities does not violate the *ne bis in idem* principle, provided that there is a substantially close connection in substance and time between the two proceedings.

[29] Trib I, 6 April 2006, T-309/03, *Manuel Camos Grau v European Commission*, § 130. On this point, see A Perduca, 'Le indagini dell'ufficio europeo per la lotta antifrode (OLAF) ed I rapporti con le autorità giudiziarie' (2006) *Cassazione penale* 4246 ff.

protection afforded by the possibility of applying to the EU Court of Justice for the purpose of voiding the act concerned under Article 263 TFEU[30] must be upheld.

The Flow of Crime Reports between National Administrative Agencies and the EPPO: A Strategic Role Still to be Played by OLAF

We have to ask ourselves, therefore, whether the problem that the establishment of the EPPO is intended to resolve is linked solely to the low priority given by national judicial authorities to combating crimes against the financial interests of the Union, or whether we should also increase the flow of information relating to these offences which runs from the national administrative agencies to the law enforcement bodies of the Member States, in order to replace these bodies with a more receptive and dynamic figure such as that of the planned EPPO. The first question was addressed by the rules and legislation arising from the original proposal COM(2013)534, particularly in relation to the structure and investigative resources available to the supranational public prosecutor. To give a reply to the second question, overlooked by the legislation now being formulated, our research has attempted to provide an initial design of the institutional and functional complexity of the phenomenon in the different Member States.

In fact, thanks to OLAF's annual report we have knowledge of the number of recommendations which, at the end of its investigations, the European body submits to the national judicial authorities, as well as the percentage of cases which subsequently lead to criminal charges. In the period spanning from 1 January 2008 to 31 December 2015, the average indictment rate was 52 per cent across all EU countries.[31] As is well known, it is precisely the dissatisfaction with this performance—considered insufficient overall, with large discrepancies among the Member States—that has represented the motivation underlying the proposal for the establishment of the EPPO. Nevertheless, what is not clear is the number of *notitiae criminis* regarding crimes against the financial interests of the European Union acquired and transferred by the national administrative authorities directly to the law enforcement bodies of the individual Member States.

Will the EPPO have the ability to become part of this flow, to connect itself effectively with national realities and become the second active player in the

---

[30] On this issue see my previous observations in D Negri, 'Le contrôle judiciaire du parquet européen dans les traités et la Charte: un "convive de pierre" face à la puissance de l'organe d'enquête supranational' in G Giudicelli-Dèlage S Manacorda J Tricot (eds), *Le contrôle judiciaire du parquet européen. Nécessité, modèles, enjeux* (Paris, Société de législation comparée, 2015) 55–67.

[31] The report is available at the following address: http://ec.europa.eu/anti-fraud/sites/antifraud/files/olaf_report_2015_en.pdf.

exchange instead of the national judicial authorities? It will be said that the type of connection will be the same as the existing one, since the underlying criterion of the so-called 'double hat' will transform the national judicial authority into the European Delegated Prosecutor.[32] In this case, it is hard to see what the added value of establishing the EPPO might be, at least as regards the crucial point of giving momentum to the investigations with a number of cases sufficient to justify the creation of an organism such as the EPPO. Indeed, as we have suggested previously, the situation risks becoming even worse due to the increased distance which is likely to be created between a deputy of the EPPO who will generally work alone and the myriad of *lato sensu* administrative bodies scattered across national territories acting as potential collectors of reports concerning criminal offences.

The key to the dilemma lies, as far as I can see, in the future role of OLAF, which must remain strategic. The EPPO should not fully absorb the competencies of OLAF, nor should OLAF staff be incorporated into that of the EPPO leading to their complete takeover of criminal investigation tasks. If it is true that the separation between the administrative enquiry and the criminal investigation results artificial as well as risky as regards the prohibition of *bis in idem*, it is also true that the overlapping between them is widespread but not complete. Almost always there is an area in which the administrative enquiry can be conducted outside of and before the emergence of evidence of criminal conduct relating to the same nucleus of facts, which could turn out to be doubly illegal. To be precise, it is the space running between the different requirements, however similar, of the 'sufficient suspicion' which leads to a supposition of 'the existence of fraud' (according to Article 5, EU Regulation 883/2013 on OLAF investigations),[33] on the one hand, and 'having good reason to believe' that a crime under the competence of the EPPO has been committed (current Article 16 of the EPPO draft regulation), on the other hand.

What is more, two requirements must be balanced here. On the one hand, the assumed administrative nature of the investigation must not be an excuse for delaying the granting to the individual involved safeguards that are suited to the substantial criminal nature of the offences the prosecuting authority is seeking to investigate.[34] On the other hand, what must be avoided is that a situation which by its nature affects the rights of the individual, as criminal proceedings do, arises

---

[32] On the model chosen for the EPPO, see K Ligeti and M Simonato, 'The European Public Prosecutor's Office: Towards a Truly European Prosecution Service?' (2013) 4(1–2) *New Journal of European Criminal Law* 12 ff.

[33] On these aspects see R Panait, 'Information Sharing between OLAF and National Judicial Authorities' (2/2015) *EuCrim* 67 ff.

[34] JFH Inghelram, *Legal and Institutional Aspects of the European Anti-Fraud Office (OLAF). An Analysis with a Look Forward to a European Public Prosecutor's Office* (Groningen, Europa Law Publishing, 2011) 134 ff. For a review of the case law on the safeguards to be ensured during OLAF investigations see V Mitsilegas, 'The European Public Prosecutor before the Court of Justice. The Challenge of effective Judicial Protection' in G Giudicelli-Delage, S Manacorda and J Tricot (eds), *Le contrôle judiciaire du parquet européen. Nécessité, modèles, enjeux* 80 ff.

without adequate justification, if we consider that the decision to open an administrative enquiry 'could not be done in the absence of sufficiently serious suspicions',[35] and therefore that even the most serious criminal prosecution could not be launched lightly.

By maintaining OLAF's prerogative to conduct administrative investigations, the EPPO system would have powers not foreseen by its establishing framework and no less essential to a more effective protection of the EU's financial interests; in other words the power to take the initiative with regard to acquiring information about the commission of crimes. Whereas the structure envisaged by the proposal for a regulation COM(2013)534 gives us a European Public Prosecutor who is merely a passive receiver of *notitiae criminis* which have already been acquired, a public prosecutor who, in other words, patiently waits for others to give impetus and provide the initial materials for his criminal investigation.

One solution to this problem could actually be to give OLAF a dual role oriented towards helping the EPPO with criminal investigations that have already begun, but above all to supporting, before the launch of criminal prosecution and precisely in order to lend it impetus, the numerous national authorities which can be the source of information concerning suspected criminal conduct, in order to exploit the consolidated experience in this area because of the close links forged over many years of activity.

It is proposed, therefore, to make OLAF an intermediary body between the EPPO and national administrative agencies, a connecting link able to move within the 'grey zone' which precedes the acquisition of reports on alleged criminal offences. On the other hand, the European Parliament recommends that the Council should clarify how to complement the actions of OLAF and those of the EPPO also in the case of 'external' investigations (Resolution of 29 April 2015). All this means that it is necessary to establish and consolidate EPPO's link with national tax or public security authorities, using OLAF as its *longa manus*.[36]

In particular, it appears essential that the initial investigative activity of these agencies, even after the institution of the EPPO, should continue to be the collection—without the use of coercive powers—of documentary evidence which can then be used in criminal proceedings. This is a flexible way of providing information which it would be wise not to reject in the context of an efficient protection of the EU's financial interests, but which could be at risk if one were to consider that the anticipated impetus to criminal prosecution removes the evidence acquired without going through the investigative measures ordered by the judicial authority.

---

[35] EU Court of Justice, 10 July 2003, Case C-11/00, *European Commission v Central European Bank*, § 141.

[36] As highlighted by L Kuhl, 'L'expérience de l'office européen de lutte anti-fraude' in G Giudicelli-Delage, S Manacorda and J Tricot, *Le contrôle judiciaire* 184, 'reste ouverte la question de savoir si l'OLAF pourrait être chargé par le parquet européen de conduire, sous son contrôle, des mesures spécifiques d'investigation (criminelle)'.

Moreover, this problem will grow exponentially if—as shown following the negotiations—the principle of the *single legal area* is not maintained and there is a return to forms of judicial cooperation based on the example of Directive 2014/41/EU regarding the European Investigation Order in criminal matters.[37] Within a similar context, the administrative investigation preceding a criminal prosecution will once again become attractive in the context of better protection of EU finances, all the more if it continues to benefit from the contacts established with the various national authorities and the evidence collecting activities of a body of inquiry that is hybrid and 'without borders', which is precisely the role of OLAF.[38]

The indications we provided in this regard during our research (culminating in a seminar held in November 2015) had some interesting echoes in the most recent versions of the proposal regarding the establishment of the EPPO. Whereas in the original draft the definition of the relationship between the supranational prosecuting body and the Anti-Fraud Office was relegated to a paragraph of Article 58 (regarding in general to 'relations with other Union institutions, bodies, offices and agencies'), which in turn referred to an agreement aimed at defining the terms of mutual cooperation, the present legislative text dedicates an Article 57a specifically to this issue. It directly provides that the relationship between the two bodies will aim to ensure the use of all available means for the protection of the Union's financial interests through the complementarity and support of OLAF to the Prosecutor's Office. In particular, the cooperation should consist in providing information, analyses (including forensic analyses), expertise and operational support; as well as facilitating coordination of specific actions of the competent national administrative authorities.

Interpreting the last form of support listed in the aforementioned reference provision is more problematic. Indeed, it alludes to the possibility of OLAF also conducting 'administrative investigations'. One the one hand, this provision needs to be coordinated with the one that forbids *bis in idem* and therefore prevents OLAF from opening an administrative inquiry in parallel with the criminal investigation into the same facts; on the other hand, it needs to be fit into the context of operations to support or complement a criminal prosecution activity already undertaken by the European Public Prosecutor's Office, in the course of which such forms of help may be requested of OLAF. It must thus be concluded that the powers of administrative investigation may be exercised not only before but also during the criminal investigation. This appears contradictory, since after a suspected criminal conduct has been reported the actions carried out under the

---

[37] *cf* S Allegrezza, 'Collecting Criminal Evidence Across the European Union: The European Investigation Order Between Flexibility and Proportionality' in S Ruggeri (ed), *Transnational Evidence and Multicultural Inquiries in Europe* (Heidelberg, Springer, 2014) 55 ff.

[38] See also the study by J Łacny, L Paprzycki and E Zielinska, 'The System of Vertical Cooperation in Administrative Investigations Cases' in K Ligeti (ed), *Toward a Prosecutor* 803 ff.

supervision of the supranational investigating body should be exclusively of a judicial nature. However, the singular attribution to OLAF of criminal investigative functions (even if complementary) masked by activities of an administrative nature perhaps betrays the European legislator's awareness of the indispensable role that must be played by the Anti-Fraud Office if we really want to achieve an efficient protection of the financial interests of the Union through the creation of the European Public Prosecutor: OLAF would thus seem to be seen as a sort of 'para-judicial' police;[39] however, it would be better to clearly define the limits and the means that may be adopted in relation to criminal proceedings in order to avoid dangerous confusions of functions of dubious compatibility with the legislative framework of the Treaties.

---

[39] An observation to this effect is made by K Ligeti and A Weyembergh, 'The European Public Prosecutor's Office: Certain Constitutional Issues' in LH Erkelens and AWH Meij P Pawlik (eds), *The European Public Prosecutor's Office* 70: 'The integrationist view supported by OLAF itself suggested, therefore, that OLAF should become the "police judicière" of the EPPO acting at the central level. It is, however, doubtful whether Article 86 TFEU provides legal basis for such a scenario'. A view in favour of transforming OLAF into a specialised agency endowed with investigative functions of judicial relevance is expressed, however, by G De Amicis, 'I Rapporti della Procura europea con Eurojust, OLAF ed Europol. Le questioni in gioco' in G Grasso, G Illuminati, R Sicurella and S Allegrezza (eds), *Le sfide dell'attuazione di una Procura europea* 652.

BIBLIOGRAPHY

Aguilera Morales, M, *Las diligencias de investigación fiscal* (Cisur Menor Navarra, Thomson/ Aranza, 2015).

Aldridge, P, 'The UK Bribery Act: The Caffeinated Younger Sibling of the FCPA' (2012) 73 *Ohio State Law Journal* 1181.

Aldridge, P, 'Two Key Areas in Proceeds of Crime Law' (2014) *Criminal Law Review* 170.

Allegrezza, S, 'Verso una Procura Europea per tutelare gli interessi finanziari dell'Unione', www.penalecontemporaneo.it 1.

Amodio, E, 'I reati economici nel prisma dell'accertamento processuale', (2008) *Riv. it. dir. proc. pen.* 1496.

Anderson M and Anderson, TA, 'Anti-money laundering: history and current developments' (2015) 30(10) *JIBLR* 521.

Asp, P, (ed), *The European Public Prosecutor's Office. Legal and Criminal Policy Perspectives* (Stockholm, Stockholm University, 2015).

Ayrault, L, 'La pénalisation de la lutte contre la fraude fiscal' (2015) 1 *REIDF* 4.

Bachmaier Winter, L, 'The Potential Contribution of a European Public Prosecutor in Light of the Proposal for a Regulation of 17 July 2013' (2013) 23 *European Journal of Crime, Criminal Law and Criminal Justice* 126.

Bacigalupo, E, Gimeno Sendra, V, Moreno Catena V and Torres-Dulce Lifante, E, *La posición del fiscal en la investigación penal: la reforma de la Ley de Enjuiciamiento Criminal* (Cisur Menor Navarra, Thomson/Aranza, 2005).

Balsamo, A, 'Il contenuto dei diritti fondamentali, in Manuale di procedura penale Europea' in R Kostoris (ed), *Manuale di procedura penale europea*, (Milano, Giuffrè, 2015) 109–164.

Bazzocchi, V, (ed), *La protezione dei diritti fondamentali e procedurali dalle esperienze investigative dell'OLAF all'istituzione della procura europea* (Roma, Fondazione Lelio e Lisli Basso Issoco, 2014).

Blumenberg A and Nieto Martìn, A, 'Nemo tenetur se ipsum accusare en el Derecho penal económico europeo' in A Nieto Martín and Diez Picazo (eds), *Los derechos fundamentales en el derecho penal europeo* (Madrid, Civitas, 2010) 397–420.

Bonetti, N, 'Gli indizi nel nuovo processo penale', (1989) *L'indice penale* 487.

Bontempelli M, *L'accertamento amministrativo nel sistema processuale penale* (Milano, Giuffrè 2009).

Böse, M, *Wirtschaftsaufsicht und Strafverfolgung* (Tubingen, Mohr Siebeck, 2005).

Buse, JW, 'Der steuerstrafrechtliche Verdacht des Außenprüfer' (2011) *Der Betrieb* 1942.

Cahn, O, *Mélanges en l'honneur de Christine Lazerges* (Paris, Dalloz, 2014).

Cahn, O, 'Le sentencing anglo-américain, avenir de l'administration des peines en France?' (2014) 36 *APC* 249.

Caianiello, M, 'The Proposal for a Regulation on the Establishment of an European Public prosecutor's Office: Everything Changes, or Nothing Changes?' (2013) 21 *European Journal of Crime, Criminal Law and Criminal Justice* 115.

Caianiello, M, 'Il principio di proporzionalità nel procedimento penale', (2016) 3–4 *Riv. Trim. dir. pen. cont.* 143.

Camaldo, L, 'La nuova fisionomia della Procura europea all'esito del semestre di presidenza italiana del Consiglio europeo' (2015) *Cassazione penale* 804.

Caprioli, F, 'Indagini preliminari e udienza preliminare' in G Conso and V Grevi (eds), *Compendio di procedura penale*, 6th edn (Padova, Cedam, 2012) 494–660.

Caraccioli, I, 'Reati fiscali: ritorna la forte tentazione di resuscitare la pregiudiziale tributaria' (2000) *Il fisco* 5.

Corrado, LR, 'Locali comunicanti? E' necessaria l'autorizzazione del Procuratore' (2013) *D&G* 264.

Damaskou, A, 'The European Public Prosecutor's Office. A Ground-Breaking New Institution of the EU Legal Order', (2015) 6(1) *New Journal of European Criminal Law* 149.

Daniele, M, 'La prova digitale nel processo penale' (2011) *Dir. pen. e proc.* 283.

Daniele, M, 'Indagini informatiche lesive della riservatezza. Verso un'inutilizzabilità convenzionale?' (2013) *Cassazione penale* 367.

De Hert P and Papakonstantiou, V, 'The new police and criminal justice data protection directive' (2016) 7 *New Journal of European Criminal Law* 1.

Debat, O, 'La Commission des infractions fiscales, les ressorts d'un désamour inépuisable' (2015) 1 *REIDF* 79.

Delmas-Marty, M, *Corpus juris portant dispositions pénales pour la protection des intérêts financiers de l'Union européenne* (Paris, Economica, 1997).

Delmas-Marty, M and Vervaele, JAE, *The Implementation of the Corpus Juris in the Member States: Penal Provisions for the Protection of European Finances* (Antwerpen-Groningen-Oxford, Intersentia, 2000).

Dell'Anno, P, 'Il processo verbale di constatazione degli illeciti tributari e il nuovo processo penale', (1990) *Cassazione penale* 435.

Di Amato A and Pisano R (eds), *Trattato di Diritto penale dell'impresa*, vol VII (Padova, Cedam, 2002).

Díez-Picazo, LM, and Nieto Martín, A, *Los derechos fundamentales en el Derecho Penal europeo* (Navarra, Cisur Menor, Thomson Reuters, 2010).

Dominioni, O, *Le parti nel processo penale (profili sistematici e problemi)* (Milano, Giuffrè, 1985).

Erkelens, LH, Meij, AWH and Pawlik, P (eds), *The European Public Prosecutor's Office. An extended arm or a Two-Headed dragon?* (The Hague, TMC Asser Press, 2015).

Eusepi, S, 'Reati tributari, sequestro preventivo e fondo patrimoniale' (2014) *Riv. Dir. Trib.* 347.

Faberi, A, 'Sui confini delle garanzie, autodifensive dell'accusato (accertamenti fiscali, richiesta di documenti, rischio di autoincriminazione)' (2013) 2 *Archivio Penale* 1.

Fall, C, Müller, E, Satzger, H and Swoboda, S, *Ein menschengerechtes Strafrecht als Lebensaufgabe. Festschrift für Werner Beulke zum 70 Gegurstag* (Heidelberg, CF Müller, 2015).

Fauvarque-Cosson, B, *Les procédures répressives contre la grand délinquance économique et financière, en Le Droit Comparé au XXI Siècle. Enjeux et Défis. Journées Internationales de la Société de Législation Comparé 8-9 Avril 2015*, (Paris, Société de Législation Comparée, 2015).

Fernández Vázquez, A, 'El Servicio de Vigilancia Aduanera: problemática sobre su consideración como policía judicial' (2009) *Boletín del Ministerio de Justicia* 1838.

Ferran, E, 'Examining the UK Experience in Adopting the Single Financial Regulator Model' (2003) *28 Brooklyn Journal of International Law* 257.

Fidelbo, M, 'La cooperazione rafforzata come modalità d'istituzione della Procura europea. Scenari futuri di un dibattito ancora in evoluzione', www.penalecontemporaneo.it 1.

Fisher, J, 'The Part 1 of the Serious Crime Act 2015: strengthening the restraint and confiscation regime' (2015) 10 *Crim. L.R.* 754.

Fontaine, B, Guyomar, M, Pesin, F and Baranger, S, 'Les procédures de contrôle sur place des régulateurs financiers: état des lieux et perspectives d'évolution' (2012) *Bulletin Joly Bourse et produits financiers* 378.

Frigo G, 'Diritto di difesa e atti di polizia giudiziaria nel processo per frodi alimentari' (1969) *Giur. cost.* 2286.

Furin N, 'Il principio della libertà dalle autoincriminazioni e la sua rilevanza in materia di infortuni sul lavoro o di malattia professionale' (1998) *Cassazione penale* 1008.

Furin N, 'Diritto di difesa, indizi, sospetti e l'art. 220 norme att. c.p.p.' (1999) *Cassazione penale* 2713.

Gagliardi, R, 'Sospetto e indizio. Presunzione e congetture' (1969) *Riv. di polizia* 720.

Gòmez Colomer, JL and Esparza, I, *Tratado jurisprudencial de aforamientos procesales* (Valencia, Tirant lo Blanch, 2009).

Grasso, G, Illuminati, G, Sicurella, R and Allegrezza, S (eds), *Le sfide dell'attuazione di una Procura europea: definizione di regole comuni e loro impatto sugli ordinamenti interni* (Milano, Giuffrè, 2013).

Grevi G, 'Attività di polizia giudiziaria degli ispettori di lavoro', (1974) *L'indice penale* 230.

Guarnelli, VM, 'Aspetti operativi e processuali dell'attività di p.g. nel nuovo c.p.p.' (1991) *Arch. n. proc. pen.* 157.

Gutiérrez Zarza, A, *Investigación y enjuiciamiento de los delitos económicos* (Madrid, Colex, 2000).

Hill, J and Ligere, E, 'The UK's new financial services regulatory structure—the shape of things to come' (2013) 28(4) *Journal of International Banking Law and Regulation* 156.

Hofmański, P, *System prawa karnego procesowego. Tom I cz. 2. Zagadnienia ogólne* (Warsaw, LexisNexis, 2013).

Inghelram, JFH, *Legal and Institutional Aspects of the European Anti-Fraud Office (OLAF). An Analysis with a Look Forward to a European Public Prosecutor's Office* (Groningen, Europa Law Publishing, 2011).

Isaguirre Guerricagoitia, JM, *La investigación preliminar del Ministerio Fiscal. La intervención de las partes en la misma*, (Navarra, Aranzadi, Elcano, 2001).

Izzo, G, 'Le sezioni Unite limitano l'utilizzabilità di dichiarazioni rese in sede ispettiva di vigilanza', (2002) *Il fisco* 1178.

Killick, M, 'Twin peak—a new series or a new chimera? An analysis of the proposed new regulatory structure in the UK' (2012) 33(12) *Comp. Law* 366.

Klip, A, 'The Substantive Criminal Law Jurisdiction of the European Public Prosecutor's Office' (2012) 20 *European Journal of Crime, Criminal Law and Criminal Justice* 367.

Konarska-Wrzosek, W, Oczkowski T and Skorupka, J, *Prawo i postępowanie karne skarbowe* (Warsaw, Wolters Kluwer, 2010).

Kostoris, RE, 'Pubblico Ministero europeo e indagini "nazionalizzate"' (2013) *Cassazione penale* 4738.

Lasagni, G, 'Cooperazione amministrativa e circolazione probatoria nelle frodi doganali e fiscali. Il ruolo dell'Ufficio europeo per la lotta antifrode (OLAF) alla luce della direttiva OEI e del progetto EPPO' (2015) www.penalecontemporaneo.it 1.

Laudati, L, 'Data Protection at O.L.A.F.' (2013) 1 *E.U. Crim* 14.

Lemoine, V, 'Les aspects policiers de la lutte contre la corruption' (2012) *Droit pénal et procédure pénale, Dossier: Les manquements au devoir de probité* 1.

Levi, 'The Roskill Fraud Commission Revisited: An Assessment' (2003) 11(1) *Journal of Financial Crime* 38.

Ligeti, K (ed), *Toward a Prosecutor for the European Union: A Comparative Analysis*, vol I., (Oxford, Hart, 2013).

Ligeti, K and Simonato, M, 'The European Public Prosecutor's Office: Towards a Truly European Prosecution Service?' (2013) 4(1–2) *New Journal of European Criminal Law* 7.

López Ortega, JJ, 'Derecho Penal y corrupción: las garantías en los instrumentos penales de investigación y enjuiciamiento' in A Jareño Leal and A Doval País (eds), *Corrupción pública, prueba y delito: cuestiones de libertad e intimidad* (Navarra, Thomson/Aranzadi, Cizur Menor, 2015) 181–198.

Lorenzetto, E, 'Utilizzabilità di dati informatici incorporati su computer in sequestro: dal contenitore al contenuto, passando per la copia' (2010) *Cassazione penale* 1522.

Löwe, Rosenberg, *Strafprozessordnung*, vol III, 26th edn (Berlin, De Gruyter, 2014).

Lupària, L, 'Processo penale e scienza informatica: anatomia di una trasformazione epocale' in L Lupària and G Ziccardi (eds), *Investigazione penale e tecnologia informatica*, (Milano, Giuffrè, 2007) 127–137.

Madauß, N ,'Außenprüfung und Steuerstrafverfahren—Anmerkung aus der Praxis' (2014) *NZWiSt* 296.

Marafioti L, 'Digital evidence e processo penale' (2011) *Cassazione penale* 4509.

Marello, E, 'Evanescenza del principio di specialità e dissoluzione del doppio binario: le ragioni per una riforma del sistema punitivo penale tributario' (2013) 12 *Rivista di Diritto Tributario* 269.

Martín García, P, *La actuación de la policía judicial en el proceso penal* (Madrid, Marcial Pons, 2006).

Martín Pallín, JA, '¿Tiene futuro el juez de instrucción?' (2001) 5 *Anuario de la Facultad de Derecho de la Universidad Autónoma de Madrid* 149.

Martín Velasco, L, 'La investigación policial en el blanqueo de capitales' in JL González Cussac, *Financiación del terrorismo, blanqueo de capitales y secreto bancario: un análisis crítico* (Valencia, Tirant lo Blanch, 2009) 235–244.

Martínez Pérez, R, *Policía Judicial y Constitución* (Navarra, Aranzadi, 2001).

Meyer, IM, 'Steuerstrafrechtliche Probleme bei Betriebsprüfungen' (2001) *DStR* 461.

Mitsilegas, V, 'The External Dimension of Mutual Trust: the Case of Transatlantic Counter-terrorism Cooperation' in C Grandi (ed) *Justice and Trust in the European Legal Order* (Napoli, Jovene 2016) 153–183.

Morales García, O and Ferreres Comella, V, 'El Servicio de Vigilancia Aduanera como policía judicial: la dimensión constitucional del problema' (2015) *Diario La Ley* 16 December 16 1.

Negri, D,'Le contrôle judiciaire du parquet européen dans les traités et la Charte: un "convive de pierre" face à la puissance de l'organe d'enquête supranational' in G Giudicelli-Dèlage S Manacorda J Tricot (eds), *Le contrôle judiciaire du parquet européen. Nécessité, modèles, enjeux* (Paris, Société de législation comparée, 2015) 55–67.

Nobili, M, *Scenari e trasformazioni del processo penale*, (Padova, Cedam, 1998).

Nowak, C, *Evidence in EU Fraud Cases* (Warsaw, Wolters Kluwer, 2012).

Nowak, C (ed), *The European Public Prosecutor's Office and National Authorities* (Padova, Cedam, 2016).

Orbaneja, EG, *Comentarios a la Ley de Enjuiciamiento Criminal* (Barcelona, Bosch, 1947).

Orlandi, R, *Atti e informazioni dell'autorità amministrativa nel processo penale* (Milano, Giuffrè, 1992).

Orlandi, R, 'Questioni attuali in tema di processo penale e informatica' (2009) *Riv. Dir. proc.* 129.

Ormerod D and Laird, K, *Smith and Hogan's Text, Cases, and Materials on Criminal Law*, 11th edn (Oxford, Oxford University Press, 2014).

Panait, R, 'Information Sharing between OLAF and National Judicial Authorities' (2/2015) *E.U. Crim* 67.

Pastor López, *El proceso de persecución: análisis del concepto, naturaleza y específicas funciones de la instrucción criminal* (Valencia, Universidad de Valencia: Secretariado de Publicaciones, 1979).

Perduca, A, 'Le indagini dell'ufficio europeo per la lotta antifrode (OLAF) ed I rapporti con le autorità giudiziarie' (2006) *Cassazione penale* 4246.

Pérez Gil, J and González López, JJ, 'Cesión de datos personales para la investigación penal. Una propuesta para su inmediata inclusión en la Ley de Enjuiciamiento Criminal,' (2010) *Diario La Ley*, 13 May 1.

Pérez Gil, J, *El proceso penal en la sociedad de la información. Las nuevas tecnologías para investigar y probar el delito* (Madrid, La Ley, 2012).

Raphael, 'Fraud on Trial—Reviewing the Roskill Legacy' (2003) 11(1) *Journal of Financial Crime* 8.

Recchione, S, 'European Public Prosecutor Office. Anche gli entusiasti diventano scettici?' www.penalecontemporaneo.it 1.

Roberts M and Hohl, A, 'The new NCA: what does it mean for the SFO?' (2013) 24(10) *Practical Law Companies* 1.

Rolletschke, S, *Steuerstrafrecht* (Munchen, Franz Vahlen, 2012).

Ruggeri, S (ed), *Transnational Evidence and Multicultural Inquiries in Europe* (Heidelberg, Springer, 2014).

Savla, S, 'Serious Fraud Office powers under section 2 of the Criminal Justice Act 1987 and Police and Criminal Evidence Act 1984' (1997) 4(3) *Journal of Financial Crime* 223.

Solaz Solaz, E, *La instrucción de los delitos económicos y contra la Hacienda Pública* (Madrid, Consejo General del Poder Judicial, 2005).

Spangher, G, *Trattato di procedura penale*, vol III (Torino, Utet, 2009).

Theile, H, 'Zur Ermittlungs- und Abschlusskompetenz in Steuerstrafsachen—Anmerkung zu BGH, Beschl. v. 30.4.2009—1 StR 90/09' (2009) *Zeitschrift für internationale Strafrechtsdogmatik* 446.

Thomson, C and Garfield, H, 'SFO enforcement: has the tanker turned?' (2015) *Practical Law Companies* 26.

Vallés Causada, LM, *La policía judicial en la obtención de inteligencia sobre comunicaciones electrónicas para el proceso penal*, Tesis Doctoral, (Madrid, UNED, 2013).

Venegoni, A, 'Il difficile cammino della proposta di direttiva per la protezione degli interessi finanziari dell'Unione europea attraverso la legge penale (c.d. direttiva PIF): il problema della base legale' (2015) *Cassazione penale* 2442.

Walker, G, Purves, R and Blair, M, *Financial Services Law*, 3rd edn (Oxford, Oxford University Press, 2014).

White, S, 'Towards a Decentralised European Public Prosecutor's Office?' (2013) 4(1–2) *New Journal of European Criminal Law* 22.

Wilk, L and Zagrodnik, J, *Prawo karne skarbowe* (Warsaw, CH Beck, 2009).

Wright, R, 'Fraud after Roskill: A View from the Serious Fraud' (2003) 11(1) *Office Journal of Financial Crime* 10.

Yeoh, P, 'Reform of financial regulations in the UK: contents and implications' (2011) 32(10) *Bus. L.R.* 244.

Zappulla, A, 'Notizia di reato' in *Enc. Dir.*, Annali vol V (Milano, Giuffrè, 2012).

INDEX